LOOKING AT LIFE
POEMS, SONGS AND STORIES

Linda Bootherstone-Bick

DEDICATION

This book is dedicated to my parents, Dulcie Estelle and Arthur Royle Bootherstone (both deceased). Not only did they give me life but also the confidence to travel in order to explore and appreciate it.

Copyright © Linda Bootherstone-Bick 2020
All rights reserved.

ISBN: 978-0-6487261-8-0

Published by M R Gudzenovs
Printed in Australia

CONTENTS

Introduction	1
An Embarrassing Moment	2
Of Course	2
Hiroshima II	4
Birthdays... (7th and 21st)	6
A Permanent Reminder...	7
The Busker	7
A Campfire	7
Manx Cat Song	8
The Confidence of Youth	10
Birthdays... (24th and 25th)	11
Africa	12
Excerpt from *Into Africa with a Smile*	13
African Odyssey	13
Birthdays... (29th, 30th and 31st)	15
Easter in Namibia	16
A Not So Fast Woman	20
The Community Arts Team (CAT)	22
CAT Among the Gum Trees	23
Paddle Steamer Come Home	24
Penong Song	26
Space Bus Shuttle	28
Lady of the West Coast	30
The 1,000-Legged Worm	32
Kitty Cat	34
Portland Whaler	36
Callana Gold	38
Tennant Creek	40
Arkaroo	42
The CAT Van	44
Timothy Tadpole	46
Little Red Riding Hood	47
Song for Bill	48
Missing You	49
The Power Song	50
The Headstone	51
See the Aymite Flood	52
A Winter Afternoon on the Aymite	53
Duck Egg Blues	54
Sunny Jim the Goat	55
Flying High	56
Birthdays... (40th)	58
The Week We Went to Alice	59
Who's Who in the Folk Scene	60
The Missus of the House	62
I'm a Flea	64
Take My Breath Away	66
I Smell a Rat	68
Driving to Dunbar	70
Affaire Chanson	71
Perish the Thought	80
A Great Result	84
Flying with Angels	85
Interview with Mr Rick Burgess	87
Ann Davison	91
Sacrifices for the Sea	92
A Mountain Scorned	94
The Wee Magic Stane	96
Women on the Rock	100
Birthdays... (47th)	102

A Sort of Sortie	103
Is it a Mountain?	104
The Siege Song	106
A Whistling Gypsy Rover	108
South Wind	110
Puff the Magic Dragon	112
Out of Africa - In an Allegro	114
Birthdays... (49th)	116
Rose of Moses	117
Morocco	118
Riding On... An Odessa Odyssey	120
Odessa	123
Birthdays... (50th)	124
A Castle in Spain	126
Grazalema	128
Castellar	130
Pole Polka	131
Andalus Lullaby	132
The Angel of Lagos	134
A Friday Night Deluge in Castellar	136
Castillejos Rant	137
Flamenco	138
The Song of the Sea	140
Song of the Sea	143
After the Sun Goes Down	144
Druid Chant	145
Gretna Green	146
Gretna Green Song	147
Travels with Sammy...	149
In Search of Earthly Treasures...	152
Johnny Won't You Come Along Now	154
Playing Music Way Out at Boghill	156
Out of the Frying Pan	157
Natural Healing Techniques	158
A Plethora of Peters	163
Limericks	163
Woad at the Wharf	164
Millennium in the Mississippi Mud	165
Highway 49	166
El Camino De Santiago...	168
Buen Camino	169
A Walk North	171
Damp Day on the Danube	173
If You Want to See a Tree	174
The Overlander	176
Who or What is an Overlander?	176
Birthdays... (60th)	179
Bent Crash Bar Song	180
A Bump in the Road	182
Elephant Walk	184
The KL Blues	186
Police Problem in Indonesia	188
On the Shore Labuan Poh	190
Ode to Indonesia	192
Epitaph for Larry	193
Baa Baa Bach	194
Patience	195
The Arctic Ale	196
Brew the Arctic Ale	197
Leaving on a Sherpa	200
Beginning Again	202
Back Into the Light	202

Two Chairs	203
The Bed	203
Port Lincoln My Home	204
Table Tennis	206
Community House	207
The Men's Shed	208
Addiction	210
May Peace and Love Be With You	211
Song of the Endeavour	212
The Trolley in the Trees	214
The Desert Breathes	214
Limericks	215
Lament for the Nauo Nation	217
A Walk in Wilpena Pound	218
Poetry Through a Lens	220
Gravestone	220
The Love of Your Life	221
Rusting Heap	222
Busy Port	223
Nearly There	223
The Land of Smiles	224
Get On With It	226
An Island Interlude	227
A Christmas Story	228
Harvest Time	230
Incident in the Andes	232
Birthdays… (70th)	233
Border Control	234
The Ruin in the Bush	235
Ode To A Faithful Friend	236
Birthdays… (72nd)	237
Koonalda	238
Nullarbor Nymph	240
I'd Rather be a Dag than a Doll	241
Going Down to Louisiana	242
Faraway Friends	244
Where Will We Be?	246
Picture of My Life	247
Other Books by Linda	

ACKNOWLEDGEMENTS

Mary Gudzenovs (Port Lincoln)	Compositor
Viola Wiedmann (Adelaide)	Editor
Dave Moss (Adelaide)	Music transcription
Ann Staunton (Port Lincoln)	Music transcription
Maxine McFarlane (Port Lincoln)	Music transcription
Colin Clegg (UK)	Music transcription
Sally Perry (Port Lincoln)	Leader of Eyre Writers Inc Night Writing Class

There are times in my life that I have been accused of 'being away with the fairies'. And, to be sure, isn't this altogether grand! When the fairies are with you, you have luck. When against you, all sorts of things happen, like strangely misplaced car keys, spectacles, house keys and mobile phones. I hope you have the fairies with you while you read this book.

Introduction

This may, at first, seem an odd format for a book: a collection of poems, songs, stories and articles, but I have a very good reason for presenting it in this fashion.

Many people have commented that I have lived a diverse and interesting life and suggested that I write a book about it. Indeed, I have already written three books about some of my travels by motorcycle in various countries (see back page) and I have also produced an illustrated poetry book with pieces that describe various places and experiences.

However, I am also a song-writer and most of my songs are about people, places and stories in my life – they are true folk songs as they describe events.

I have also written short stories based on my life experiences and items for shows that I have presented in schools in Australia and Spain on various themes. Some of these stories are autobiographical and some not. I leave it to you to decide which!

While I was living in Spain, close to Gibraltar, in the 1990s, I was always looking for a way to earn a living and I hit on the idea of interviewing some of the colourful characters who passed through that part of the world and selling these as articles to the local paper – *The Gibraltar Chronicle*. So, these are also included as they show the diverse ways in which people live their lives – myself included.

Coming to live in Port Lincoln South Australia in 2010 I joined the Eyre Writers for a while and went to the evening sessions run by Sally Perry. I have found an exercise book used at these meetings and in it are some interesting short pieces we had to write in 10 minutes on a subject Sally suggested, and, as Sally loved limericks, there are some written in that format too. These pieces have been included as short fillers.

I have tried to present the material in roughly chronological order, as they occurred or were written during my life but this is not strictly adhered to.

It has been an interesting exercise finding the material and formatting this book and I have needed especial help with presenting the songs as, only playing by ear, I have not enough knowledge of writing music to be able to present, by myself, the songs in a format that other people can play. With many hands and ears on the work, the music is open to Interpretation!

I do hope you enjoy this book as much as I have enjoyed putting it together.

An Embarrassing Moment

My mother was a shorthand typist and the office in which she worked had several men who were very into football (known as soccer in Australia). Her boss was even a member of the *Crystal Palace Football Club* in South London and informed her that they would soon be holding a dance and would she like to come and bring her daughter.

I was 14 at the time, very interested in dressing up and hopefully attracting boys. I was at a girls' school so they were relatively unknown creatures but supposed to be worth attracting.

The fashion at the time was for pinafore dresses, tight around the bust and waist but with full skirts and in order to have those full skirts standing out as much as possible, we trendy girls sewed net petticoats. Every week a shilling of my pocket money went to buy yet another yard of net, in a different colour and I duly gathered it and sewed it onto my petticoat.

My best dress was purple and white check, very fetching, and with the petticoat beneath I was ready for any dance, football or not.

The night of the dance came and I accompanied my mother to the hall. I nervously sat beside her as the music began and furtively viewed the boys. Wonder of wonders, one came toward me and asked me for a dance. It was a jive – we went to the centre of the floor and he twirled me around. I was delighted!

Then ping and woosh! I tripped. Horrified I looked down and saw my deflated skirt hanging limply and, around my ankle, a full circle of multi-coloured foaming net.

I will never know why but I had fastened it with a button, not elastic and the button had failed.

My cheeks blazing with embarrassment I stepped out of the rainbow circle, stooped down to gather it up and rushed to the toilet, wishing the ground would open up and swallow me.

It was a long time before I dared to emerge and sit in shamed silence beside my mother who, I believe, was trying very hard not to laugh. My dress was now hanging straight, deflated on my legs.

Amazingly, the young man very kindly and politely approached us again and renewed his offer of being my partner but I was just too embarrassed and shook my head. He walked away.

Well, that taught me a lot about dressmaking, if nothing else!

Of Course

'Enough,' Dulcie said to herself. 'Time for a cup of tea.' She moved to the stove to put the kettle on then sat down at the table in the breakfast room. She had done the washing and made the evening meal, stew of left-overs big enough to feed all the family if they came home for dinner.

Her husband, Roy, was in, working in his office getting ready for Monday's business appointments. Janet and Philip were out with their friends and Linda was somewhere on her motorbike. She was the traveller in the family and Dulcie wondered, for the hundredth time, where she got the travel bug from.

Pouring the hot water on the tea leaves in the pot she continued that train of thought. 'She certainly doesn't get it from me: I've never been out of England. I had a few holidays around this country in the car with Roy and the family when they were small and that's all.'

Roy had only been overseas with the RAF during the war, training in Canada then stationed in Egypt for a while.

She remembered, with a shudder, how she had nearly lost him when his plane was shot down but luckily he had survived and come home. Marrying immediately he settled easily and didn't want any more adventures. Linda was the adventuress, often going on the Continent with her motorcycle friends.

Sipping her tea, Dulcie thought about how boring her life must appear to her daughter. Working as a shorthand typist during the week and just doing housework at the weekend in their suburban home. It was a nice house, old fashioned semi-detached three stories high with a large garden, having a vegetable patch and an orchard.

She had friends at work, played a bit of badminton and she and Roy enjoyed wine tasting with the local wine society. A trip to the movies in London occasionally or to the museum and art galleries there and maybe a drive in the Surrey countryside. What more could a 45-year-old want? She had a slim, diminutive form (5 foot), was in good health and her dark brown, curly hair was only just becoming streaked with grey.

Aha! Sounds of life in the hall and then Linda, in her motorcycle gear, burst through the breakfast room door followed by two young men, likewise attired. Dulcie didn't recognise them.

'Hi Mum,' Linda said, smiling widely. 'I'm home. These two guys are Jean and Pierre - they're French and I found them at the roadside. They had just fixed a puncture and were on their way to Dover, but now it's too late for them to catch their ferry and they need somewhere to stay for the night.'

Dulcie looked at the two young men, lean and handsome with dark hair and a very French style. The taller of the two stepped forward and put out his hand.

'Bonjour, Madame.'

His flashing brown eyes looked into hers.

Dulcie put out her hand.

'Hello and welcome,' she said, stepping forward for a hand shake.

However, the young man took her hand and brought it to his lips. 'Enchante, Madam,' he said softly.

Linda was fidgeting impatiently.

'Mum, they can stay, can't they?'

Dulcie felt herself blushing and at once drawn into the world of international friendship that her daughter so easily inhabited. For that moment she shed her urban housewife aura and became an English Lady.

Turning gracefully to her expectant daughter she replied regally,

'Of course.'

Hiroshima II

During my early childhood, whenever Dad took us out for a family drive, I was fascinated with how he changed gear, accelerated and braked and I was always leaning over Mum's shoulder, firing questions at Dad, as she sat in the front passenger seat. I couldn't wait until I was old enough to drive and own my own car. I was keen to be out exploring our country.

When I was sixteen, still at school and studying for GCEs Dad found a wrecked Bond Minicar for £25. I had been diligently saving my pocket money, had a book full of 2/6d Post Office saving stamps and eagerly cashed them in to purchase this wonder.

It looked as if it had gone under the back of a lorry and, as I later found out how bad the brakes were, it probably had. The windscreen was smashed and flattened, there were holes in the wings where the mirrors had been ripped out and other various dents but, on the whole the body was good and the 197 Villiers two stroke engine was healthy. There was one wheel at the front on which the engine was mounted and two wheels at the back. Just one bench seat and a space behind for luggage and the battery.

This possession provided a whole new learning curve for me in crash repairs and maintenance. Firstly we located another windscreen. Then out came the fiberglass for patching and the technique of using wet and dry paper to rub down the paintwork. In between swotting for exams, I was in the garage patching and painting my prized possession with Dad as my able instructor. The car was given coats of rust preventer, undercoat and two shiny top coats, all brush-applied but with such fanatical preparation that it look spray-painted. The main body was black, the wings red with yellow beading. The piece de resistance was a white skull and crossbones on the bonnet and two white ban the bomb signs on the rear. It was the time of the ban the bomb marches and although I did not actually attend them myself I was a supporter and the car was named Hiroshima II.

As it did not have reverse it only required a motorcycle license to drive for which I could apply at age 16 so, with L plates attached I started driving lessons with my brave father.

To start the engine I had to pull a lever inside the car which was attached to the engine, mounted on the front wheel and acted like a kick starter. It needed a strong left arm to pull and could give a healthy kick back. It also was a reluctant starter. The gear change was column mounted and it had three gears. The brakes were in the usual position on the floor next to the clutch but they were drum brakes connected by rods which tended to bend and were therefore not very effective.

My father was a very patient teacher and gave many lessons to me and my best school friend, Lynn Fillmore, who was also anxious to learn. Finally he deemed me proficient enough to take the test so off we went to the testing station. The examiner took a horrified look at the car and reluctantly climbed into the passenger bench seat beside me. I pulled and pulled on the starter lever but the car refused to start. The examiner gladly climbed out and said I would have to reschedule a test as he couldn't waste any more time. So, three weeks later I tried again and fortunately Hiroshima started and I passed. Hooray! At last I was free to roam the roads.

I learnt how to de-coke the engine, mix the two stroke fuel and how to drive in all conditions. She had a retractable hood but no side panels or heater so a hat, thick coat and gloves were regular winter outfits.

    This brave little car took Lynn and me all round Cornwall during school holidays and drove us up to Biggin Hill where we joined the *Saltbox MCC* and I became involved with motorcycling, after all I already had the license to ride one. I had to take another test for a car licence which I did when I later bought a Morris Minor convertible.

    Hiroshima, however, was my entry into the world of travel and will always be remembered with fondness along with my brave, patient father.

Birthdays I Will Always Remember (7th and 21st)
(or, If you're going to get older you may as well have fun doing it)

My very first birthday recollection was, I think, of my 7th. We lived near Ruislip, Middlesex and my cousins and local childhood friends were invited. I was wearing my best dress, a little yellow chiffon number with puffed sleeves, a fitted bodice and full skirt. However this feminine appearance was belied by an unlady-like display of my knickers as I demonstrated to the guests how good I was at handstands and cartwheels. My cousin Michael, who always had to go one better than me, started his cartwheel display and in doing so, his well-shod heel connected with my forehead. Blood spurted forth – all over my yellow dress, turning it a sickly orange.

Parents panicked and I was whisked off to the nearest doctor in the family jalopy. As the wound didn't hurt too much and as it made me the centre of attention, I began to enjoy the experience and was somewhat miffed when the cut wasn't deemed deep enough for stitches. That would have made me a real hero! However, I made do with a big bandage and was looking forward to my triumphant return. But my dramatic re-entry was dampened by the scowls of my cousin who had been severely reprimanded for showing off and hurting me. Even worse, the local kids had all gone home, having eaten my favourite jellies and the fairy cakes with all the hundreds and thousands on them. So much for stardom!

The first really significant celebration was for my 21st. In those days 18th birthdays went unmarked. At the time, I was heavily involved with the motorcycling fraternity and my parents decided that to save any cultural clashes it would be more prudent to have two parties. One for family and relatives, a respectable cheese and wine affair, was held on the Friday night at our home in Sanderstead, Surrey, and on Saturday night I hired a hall in Selsdon for my more rumbunctious friends. These consisted of members of the *Saltbox MCC* (Biggin Hill, Kent) and the *Knightriders MCC* from Caterham. I had two bands, both of which contained friends of mine, and we jived, twisted, rocked and rolled to Beatles tunes until midnight. We were not particularly a drinking crowd in those days but a good time was had by all. Presents I remember from that time were a bottle of Balenciaga 'Quadrille' perfume from my parents and a slide projector.

A Permanent Reminder Of A Temporary Feeling

A Permanent Reminder of a Temporary Feeling, a song by Jimmy Buffet which describes some of the many ways that we go into something impulsively without thinking about the long term implications.

He cites a wedding in Las Vegas at the end of a fluid filled night at the pub meeting a good-looking stranger. Having a wild night and getting pregnant and many more kinds of unthinking behavior. In the case of tattoos many young people have one done when drunk and when their peers persuade them it is the thing to do. Not realizing that many prospective employers frown on them.

Tattoos remind me of my Rhodesian friend who had a small butterfly tattooed on her shoulder in the vain attempt to try and lesson the reaction that her husband would make to their daughter when he found out that she had just had a tattoo on a delicate part of her body.

I would not like to make such a commitment knowing that fashions and feelings change and it is an expensive and painful process to get them removed.

The Busker

Paddy Dougan took his cap from his head of unruly red curls and placed it on the pavement at his feet. His down-at-heel boots looked on in hope of their resurrection if the shopping crowds threw their pounds in the waiting cap.
Paddy undid his worn fiddle case and, taking the beloved instrument out, rosined up the bow and, with his nimble fingers, drew it rapidly across the strings.
As the jigs and reels filled the air his dancing, blue eyes lit up with joy and his empty belly was forgotten.

A Campfire

The sun is setting, soon to be lost between the trees. The fading light necessitates quickly foraging for fuel. Dry leaves and twigs for a start then larger limbs and lastly, a trunk or two from a fallen tree, hurriedly chopped with an axe.

Who has the matches? … Ah, here.

Eager faces huddle around as the first spark strikes. Will it take among the leaves?

A wisp of smoke follows the first tiny flame and then there is the crackle of burning twigs and, finally, the fire spreads and a warm glow ensues.

At last we can place the billy.

Manx Cat Song

Linda Bick &Traditional

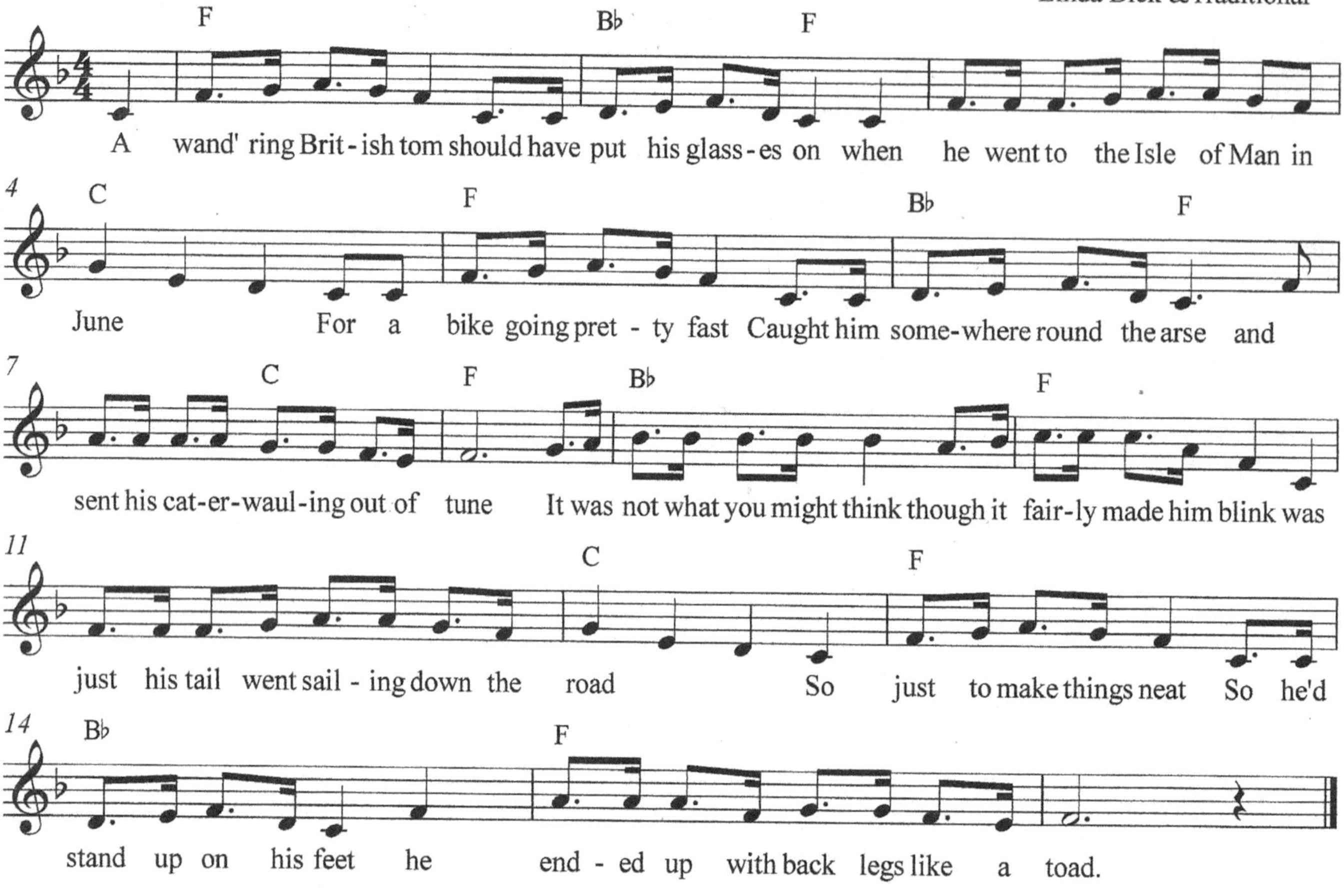
F Bb F
A wand' ring Brit - ish tom should have put his glass - es on when he went to the Isle of Man in
4 C F Bb F
June For a bike going pret - ty fast Caught him some-where round the arse and
7 C F Bb F
sent his cat-er-waul-ing out of tune It was not what you might think though it fair-ly made him blink was
11 C F
just his tail went sail - ing down the road So just to make things neat So he'd
14 Bb F
stand up on his feet he end - ed up with back legs like a toad.

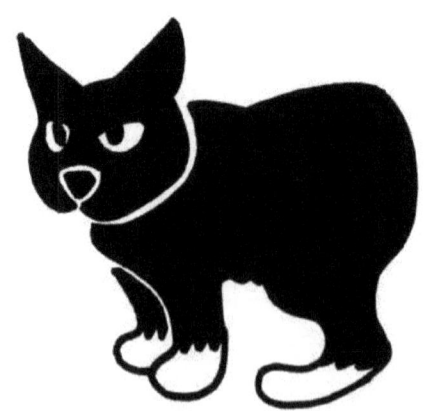

A wandering British tom should have put his glasses on
When he went to the Isle of Man in June
For a bike going pretty fast caught him somewhere round the arse
And sent his caterwauling out of tune
Twas not what you might think, though it fairly made him blink
Was just his tail went sailing down the road
So just to make things neat, so he'd land upon his feet
He ended up with back legs like a toad

The idea caught on pretty quick, people thought it rather slick
To own a cat that didn't have a tail
They put on quite a pose, started winning all the shows
And even started getting some fan mail
But every now and then the strain breaks through again
Some poor kitten finds he's got more than his share
So he holds his tail up high pointing upwards to the sky
For he knows that it's much safer way up there!

I went to the Isle of Man for the Manx Grand Prix in the 1970s and, whilst there saw the Manx Cat Museum where they explain that a strain of cats developed that didn't have full tails. I'm not sure why. However, a cat uses its tail for balance and when they didn't have one their back legs become stronger to compensate. This song is my explanation of the cause of the tail-less breed.

The Confidence of Youth

In the 1960s in the UK I belonged to the Saltbox Motorcycle Club (Biggin Hill, Kent) and many members would go to motorcycle rallies held both in the UK and on the Continent. The favourite winter rally was *The Elephant Rally* held at the Nurburgring in Germany in January when the weather was likely to be very cold with ice and snow on the roads. This meant that only true enthusiasts would attend and especially enjoy the camaraderie when finally meeting up with friends from different countries and drinking schnapps!

It was wiser to go on three wheels (motorcycle and sidecar) as the roads were likely to be slippery and therefore I had elected to go as passenger in the sidecar of one of my friends rather than take my own motorbike.

So, a group of us set off for Dover to catch the midnight ferry to Ostend. We would dock about 4am and then ride through Belgium and into Germany to reach the rally site later that day.

As we queued at customs before embarking I suddenly realised that I didn't have my passport! Usually kept in my jacket pocket I remembered, too late, that I had changed jackets. So the others boarded without me and I was left alone on the docks at midnight.

I checked at the railway station and was told that the next train to London wasn't until 6am. What to do? Well, fortunately there was a lone taxi driver parked outside a small shed where drivers waited for fares out of the cold and could make a brew. Seeing me looking lost he invited me in and offered me a cup of tea. I ended up spending all night playing cards with him and drinking tea. Desperate to go to the toilet I was too embarrassed to go out and squat behind the shed. My bladder was bursting when I finally found a toilet on the train. (It wouldn't have lasted that long now!)

I took the train to London, then one to Croydon and finally a bus home to Sanderstead. I immediately phoned the Automobile Association to get a weather report for Belgium and Germany and they said fine and the roads were clear so I wheeled my BMW out of the garage, hopped on to it and just made the midday ferry from Dover, making sure I had my passport with me.

It was a long, cold ride but I finally arrived at the rally site and enjoyed the looks of amazement on my friends' faces. There was plenty of schnapps handed round that night and it didn't take me long to fall asleep despite the sub-zero temperature.

The things we can do when we are young!

Birthdays I Will Always Remember (24th and 25th)

The next birthday I recall was my 24th, celebrated in a flat in Bondi (Australia) with my flat mates and fellow travellers Angie and Jacky Griffin, a few members of the Willoughby (Nth Sydney) MCC and a crowd of some pretty wild Kiwis (New Zealanders) one of whom had shaved his head completely for a bet. In those days it wasn't such a common thing to do and we all thought he was quite outrageous. They thought we were a bit weird too, three women with motorbikes, one of which was parked behind the sofa. I don't recall any special presents that birthday but the following year – my 25th – I decided to buy myself one – a brand new BMW R60/5 – the only new motorbike I'd ever owned.

By this time Angie, Jacky and I were in Perth (Western Australia) and mixing with the motorbike boys there. I was courting the secretary of the *WA Racing Club*, Terry Bick, and racing his Desmo Ducati, and we also had friends in the *Touring Club of WA.* Funnily enough you couldn't officially belong to both of these clubs at the same time; Road Racers and Tourers appeared to be a separate breed, but we managed to get them all together to socialise occasionally and my birthday was a good opportunity.

I was running in my bike and was anxious for a trip. We persuaded the racing mob to come with us in their ute (pick-up). This we loaded with beer and ice and headed off to Margaret River, a beautiful seaside area a few hours south of Perth. The party consisted of about a dozen of us. I was currently singing with an Irish boy (Paddy) and he and his friends were pillioned on the back of various bikes, with his guitar stowed safely in the ute for later use. Angie and Jacky were riding their own bikes and Angie's boyfriend, Geoff, was riding 2-up with a Scottish friend Andy. They had perfected the technique of swapping rider and pillion positions whilst still in motion so this was an interesting spectacle to behold, at a safe distance.

At Margaret River we set up camp on the beach and then all jumped into the back of the ute to negotiate the sandy track into town to find the local pub. There we more or less took over a private party in the lounge and entertained the stunned people by singing Irish Folk songs in the intervals between their quartet playing for ballroom dancing. We joined in that too, me tripping over Terry's feet as he tried a romantic waltz in his big motorcycle boots. When the party came to an end we made our drunken way back to the campsite and spent the next day having a hair of the dog by the sea.

During 1974 and 1975 I rode my 500cc BMW motorcycle down through Africa. The map below shows the route that I took.

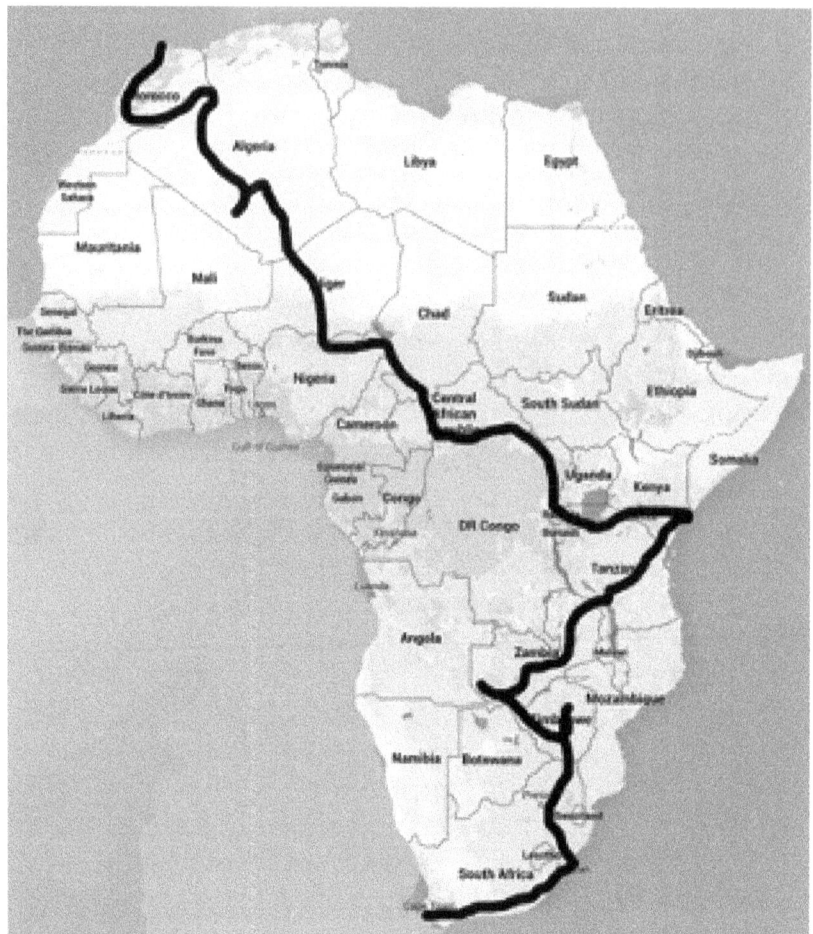

Africa

You have shown me your beauty and your turmoil.
I have been shocked by your violence and soothed by your tenderness
I have revelled in the magnificence of mountains and wide vistas of valleys, lakes, and rivers
In dense forest I glimpsed the fleeting brilliance of butterflies and heard screaming monkeys and roaring lions
I have wondered at rain-bowed waterfalls crashing into deep chasms, sunsets blazing over blood-red earth or sinking slowly into western bays
Your teeming towns and cities are alive with many-coloured people, languages, and songs
Your heart is a beating drum sending its message to the world and bewitching me

Excerpt from *Into Africa with a Smile* (Linda Bootherstone – 2015)

The air was hot and sticky, only to be expected in this tropical climate. Thick vegetation each side of the track prevented any view of the surrounding countryside; it was like riding through a never-ending tunnel of green. Hour upon hour I had been battling the rocky, potholed surface that passed for a road. For a little while I managed to pick up speed to 25 mph and then came to a halt surveying a particularly rough patch through which to pick my path.

A rustle came from the bushes and then, suddenly, a dark figure rushed out into the open, running towards me. The man was semi- naked with flashing eyes and a mop of wiry African hair. He approached waving a panga and screaming. I sat frozen, astride my heavily-laden motorcycle. On this particularly rough stretch I could not just open the throttle and go. Heart beating wildly I sat, awaiting my fate as the man came closer, gurgling unintelligible words.

As calmly as I could I fixed a broad smile on my face and thrust forward a gloved hand in a gesture of friendship, 'How do you do? My name is Linda. I'm so pleased to meet you and it's a lovely day isn't it?'

The African stopped his gesticulating with the lethal looking implement and ceased his cries. He looked at me with an expression of pure amazement then turned and disappeared into the jungle.

Shaking like a leaf I fixed my attention back onto the track ahead and gingerly began a tentative forward motion.

'What on earth am I doing here?' I asked myself.

An African Odyssey

Finding facts to start the journey
Equip the bike and say farewells
Leaving the shores of Mother England
What lies ahead no-one can tell

Morocco with its wool jelabas
Spice-filled markets, mountains high
Through the snow then down to desert
To palm trees and a star-filled sky

Sahara sand is next to battle
Corrugations do their worst
Blue-clad Tuaregs driving lorries
Help transport a bike that's bust

Leaving camels and silver crosses
Black figures now appear instead
Smiling ladies in coloured cotton
Balance baskets on their heads

In a land of changing conflicts
Fort Lamy is the place to be
Where fighting men from round the world
Give the French Foreign Legion their loyalty

Camped beside the Ubangi river
Prized possessions go astray
But heading on into the jungle
Butterflies flit and monkeys play

As rain falls down the mud gets deeper
Log bridges span the swollen streams
Each day is a constant battle
And bitumen roads are in my dreams

Are there gorillas in the mist?
In volcanic country with mountains high
Serengeti's wildlife banned for BMs
But now sealed road I can espy

At City Park the travellers gather
There's many a tale that's tall and true
With the jungle dangers now behind
It's southward to adventures new

Mt Kenya conquered, the east coast beckons
Coral reefs and graceful dhows
Pole Pole is a haven
But there malaria lays me low

Meershaum pipes in Tanzania
Then elephants and a copper mine
Lusaka police are causing trouble
But I escape without a fine

Between black and white the border runs
The smoke that thunders so they say
Uneasy peace on either side
While rainbows shine amidst the spray

At last Rhodesia smiles a welcome
Southern Africa a change indeed
A broken valve then halts the progress
But soon is fixed by friends in need

A job at last but not for long
With BM fixed I take the road
To find the city of gold and diamonds
And to its portals I am towed!

Durban dazzles with its friendships
Pilot boats and breakfast runs
BM rebuilt, I leave with sadness
To forsake the laughs and fun

Can I now shout at the devil?
As my trip is near its end
Like an ostrich ignore the future
And put my head down in the sand

Table Mountain shouts the message
A ship awaits me at the quay
Now time to bid Africa adieu
Will I return another day?

Birthdays I Will Always Remember (29th, 30th and 31st)

The next birthday of note was my 29th, spent in Durban, South Africa, after I had completed my Trans-Africa trip. I was staying with some Saltbox MCC members, including Les Fleming, who were renting a beautiful house in a very posh suburb. Mike Hailwood (World Champion Motorcycle Racer) lived just up the road. One of our rich neighbours who had a swimming pool, found that my birthday and her husband's coincided so we had a joint party at their place. It was the first time I had seen floating candles in a pool, and, with November being a warm month, the evening was balmy and we had a Braaivleis (BBQ) on the patio. To complete the ambience there was a row of beautifully gleaming, vintage bikes parked on the immaculate lawn, as her husband and his friends were avid collectors. I had prudently left my tatty, rusting BMW at home!

As a complete contrast, my 30th birthday was a complete flop. Back in Blighty, I was living with my South African boyfriend, Devon, in a pokey bedsit in Balham (Gateway to the South). November in the UK is horrible, cold, damp and fog-ridden. The heating system in the flat relied on a 10p meter and we were always running out of coins. I didn't have many close friends in that area and the only one I knew, Don Dew of Tridon Spares, came round to this grotty flat with a bottle of wine which we shared in the depressing surroundings, trying to be jolly. Devon gave me a steam iron for my birthday present and I nearly flattened him with it. Its amazing the relationship lasted as long as it did.

However, the next year, my 31st, made up for this lapse. By this time I was out of Britain and back in Africa. Leaving the dreaded Devon behind in Cape Town, I had ridden the BMW up to Windhoek, Namibia, and made some good new friends there. I was sharing a flat with Peter Murphy, another Africa overlander, and we invited everyone we knew in Windhoek and Swakopmund to the party. I must admit I was a bit naughty and told everyone I was 21. I'm not sure if they believed me but I received some great presents. The ones I remember were some Fenjal Jasmine Bath Oil (very necessary in the ultra-dry climate) and a German Black Forest cake. There were many different people at the party and some had travelled quite a long way and became too drunk to drive home. I woke up to find my double-bed full of bodies squashed together like pickled sardines. The Black Forest cake, especially saved for Sunday lunch, ended up being splattered all over my face when I tripped while carrying it into the lounge. A hilarious photo session ensued, with more people being anointed with chocolate and cream.

Easter in Namibia (1977)

'And don't, for goodness sake, forget the Guinness!'

Isn't it amazing how it takes as long to pack for four days as it does for six months, especially if you are heading into the desert.

We were leaving the teeming metropolis (one main street) of Windhoek, capitol of South West Africa, (now known as Namibia) for the Easter weekend to tour as much as possible of the surrounding countryside. There were four of us, two boys, Devon and Peter and two girls, myself and Pat.

The vehicle we were using was Pete's 1964 long wheel-based Landrover that had already proved itself by doing the overland trip from England through to South Africa. Pete said if you looked closely you could see the bullet holes from the dash through Angola when the fighting was on in 1975.

On Thursday night, having stowed the precious Guinness carefully at the bottom of our huge pile of luggage, we filled up with diesel and water and headed off towards Karibib, about 100 miles away. The road is tarred and not very interesting as the land is flat and dry with little vegetation, only a few tsummas on the side of the road. These are sneaky little plants bearing fruit which looks and smells like melon but which are so bitter they are impossible to eat and even the Bushmen leave them as a last resort for water.

The local pub at Karibib was alive with locals and people travelling through for the weekend. We met up with some friends and spent the evening entertaining the public with guitars and banjos and much singing.

Next morning we carried on westward for about 50 miles and then turned off toward the towering peak of Spitzkop, standing up like a dog tooth on the flat horizon. It is a popular climbing area but very treacherous because the rock is crumbly and quite a few climbers have been trapped when they have lost their footholds. Not being experts we just pottered around the foot-slopes taking pictures. It was a lovely area- the sandy coloured mountain contrasting well against the blue sky and a few trees for shade under which we made a cow dung fire to prepare our lunch. Tea and hot cross buns.

Leaving Spitzcop behind, we drove on for the coast. As there is an almost perpetual sea mist on that part of the coast we were rapidly donning clothes and the change from shorts and T-shirts to jeans and jumpers was accomplished by the time we reached Cape Cross where the Portuguese explorer Diego Cao originally landed. There is a large seal colony which is interesting to watch but a bit smelly.

We headed north up into the area which is known as the Skeleton Coast. The title is actually given because of the skeleton formation of the coastline which makes it difficult to navigate, thus forming a natural barrier for diamond thieves approaching from the sea. However, the name is also appropriate because of the number of seal skeletons scattered on the beach. It is a natural graveyard for the thousands of seals that have finished their life-span. There is no vegetation or fresh water for miles inland and any trespassers who escaped death by shipwreck on the treacherous reefs would not survive long on shore. There were plenty of wrecks in the area and the sea mist made the place chill and foreboding.

We were glad to find some of our friends from the *Anglo Mining Company* camping along the shore-line. It was cold, damp and windy but the company was good and, after we put up our tents and got the stove on the go, we settled into a bottle or two of the Guinness. This, I may add, had been especially railed up from Cape Town, 1000 miles away.

The BBQ was made by digging a trench in the sand, putting driftwood inside and burning it down to coals. One of the girls made some batter and was deep-frying the cockles they had collected during the day – delicious! Despite the howling wind and bleak grey sand, which wasn't conducive to anchoring tent pegs, we all managed a good night's sleep.

After a quick look at some of the more accessible wrecks we headed inland, out of the mist toward the Brandberg mountains. These mountains form a ring, similar, I thought, to Wilpena Pound in South Australia. They are not very high and provide some good walks as well as more serious climbing. They are also the home of *The White Lady*, a bushman rock painting that has been the subject of speculation since it was discovered in 1918. The figure is larger than the surrounding ones and the lower part of the body is white. There are some theories that it could have been a visitor from another race or planet, but nothing has been satisfactorily explained.

Since we didn't reach the mountain until the evening and camped as the last rays of the sun were disappearing in a thundery looking sky, we just had a quiet night by the campfire and set out to see the *White Lady* the next morning.

The rock paintings took about half-an-hour's walk to find and were surrounded by a metal frame to stop people touching them and wearing away the paint. We signed the visitors' book that was chained to the fence and came away with no better ideas as to the painting's origin than the experts.

Our lunch of pickled fish and cabbage was rather rushed as we had many more miles to cover to find the *Petrified Forest*. This we found well marked on the tourist map but with hardly any signposts on the road. There were some really good specimens of petrified trees and, also in the area, some of the strange Welchitchia. This is a unique plant, the only one of its genus which is found only in the north of Namibia and southern Angola. It can a grow a body of up to two metres in height and, at first glance, seems to be surrounded by a mass of narrow leaves. In fact there are only two leaves but, in time and the desert wind, they have been shredded into ribbons which can be two metres long. The plant looks as ancient as it is; some of the plants still living today date back to the birth of Christ. The age of some young ones has been accurately fixed at five to six hundred years.

The area was fascinating but we still had some miles to go to a deserted farm, Twyfelfontain, known for its rock paintings and engravings. We were now in Damaraland and the roads had deteriorated to gravel. When we took the turning off toward the farm we found ourselves driving along a sandy track through dry creek beds. The sun was setting and the colours of the red soil highlighted by the golden rays were set off against the deep shadows and the black sky. There are many electrical storms and threatening skies at this time of year but the rains have passed and it is rare that any storm breaks.

Again we were late camping, in a sandy river bed, and I may add that there was such a strong wind blowing along the creek that my tent fell down twice during supper but, after anchoring it with a few very hard to find stones, it stayed up for the night.

Goodness, it was Monday already. We had to be back in Windhoek that night and we had 600 miles to do plus quite a few more things to see. The farmhouse, deserted for 25 years because of drought had not much to offer but a pile of empty beer cans deposited by less thoughtful tourists.

We quickly checked out the farmer's gravity-feed water system by following the pipe up the hill behind the house. The farmhouse looked tiny in the valley and the surrounding hills seemed to protect it. A pity the weather wasn't kinder to a family who must have worked so hard before having to give up.

Not having much time we had to leave searching for the rock engravings and followed a signpost leading to the *Burnt Mountain*. This is another mystery to scientists and visitors. It is a relatively small hill of 200mtres. In fact it looks like a slag heap of charred stones and ashes. The formation is completely different from the surrounding hills, it's crudely shaped red rocks inexplicably streaked with vivid areas of black, white and grey. Just a little further along was a dry river bed with steep sides, like a small gorge and, for a few hundred yards, the rock was of a tubular, vertical formation that give it the name of *The Organ Pipes*. There was a tree growing close to the rocky sides and we traced its roots up the rock face to where they ended, its search for water two feet higher than the tree itself.

We had to leave as time was marching on towards noon. Oh, to have four weeks to explore instead of just four days! Half way home we drove past a range of hills so weathered that they were standing like pedestals, one so narrow and pointed it was called the *Fingerklip*.

By afternoon tea time we had all had enough of the mad dash for home and got out to stretch our legs and have some tea and sandwiches on the verandah of a quaint country town hotel. The last tourist attraction on our route was just a few miles down the road and certainly took some finding. At a tiny hand-painted sign we turned left along a narrow grassy track. We were now in much wetter country with grass and grey rather than red soil. This fact was made more obvious by the giant grey anthills.

At the end of the track we had to park the Landrover and started walking, over a little running stream – a very rare sight in SWA – and across some expanses of flat stone, gently sloping downhill with a trickle of water on them. We were following a white, dotted line painted on the rock and eventually found what we were looking for – the *Dinosaurs Footprints*. These were surprising small, only about 12" long and 8" wide and shaped rather like a maple leaf. The ground had obviously originally been mud and the foot-prints were clearly marked. About a dozen of them headed off down the slope and into the grass. We were amazed. After close inspection we unanimously agreed that they couldn't have been faked. Whatever the type of dinosaur they were definitely footprints, genuinely formed.

With a last awe-filled look, we wandered back to the Landrover and set out on the last leg of the journey, arriving at Windhoek well after dark and feeling very tired but satisfied that we had made the most of our four-day holiday.

The most impressive thing about the whole trip was that all the tourist attractions were not commercialised in any way. Indeed, had it not been for the instructions and maps from the Tourist Bureau in Windhoek, we would have been hard-pressed to find them. It is a credit to the SWA government and tourist industry that there aren't any little men on a gate holding out their palms to be crossed with silver before you can view these things. Also there are no ice-cream kiosks or organised camping areas so you have to bring your own supplies making you more aware of the isolation and life in the bush.

There is much more to be seen in the dramatic and colourful land of Namibia. I did some other trips during my year there and was equally impressed. I hope that, despite political difficulties, the land will always remain accessible for all people to explore and admire.

NOTE:
This article was written in the late 1970s, I'm sure things have changed considerably since then.

A Not So Fast Woman

In 1969, while living in Sydney, I met Sandra Davis who rode a 350cc Yamaha. She, her sister, and I entered a road safety competition and won awards, one of which was donated by Ryan's Motorcycles, in Parramatta. Not long after this Sandra brought my attention to a race-meeting at Oran Park circuit which included a women's race the *Powder Puff Derby*.

'Why don't we enter?' she asked.

'But I have never raced and have only my old BMW,' I protested.

However, a chat to Ryan's Motorcycles produced a 250 Suzuki. I applied for a racing licence and we entered the race.

On the day there were about ten entries by women on various sized machines. The hot favourite to win was Peggy Hyde on her 500cc Kawasaki, already a racing legend.

With only a few laps practice on the Suzuki I was pretty nervous but, when the race began, I just chased Sandra - Peggy was well ahead but Sandra and I were in second and third place, the commentator getting excited at our close positions. With her extra 100cc Sandra outran me on the straights but I caught up on every bend and finished very close behind her at the end of the race.

As it happens the reason that I was going so fast into the bends was the fact that my throttle was jamming (apparently the Teflon slide didn't like the damp conditions) and I was frantically trying to close it while using the brakes for all they were worth.

I did not race again in Sydney but when I went to live in Perth I was introduced to Terry Bick, the secretary of the *WA Racing Club* and he, impressed by my previous racing experience, was happy to lend me his 250 Ducati to race at Wanneroo Park. This was a fast racing-bike and I was terrified each time my boot scraped the ground on corners.

As there were many different sized bikes and levels of skill the races were usually 'handicapped'. This meant that the slowest rider went off first and the others spaced out according to their lap times, previously recorded during practice. I did actually win one race in this fashion.

I later bought my own 250 Yamaha to race there and on some of the 'round the houses' circuits. These were in small country towns such as Kattaning and Collie where we mapped out a course using hay bales to block entering roads. Some of the pedestrians and dogs didn't always realise the races were on and would walk out on the track causing some hairy moments. There were three other women racing at this time and we all had a great day out at the circuits, racing with the men and enjoying sharing the kegs of beer at the end of the meetings.

Terry recently reminded me of an incident at one of these meetings at Kellerberin. There were about 18 competitors lined up at the start in three rows of six. I was positioned in the front row on the far left and was riding Terry's Ducati. Like all the other bikes this needed a racing bump start.

When the flag dropped I ran forward, pushing the bike, but when I jumped aboard I lost my balance, the bike fell to the right and the rest of the line of riders went down like nine-pins. There was chaos as the later rows tried to miss the fallen bikes.

Terry rushed over to help me and the other riders pick up our machines. He was laughing fit to bust while I was red with embarrassment. The race was restarted and I finished well down in the field, feeling very ashamed. However, Terry assured me that it was great entertainment for the crowd and I was forgiven.

Not long after this, I left Australia for a few years and my next attempt at racing was when I returned in the late 1970s and was given a chance to enter a vintage and veteran race at Mallalla circuit, South Australia. My friend, Andy Scott, had a 350cc Matchless which was easy to ride and he said he would bring it up from Mt Gambier on the day, so I renewed my racing licence, dug out my leathers and bought a new helmet.

When I met Andy at Mallalla I was horrified to see that, instead of the harmless Matchless, he had brought a BSA Gold Star in full racing trim with clip-ons and rear sets, not at all set up for me!

However, off I went for practice, finding that with my smaller foot my toes didn't reach the gear change lever and I had to move my foot forward off the peg, and change with my heel. During practice I felt there was something wrong with the clutch and we used the time before the race to investigate but couldn't find the fault.

When the race started, being the only woman I felt very conspicuous and, as the race progressed, was horrified to find I had no drive for engine braking and was going into the bend practically in neutral so I had to retire. It turned out that the cush drive had failed.

Well that was my last attempt at road racing. I am glad that I had the opportunity to try but am quite happy to be an international tourer instead.

The Community Arts Team (CAT)

The official description of the *Community Arts Team* was:

'CAT is a four-member team of multi-skilled people who, by working in workshop situations with adults and children introduce them to creative skills, whilst exploring themes that are relevant to the community. For many isolated communities CAT is the only group that provides multi-art workshop activities.'

In 1980 I was living in Adelaide, South Australia, and working as a driver for *Pacific Films*. I had just bought my own house, had a regular boyfriend, was on the committee of the local folk club and had recently formed the Australian division of the *Women's International Motorcycle Association* (WIMA). So, I had a pretty settled lifestyle.

However, I had heard about this team of touring artists and was also advised that one of the women members was leaving and they were looking for a replacement. So, I went for an interview and, much to my surprise was chosen. I think it was for my singing and songwriting skills as, unlike the other members, I had no teaching certificate or experience working with children.

The team was leaving in two weeks' time for a tour on the West Coast and they wanted me to join them. I hurriedly gave very short notice to *Pacific Films* and, at the appointed time, jumped into the Cat Van (an old Ford Transit) with three other people that I hardly knew and many instruments and props for the three-week tour. Talk about thrown in the deep end! However, this began a three-year experience involving many tours in the outback in small isolated, one-teacher schools, area schools and aboriginal reserves. When working with aborigines we were fortunate enough to be shown many places that were connected with Dreamtime legends. We mainly worked in South Australia but also did tours in the Northern Territory and, one time, spent six weeks in Portland, Victoria working with schools to celebrate the sesquicentenary of that area.

The pay was pitiful and we were billeted in the community or slept in the schools whilst on tour.

My time with CAT proved to be the best education I could get in working in schools and meeting diverse people and proved to be the basis for many other shows that I did in later life. It also honed my songwriting skills. I will be eternally grateful to those early members of the team who selected me.

Following is a selection of some of the songs we wrote while on tours and published in the song book *Cat Among the Gum Trees* with an accompanying audio tape.

The team at that time, as illustrated opposite comprised Julie Mann, Rick Petersen, Cate Burke, and myself, Linda Bick.

The goat's name is Sunny Jim.

Illustrations in the songbook are by Cate Burke.

CAT AMONG THE GUM TREES

Paddle Steamer Come Home (1980)

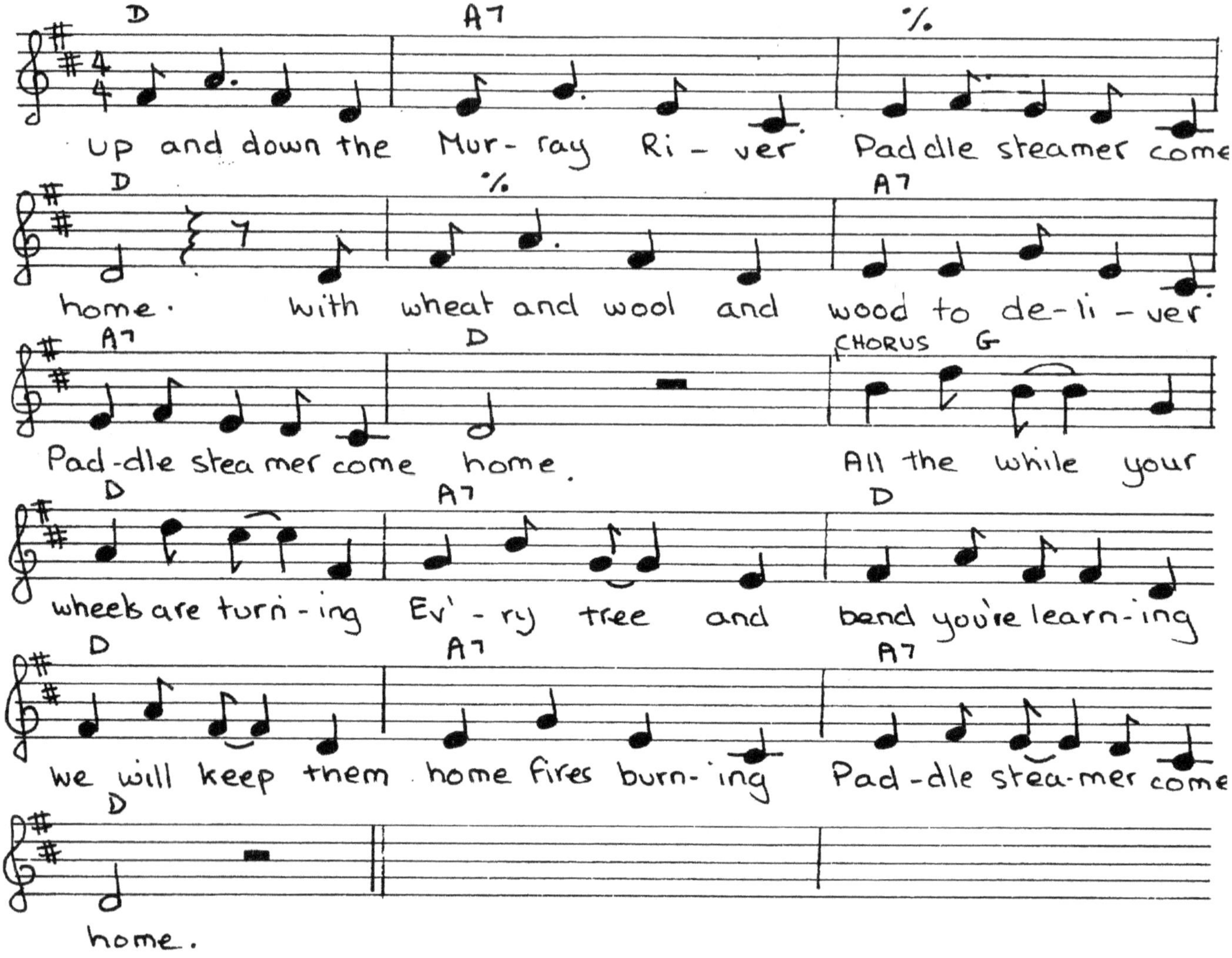
D A7 %
Up and down the Mur-ray Ri-ver Paddle steamer come
D % A7
home. With wheat and wool and wood to de-li-ver
A7 D CHORUS G
Pad-dle stea-mer come home. All the while your
D A7 D
wheels are turn-ing Ev'-ry tree and bend you're learn-ing
D A7 A7
we will keep them home fires burn-ing Pad-dle stea-mer come
D
home.

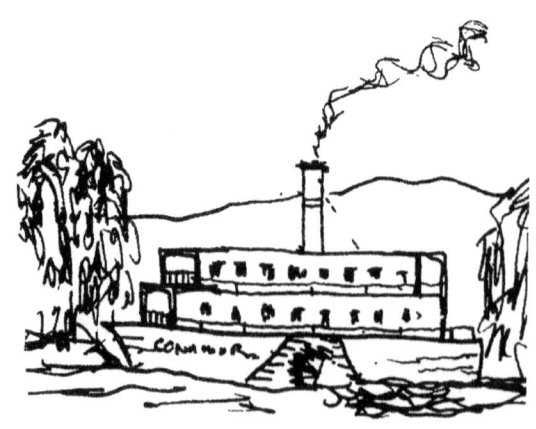

Up and down the Murray River
Paddle steamer come home
With wheat and wool and wood to deliver
Paddle steamer come home

Chorus
All the while your wheels are turning
Every tree and bend you're learning
We will keep them home fires burning
Paddle steamer come home

Out of of Mannum you will wander
Paddle steamer come home
Past Swan Reach, Morgan and Mildura
Paddle steamer come home

Chorus

You'll race the other for first landing
Paddle steamer come home
With pressure up you'll leave 'em standing
Paddle steamer come home

Chorus

Now no more your boiler's steaming
Paddle steamer come home
You lay in dry dock lazily dreaming
Paddle steamer come home
Of the times your wheels were turning
Every tree and bend you were learning
We'll keep them home fires burning
Paddle steamer you're home

Paddle Steamer Come Home was originally written for a song competition at Mannum in 1980. This song came in very handy for *River Craft* in Mildura in 1981. CAT were the shore team based on a riverboat performing at community clubs, kindergartens and schools. On the final day a model paddle steamer was 'launched' attached to some helium balloons and was later found by a farmer at Balranald... and came home.

Penong Song (1981)

Chorus
Why don't you come along to old Penong
When the wind is blowing high
You'll see them sails with dusty tails
Turning in the sky
If you can't sleep, well don't count sheep
Cos that's a waste of time
But the windmills there that ain't so rare
They're a dozen for a dime

The Nullarbor Plain just ain't the same
Since they tarred the road
But I guess it's for the best
When carrying a load
The truckies agree they'ed rather see
The tar than flaming dirt
For away they go, the tyres don't blow
And nobody gets hurt

Chorus

Ceduna's tanks just draw a blank
When it comes to Penong town
Our water's fine, it's just sublime
You keep on drilling down
With just a shower or old wind power
We keep the town alive
Folks of the west, some of the best
They know how to survive

Chorus

This is a fun song about the one thing that Penong has a lot of – windmills!

Space Bus Shuttle (1981)

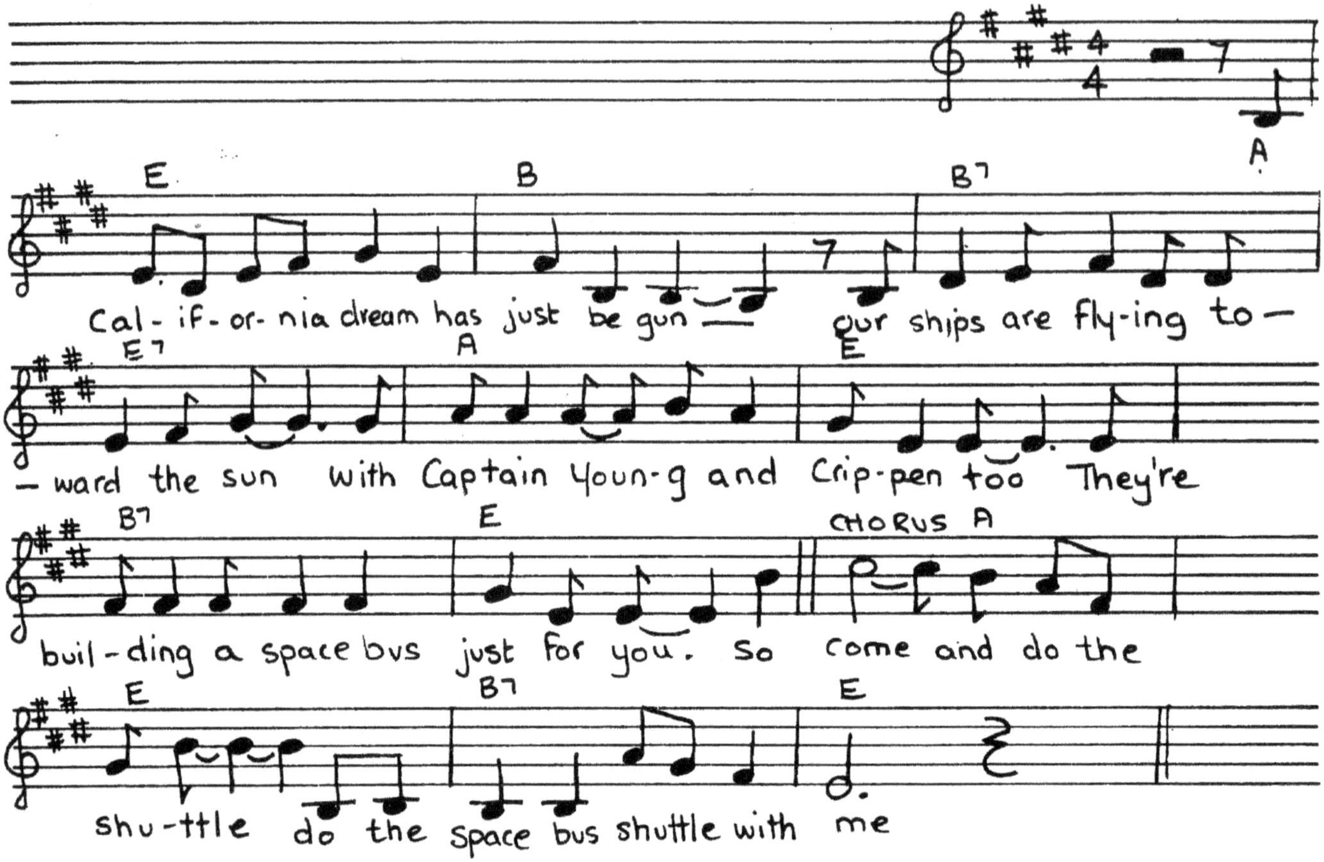
A
E B B7
Cal-if-or-nia dream has just be gun our ships are fly-ing to-
E7 A E
-ward the sun with Captain Youn-g and Crip-pen too They're
B7 E CHORUS A
buil-ding a space bus just for you. So come and do the
E B7 E
shu-ttle do the space bus shuttle with me

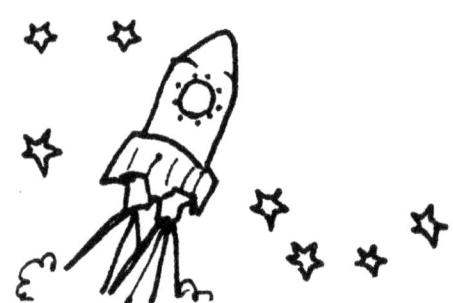

A California dream has just begun
Our ships are flying toward the sun
With Captain Young and Crippin too
They're building a space bus just for you

Chorus
So come and do the shuttle
Do the space bus shuttle with me

A light glimmers brightly in the sky
We know it's Columbia flying by
With boosters bright she left the ground
For fifty four hours she's flying around

Chorus

The time has come for her return
With fingers crossed we stand and yearn
To see our heroes safe and well
Hooray for Columbia The Southern Belle

Chorus

How sweet she glides down to the ground
The people cheer for miles around
For back to earth she found her way
And lives to fly another day

Chorus – Twice

CAT were on the West Coast at the time of the Space Shuttle launch. Donald May at Nunjikompita was a keen fan of the project and wanted to have a song written to commemorate the event. Thanks for the inspiration Donald.

Lady of the West Coast (1981)

Lady of the West Coast, town of sun and sea
By your sparkling waters lazing dreamily
Just by chance I found you, though I'd oft times passed you by
Saw a streak of silver beneath a bright blue sky

Rest for the weary traveller with many miles ahead
You break the long, hard journey with shelter and a bed
For the east-west road is lonely and the townships they are few
And seldom smiles along the way a lady such as you

Lady of the West Coast, your courtiers gather near
The farmers bring their children so that they may share
The laughter in your schoolyard, your fields of sport and play
See the sunset on the jetty at the closing of each day

Ceduna, town of sadness, Ceduna, town of joy
Your lovely heart is growing with the folk that you employ
But never lose your beauty and never lose your grace
Please remain the Lady with a smile upon her face

Ceduna is a main overnight stop on the road from Adelaide to Perth. CAT worked there for *Come-Out '81* and for the first time had the chance to really know the town. The song is a tribute to Ceduna, it's people and those from neighbouring areas.

The 1,000-Legged Worm (1981)

Said the thousand-legged worm as he gave a squirmy squirm
Has anybody seen a leg of mine
If it can't be found, I'll just have to hop around
On the other nine hundred, ninety nine
Hop around, hop around, on the other nine hundred, ninety nine
If it can't be found, I'll just have to hop around
On the other nine hundred, ninety nine

Said the spider to the fly, as he came buzzing by
Won't you please drop in and see this web of mine
If you stay to lunch, I've a kinda hunch
You'll be here for a very long time
You'll be here, you'll be here, you'll be here for a very long time
If you stay for lunch, I've a kinda hunch,
You'll be here for a very long time

Said the pretty butterfly as she fluttered to the sky
I really have a very busy day
All the flowers, you see, need a visit from me
And I have about a hundred eggs to lay
Eggs to lay, eggs to lay, yes, I have about a hundred eggs to lay
All the flowers, you see, need a visit from me
And I have about a hundred eggs to lay

The first verse was inspired by a snippet of a Canadian song I heard about a 1,000-legged worm who had lost a leg. We used this song as a music and movement exercise and found it a fun game for adults and children alike.

Kitty Cat (1981 – Bick/Petersen)

Kitty cat, kitty cat, what are you looking at
Kitty cat, kitty cat, what do you see?
I see a Mummy sheep and a baa lamb too
And I've asked if she will play with me

Baa said the lamb, baa, baa, baa
Mum says I can play but I can't go far
We can go to the wood if we're very good
But she says that we can't go too far

Kitty cat and Baa lamb, what are you looking at
Kitty cat and Baa lamb, what's all the fuss?
We see a kangaroo and a joey too
And we've asked if he can play with us

Hop went the joey, hop, hop, hop
Mum says I can play while she goes to the shop
While I'm out of her pouch there's so much she can hold
But we must be home again before it gets too cold

Kitty cat and Baa lamb and Joey played together
They saw a bird flying in the sky
Won't you come and play with us they called to him
But he laughed at them as he flew by

Tweet, went the bird, tweet, tweet, tweet
It's nice of you to ask but I'm hopeless on my feet
I'd really rather fly way up in the sky
But I'm glad we had the chance to meet

September '81 saw CAT working with kindergartens in Port Augusta and for each kindergarten we wrote a song to compliment their short performances. This song was for Quorn Kindergarten and is about baby animals.

Portland Whaler (1981)

Called by the sea to follow the whale
Through storm and calm and sickening swell
Back to the bay to be safe once again
And lie in the arms of my Mary

High the waves ride by our flimsy craft
Like tiny arrows our harpoons dart
How small our cries sound lost in the wind
So far away from my Mary

But a man must live and earn his bread
To raise his family, build his home
And so many hardships lie ahead
In this land I have now made my own

Many's the bones lie in Portland Bay
Of whale or mariner losing the day
And the time may come when I go the same way
And say farewell to my Mary

But a man must live and earn his bread
To raise his family, build his home
And so many hardships lie ahead
In this land I have now made my own

Many's the bones lie in Portland Bay
Of whale or mariner losing the day
And the time may come when I go the same way
And say farewell to my Mary

Portland was the first settled place in Victoria, when Henty landed in 1834 with his Merino sheep. However, before he arrived William Dutton had his whaling station already established. It was a hard life, especially in the long cold winters, as CAT found out when they worked there in June 1981. This song was written for a performance by *Portland South Primary School* during the sesquicentenary.

Note: I have used this song for other whaling operations in southern Australia.

Callana Gold (1981)

Chorus
There where the mountain goat skips to the hills
There where the sheep and the cattle roam free
Through dry, dusty summer and cold, frosty winter
Out west of Callana the gold calls to me

Each pan is inviting, it's promise exciting
We'll seive and we'll sluice there all through the long day
With pick and with shovel we'll dig and we'll grovel
For now the gold fever is with us to stay

Chorus

With heartbreak and hope our constant companions
We'll dig as our sweat drips down from our brow
Each inch of the claim turns under our shovel
The seam's nearly done but we can't leave it now

Chorus

And when the seam's done, we'll lay down our shovels
And head for the bright lights of Adelaide town
Our memories are safe with the gold in our pockets
Each smile and each joke, each tear and each frown

Chorus

Maureen and Barry Wright are well known in the Riverland for their *Murray River Charts*. However, they also had a gold claim in an isolated spot near Callana. While CAT were working at Marree School we had the oportunity to visit them and pan some gold for ourselves. It was a rewarding experience, although not in the monetary sense. This song is dedicated to them, and all hopeful prospectors. Maureen and Barry now live in Burra, South Australia.

Tennant Creek (1982)

Chorus
Tennant, Tennant, Tennant Creek
We only stayed there for a week
But we found life was oh so sweet
in Tennant, Tennant, Tennant Creek

The pirate out at Kagaru
He stole our van and treasure too
We all set out to track him down
And ran that villain out of town

Chorus

We went to Pebbles for to see
If we could find some space debris
The Martians must have lost their way
And thought that they would stay a day

Chorus

At Warrego there underground
There's big strong miners to be found
They live on steak and eggs and mustard
And great big bowls of spaghetti custard

Chorus

Out at the dam it has been seen
A monster, slimy, small and green
For those who don't believe their eyes
It's Leon Steele there in disguise

Chorus – twice

In January 1982 CAT went to the Northern Territory to do some holiday programs at Tennant Creek, Warrego and Elliot. Though hot and sultry we had a most enjoyable time and as told in the song had many adventures.

Arkaroo (1981)

He comes down through the valley
To the shores of old Lake Frome
Leaves behind mountain ridgetops
The Gammon Ranges are his home
He drinks deep of the water
Leaves the lake a dry salt pan
Then returns to the hillside
The best way that he can

Chorus
Arkaroo, Dreamtime serpent
We follow now your track
Each waterhole a symbol
Of your long, hard journey back
Arkaroo, may your legend
For evermore be told
But your people keep their secrets
As the mountains keep their gold

He lays down in the flowers
His bloated body weak
At Nooldoonooldoona waterhole
The Dreamtime warriors meet
They roll rocks down the hillside
To stop his slow return
But he trundles up the valley
To reach his native home

Chorus

The Adnyamathana Tribe in the Flinders Ranges have a legend about the Dreamtime serpent Arkaroo. He came down from the Gammon Ranges to drink at Lake Frome, thus leaving it the dry salt pan we know. Having drunk so much he needed to go to the toilet on his return journey and wherever he stopped to relieve himself there is now a waterhole.

The CAT Van (1982)

The CAT van sure has travelled around
It's been in and out of many a town
Through heat and dust, drought and flood
It takes us on our way

Chorus
In the CAT van, in the CAT van
We ride along in the CAT van
In the CAT van, in the CAT van
Just another few miles in the CAT van

We've been to the South, way up to the North
Both East and West we've set our course
Over highways smooth or bumpy track
It takes us on our way

Chorus

There's a smiling face in every place
A room to unpack the old suitcase
There's many a friend we've made for life
As we go on our way

Chorus

And when at last she rolls to rest
We're sure that she has done her best
A van well known both near and far
She took us on our way

Chorus – twice

The CAT van with 'Spike' the cat, and mice painted on it was an old Ford Transit owned by CAT for five years and was reaching the end of its days. At the time of making the tape CAT were negotiating a replacement. However, the old van is remembered fondly as it took us many miles and into many communities. We hoped that the next one would do the same.

Timothy Tadpole

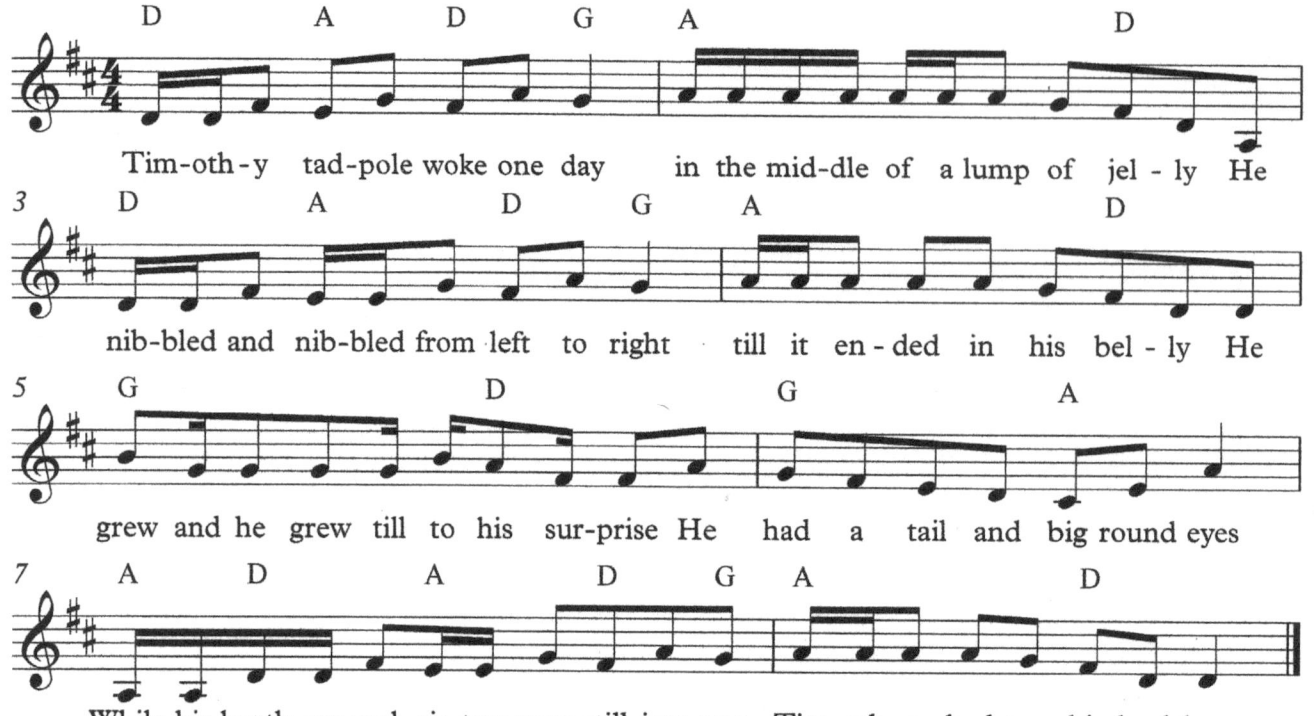

Timothy tadpole woke one day in the middle of a lump of jelly
He nibbled and nibbled from left to right 'til it ended in his belly
He grew and he grew 'til to his surprise he had a tail and big round eyes
While his brothers and sisters were still just eggs
Timothy had two big back legs

He swam around the lily pond its charms he was exploring
And in a while he found he had two big strong arms a-growing
His tail began to disappear but Timothy laughed, he had no fear
For when the swimming had to stop
Timothy found that he could hop

Now Timothy tadpole is no more...... he's turned into a froggy
He hops around the lily-pond in mud all wet and soggy
He found a lady frog one night and croaked at her in sheer delight
Now they've made the lily-pond their home
And spawned some tadpoles of their own

Another song written while working in the CAT team with kids.

Little Red Riding Hood

Julie was a hoody; all the gang wore hoodies, it was cool. But she didn't opt for those dull black or grey colours, no, hers was bright red. Of course it meant she stood out in a crowd – not much good for shop-lifting.

Anyway, today Mum had told her she had to take a casserole over to her Gran's house. It meant crossing the common and past a small patch of trees where the boys often hung out having an illicit smoke but she wasn't worried – might have a drag herself but not that marijuana, she'd tried it once before and it made her feel sick.

Putting on her hoody, off she went, whistling a bit through her brace encased teeth, Hey ho.

Damn, there was that creepy John character from the local high school. She'd heard he was on probation having been caught stealing. Good looking, he really fancied himself and she knew tales of his exploits with some of the local girls.

Good, he'd turned off; she didn't have to face him.

After about ten minutes she arrived at Gran's house. She knocked politely on the door but simultaneously pushed it open as she knew Gran never locked it anyway, which infuriated Julie's Mum.

Julie entered calling as she walked through the dim hallway, 'Hi Gran, it's me, Mum's sent some lunch.'

Silence. The usual sound of Gran's cheerful voice did not come back to her. Julie's step quickened, she entered the kitchen. No Gran. She placed the casserole dish on the table and turning, reentered the hall and bounded up the stairs. Gran was lying motionless on the upstairs bedroom carpet, a broomstick beside her. Julie bent to examine her and found her head was bleeding from a wound on the side of her skull. She appeared life-less.

Julie drew back, stifling a shriek. She looked wildly around the room, who could have done this?

Then she heard a movement on the landing and turned to see the large form of John, the creep, blocking the doorway.

'Silly old cow,' he shouted. 'I didn't mean to kill her but she came out at me with the broom as I was looking in her jewelry box. I just grabbed the first thing to ward her off.'

The copper bust of Beethoven, Gran's favourite composer, lay a few feet away on the floral patterned carpet. Horrified, Julie stood trembling, hoping this was all just a dream.

John was still staring at her.

'And as for you,' he said, 'Well, I can't let the witness get away...'

Song for Bill

Fire glows and my love grows, come sit here by my side
Raindrops fall outside the door far from our fireside
Come take my hand and talk to me, tell me how you feel
Where you've been, the things you've seen
And what makes your life real

Records play the hours away, guitar sings quietly
My heart's in tune inside this room when you are here with me
The fire dies but in your eyes I see it light again
I'll pause awhile to make you smile
I'm glad you are my friend

Let's sing our songs and play our tunes and set our spirits free
For I will come and dance with you if you will dance with me
For I just want to hold you tight and love you tenderly
And maybe in the morning g light
You'll find you're loving me.

I did have a long term relationship in the 1980s and this song was written at the beginning of it.

Missing You

Sand dunes high and beach of shells
Waves that form in rock pool wells
Swirling winds on cliffs afar
Whisper I'm missing you

Foreign places, strangers names
Chatting children playing games
Coloured kites and parachutes
Whisper I'm missing you

Tyres treading many miles
Petrol pumps and team mate's smiles
Telegraph poles with singing wires
Whisper I'm missing you

And when at last I turn my face
Back to join the human race
I'm grateful for the things I've learnt
But I'm glad I'll be seeing you

While working in the Community Arts Team we travelled all around the out-back and were away from home for weeks at a time. We all missed our friends and partners while we were away.

The Power Song

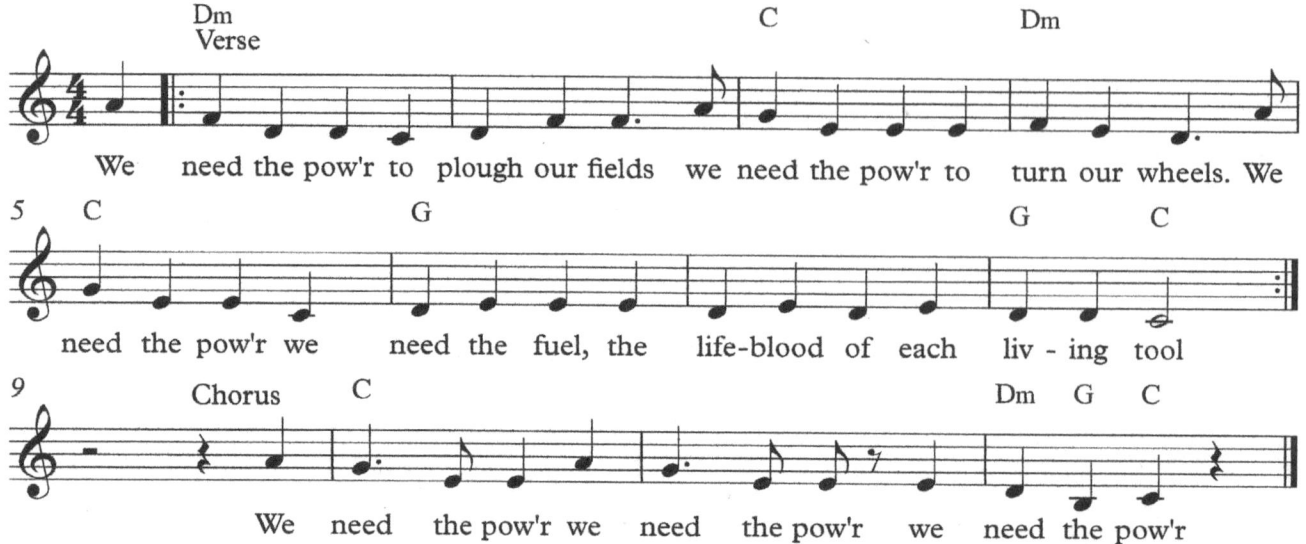

We need the power to plough our fields, we need the power to turn our wheels
We need the power, we need the fuel, the lifeblood for each living tool

Chorus:
We need the power, we need the power, we need the power

Man's arm was weak, the horse was strong until the steam power came along
But wood must burn and trees must die and forests fall to our greedy cry
Chorus

Dig deep, dig deep and rend the earth, rip out her treasures hid at birth
And what if men should perish too, the great machines must have their due
Chorus

A strike! Black gold flows from the ground but man's need grows, more must be found
While oil rigs drill both land and sea can nuclear power find eternity
Chorus

We have the sun to warm the earth, to give us light to give us birth
With wind and water still to employ, let's harness nature, not destroy

We have the power to use the power not bleed the power

When working with the Community Arts Team in a school on the West Coast, they wanted us to teach the types of power we had used over the ages. I remember taking the record with Jethro Tull's 'Heavy Horses' to play to them too.

The Headstone
'Eliza Kennedy – Her charity covereth a multitude of sins'

Eliza came from a poor family. Her father was a drover, away for months at a time and a heavy drinker when home and her mother had to take in washing to keep the family clothed and fed. There were seven kids altogether. Finally, when Eliza was sixteen her mother died in yet another childbirth and Eliza was left looking after the brood. Her father upped and left again – and never came back.

Eliza was a pretty girl and there were several young men in the area but also some older ones. She began to realise that her charms were valuable and her situation was dire so she began to charge for them.

Other girls became aware of the new dresses and her better circumstances and began asking questions. Eliza realised that she could perhaps bring them on side and, to cut a long story short, set up a brothel actually helping many women who, through one reason or another were in need of her aid.

Her clientele included bankers, politicians and even men of the cloth. However, one dreadful night a bloodcurdling scream was heard coming from her private rooms.

When the other women rushed in they found her spread-eagled, naked, on the bed, blood gushing from her slit throat.

The culprit was never found but most of the town mourned her and took a collection for a decent burial and a tombstone upon which was inscribed the following:

'Eliza Kennedy. Her charity covereth a multitude of sins'

See the Aymite Flood (Port Vincent, Lousiana, USA, 1983)

While in America in 1983 I rode down to Louisiana to visit my friend Debby Anselmo who I had last seen where I met her in South West Africa (Namibia) several years before.

Debby lived in a small village called Port Vincent and her house was, like Australian Queenlanders, built on stilts as it was beside the Aymite river, a tributary to the mighty Mississippi.

She said that anyone who lives in the river basin expects to be flooded and the previous April there had been a big one and the water had come 3' inside the house causing massive destruction. While I was there is started to rain and Debby said, 'Here we go again, we must evacuate to my mother's house in nearby Baton Rouge.' So I followed her car, on my bike and we were safe.

A few days later we returned and had to swim the last 100yards into the house yard. The water had come half way up her steps. After another few days we went back to clean up, washing the mud away.

Since then she has had the house raised even higher but the threat of floods is always there.

Whilst there I wrote this poem:

Water's rising, running high
See that debris floating by
Banks are swollen with its watery blood
People crying – see the Aymite flood!

Raindrops beating out a steady tune
Five more inches done fell since noon
Bullfrog croaking from his Cyprus log
People crying – see the Aymite flood

Thunder crashing, lightning flashing
People dashing for higher ground
Muddy river even bigger
Creeping outward for miles around

Water seeping through the bedroom floor
Just repeating many times before
Homes are drowning beneath the mud
People crying – see the Aymite flood.

A Winter Afternoon On The Aymite

Release the rope, push off gently into the stream
Let the flow take us in its persuasive hold
A touch of throttle to resume control
And take direction up or down
Soft sound of water slapping the bow
The burbling motor widely spreads a wake
Of smooth, green brown water
Breaking into chuckling bubbles
A winter sun shines low and silvery
Through the bare branches
Accentuating the grey-green lace
Of Spanish moss draping the trees
Amongst fallen trunks and limbs
Bow-beaked ibis wade on spindly legs
And prouder blue heron
Spread their smoky wings for flight
We amble on past banks where jutting Cypress knees
Proclaim their domination
While the remaining splendour of jewelled leaves
Reflect in rippling mirrors at their feet
Stilted houses, wooden shacks and lazy landings
Denote man's presence in this timeless world
A duck decoy, plastic bottle and nylon line
A hopeful fisherman waving as we putter by
The flap and cry of wood duck taking flight
Breaks the bayou's spell
And a splash nearby draws the eye
To the kingfisher skimming low
As the sun lowers the chill breeze
Turns us homeward
Tie the rope and step ashore
Leave the Aymite river to its reverie once more

Port Vincent, LA (Geaud's country), December 1999

Duck Egg Blues

Well, I woke up this morning and what did I see
Sitting on the concrete as large as can be
It was a duck egg – ah, I've got the duck egg blues
Well you're gonna wake up to the duck egg blues

You give 'em some grain and you give 'em some grass
You just lay back and sit on your arse
Wait for them duck eggs – ah, I've got the duck egg blues
Yes, you're gonna wake up to the duck egg blues

Well, I've eaten them boiled and I've eaten them fried
There's all kinds of ways that I have tried
To eat them duck eggs, ah, I've got them duck egg blues
Well, you're gonna wake up to the duck egg blues

Well, here's the reason I'm feeling so blue
It's the noisy old things them ducks have to do
To make them duck eggs – ah, I've got the duck egg blues
Well, you're gonna wake up to the duck egg blue
Yes, you're gonna wake up to the duck egg blues
Quack, quack

When I lived in Adelaide I kept some ducks in the back garden, mainly Khaki Campbell's but the odd Muscovy. They all had names beginning with D… Daisy, Donald, Demelza, Darcy, etc. they gave us hours of amusement watching their waddling back and forth across the lawn and squabbling amongst themselves. But what a noise they made when they did so!

Sunny Jim the Goat (1985)

He's as watchful as a cat and as stubborn as a mule
And though he has his funny ways, he's nobody's fool
He's as playful as a kitten and as stealthy as a stoat
He has pointed horns and long white hair, he's Sunny Jim the Goat

He likes to have his meals on time gets cranky when they're late
When he's finished up the pellets he'll nibble at the gate
He'll see the dogs out fighting and watch the ducks afloat
But food is the main interest of Sunny Jim the goat

Whilst walking to the park you'll see him chewing at the trees
In spring his fancy turns to food and he's not so hard to please
For not even will a thorny rose stick in this boy's throat
And you'd better keep your grapevines trimmed
Near Sunny Jim the goat

Whilst living in Adelaide I had a goat that was an Angora cross. He had wonderful fleece which I used to spin but he was very naughty!

Flying High

In the 1980s, I was living in Adelaide. I had finished my term with the CAT team, had come back from a tour of America and decided to go to University to acquire a BA degree to give myself some 'cultural capital'. I also wanted to learn to fly. My father had been a fighter pilot in WW2 and, as a child, I had dressed up in his RAF pilot's uniform and now felt ready to earn my own wings.

I had some money saved so, in between lectures, I took myself off to the Parafield airfield and found a flying school to take me on. I soon discovered that, always prone to motion sickness, in the small Grumman plane I felt airsick and it was no use me taking tablets as they would make me sleepy in the pre-flight briefing and I would miss learning. However, I carried on regardless and finally made it to the point at which I could go solo.

What a terrifying moment! Actually being in the plane alone without the instructor to advise me. Well, I took off ok – that's the easy bit – went round the circuit and came to the final leg, informing the tower that I was landing. That's the difficult bit.

Down I came, flared and hit the runway with an almighty wallop, bounced up and came down again with another heavy thump and bounce. Oh no! you are instructed not to try again but put the nose up, give lots of throttle and go around again. Heavy landing damages the landing gear.

So, pointing the nose skyward, engine roaring I prepared to do another circuit.

'What if I can't do it? What it I go round and around 'til the fuel runs out and I crash?'

I informed the tower of my go round and, though shaking like a leaf, managed to calm myself and concentrate.

Here we go, on the final leg, throttle off, flaps down then gently flare.

This time a perfect landing. Phew! I taxied into the parking bay, dismounted from the cockpit to enter the terminal. My latest instructor (young male) far from offering congratulations (and to buy me a celebratory drink) just asked me why I didn't land the first time.

Well, that was it! I was very upset with that flying school who had just given me a stream of young male instructors who were really using me to up their own flying hours and who laughed at me when I said I felt sick on manoeuvers.

I hunted around the other flying schools until I found a mature female instructor who had been a high school teacher before turning to flying. This school had high wing Cessna rather than the low wing Grummans that I was used to so I had to learn a different feel for the aircraft but my teacher was much more patient and considerate of my airsickness and I went on to achieve my Private Pilots licence, only the restricted one as I had run out of money to go on to learn navigation. However I was now a qualified pilot and had my wings.

Between studying I was in a folk band and when doing dances and other gigs we had a friend, Jacko, who was our sound man, in charge of the PA. He was impressed that I could now fly and take passengers so asked if he could come up with me. You need to keep your sound man happy so I was pleased to take him.

So, on a clear day we went to the airfield and he climbed in while I did the pre-flight check, then off we went, a smooth take off and perfect weather. As we went out on the run up the coast the wind picked up and I started to feel a little sick. No good telling your passenger that.

Ah, I thought, I'll do some manoeuvers to keep myself concentrating and perhaps I will feel better.

'Jacko,' I said, 'we are going to pretend to have an engine failure, I'll turn off the throttle and you can look around and see if you can identify an emergency landing spot. And if you have any false teeth take them out now,' I joked.

He looked a bit concerned but peered out of the window as I knocked off the throttle and went into a glide as we started losing height. When we were down to 500' and Jacko was looking panicky, I opened the throttle, put the nose up and regained height. I heard Jacko breathe a sigh of relief.

My flying time was nearly up and I was feeling even sicker so we turned back to the airfield. Jack was looking happier and I was looking forward to terra firma. Despite a slight crosswind I came in to do a perfect landing and pulled up thankfully by the terminal.

'Jacko, go in and order me a coffee, I just have a few things to finish off here'.

He jumped out, beaming, and I sat swallowing hard until it felt safe for me to alight without vomiting. Then smiling broadly I joined Jacko inside and wallowed in his praises. He never knew of my motion sickness and the worry that I had that I wouldn't be able to get us safely down.

Left: Grumman aircraft.
First solo.

Below: Cessna. Final test for Pilot's Licence

Birthdays I Will Always Remember (40th)

The next grand occasion was my 40th. By this time I was a 'respectable' house owner in Adelaide, South Australia with my friends including not just the motorcycle fraternity but all the South Australian folkie world too. I was playing in several different bands and knew many people. Again, it was worthwhile having two parties. On my actual birthday which was mid-week my closest friends and I went out to a restaurant for dinner. These included my writer boyfriend Bill, my singing partners and two WIMA members, one my housemate and one the vice president (as she was heavily into vice). I have photos of me looking very elegant in a white crepe dress and a rose in my hair posing beside the dinner table laden with food and good Australian wine. On the Saturday night we invited everyone else. Mick Sturgess was in Oz at the time and also made it to the Ceilidh that we held on the back lawn. My band *Green Gilbert* and all the other musicians ran a folk dance and quite a few newly-planted saplings suffered the tramp of flying feet. The neighbours who had been diplomatically invited, enjoyed themselves and one, who had just launched his home-built yacht, invited us out sailing the next day. This proved to be not a good idea. Only Bill was able to help crew. The rest of us, including Mick Sturgess, held grimly to the rail whilst throwing up all the birthday food and drink into the ocean.

* * *

Going up to the Top Half Folk Festival in Alice Springs (1980 I believe) four of us folkies from Adelaide went in Pete Mogford's old car up the then unsealed highway. The car was always breaking down, however, we made it to the festival and had a great time.

The Week We Went to Alice (Bick/Cook)

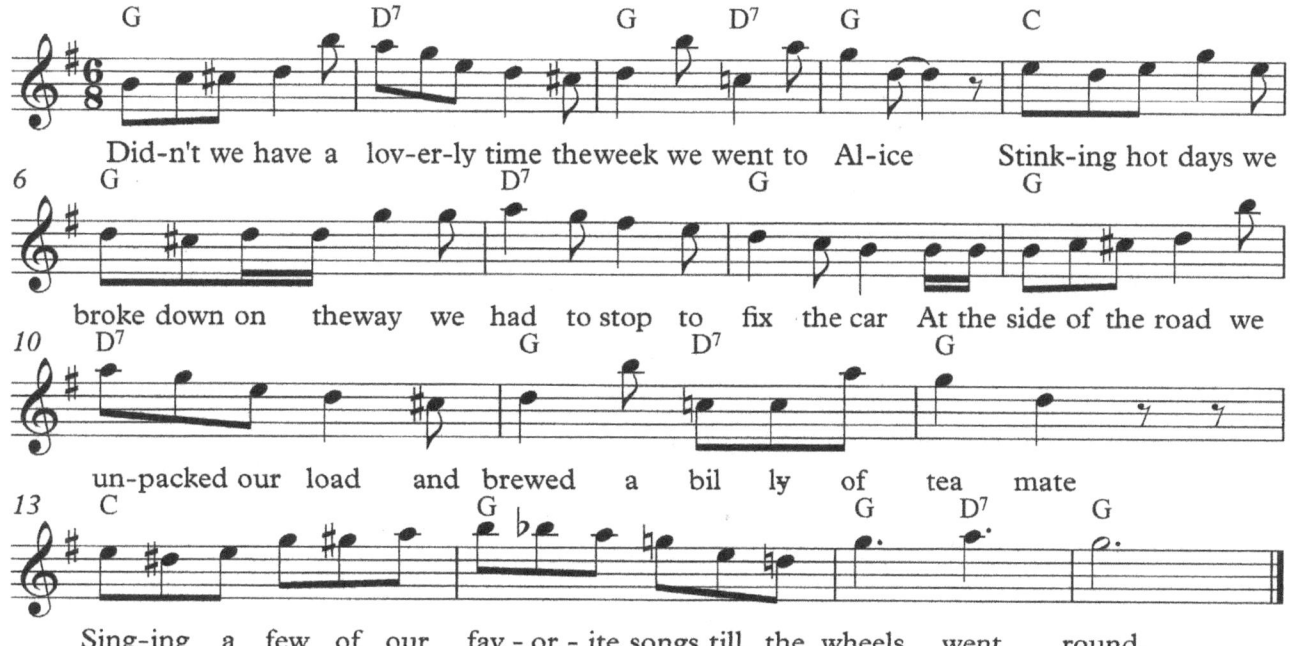

Didn't we have a lovely time the week we went to Alice
Stinking hot days we broke down on the way
We had to stop to fix the car
At the side of the road we unpacked our load and brewed a billy of tea, mate
Singing a few of our favourite songs 'til the wheels went round

Do you recall the thrill of it all when we broke down outside Pimba
The engine got hot, we near blew the lot
We had to wait for it to cool
Then with a laugh we pushed it to start and headed off to Spud's place
With a shout and a cheer we got to the beer when the wheels went round

Wasn't it nice eating weevils and rice and burning up the jaffels
Ryvitas and cheese went down with ease
The marg was running all over the place
We had to be quick cos Peter felt sick, he didn't think much of our cuisine
So with noodles and fish we made him a dish to make his wheels go round

Jacky and me we finished our tea and went to take the tent down
Jumped in the car, Pete said 'Aha!
We have to take the manifold off'
Wouldn't it be grand to have cash on demand and buy a brand new engine
But with spanners and oil we just have to toil to make the wheels go round

Who's Who in the Folk Scene

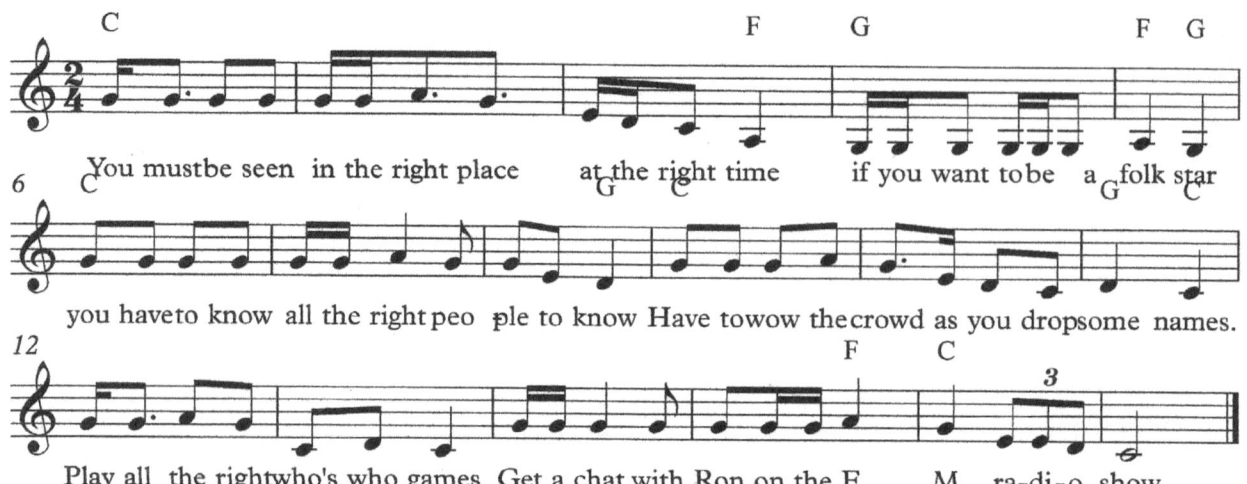

You must be seen in the right place at the right time, if you want to be a folk star
You have to know all the right people to know
Have to wow the crowd as you drop some names, play all the right 'who's who' games
Get a chat with Ron on the FM radio show

You have to grow a beard and get a Martin, especially a twelve string
You'll get nowhere with a tatty old Yamaha
You must wear your trousers loose and old, they're even better if they're holed
With a velvet waistcoat man, you're going far

You have to put your tracks down in the studio 'Every folkies doing it'
Take six months to get your record made
Your mixing must be loud and clear, 10,000 watts so all can hear
And most of all you must be getting paid

You must have played at *Traitors' Gate* on Saturday, buy a drink for Jenny
Dan O'Connell's gives you ten points on the scale
But you know you've made it to the top, you're the crème de crème of the whole damn lot
When you've drawn a crowd at the fountain in Rundle Mall

Come join our little folk scene here in Adelaide
It's friendly but you'd better watch your style
What's what, who's who and don't be late
At the *Cumberland Arms* or *Traitors' Gate*
At the Celtic dance you'll always wear a smile

A tongue in cheek look at the folk scene in Adelaide in the 1980s.

Jenny Arger and Derek Moule ran the *Traitors' Gate Folk Club* in Adelaide, which was mainly held in the Earl of Leicester Hotel. It was considered to be the best folk venue and regularly showcased top class national and international folk singing stars. The club ran for about 10 years in the 1980s.

The Missus of the House

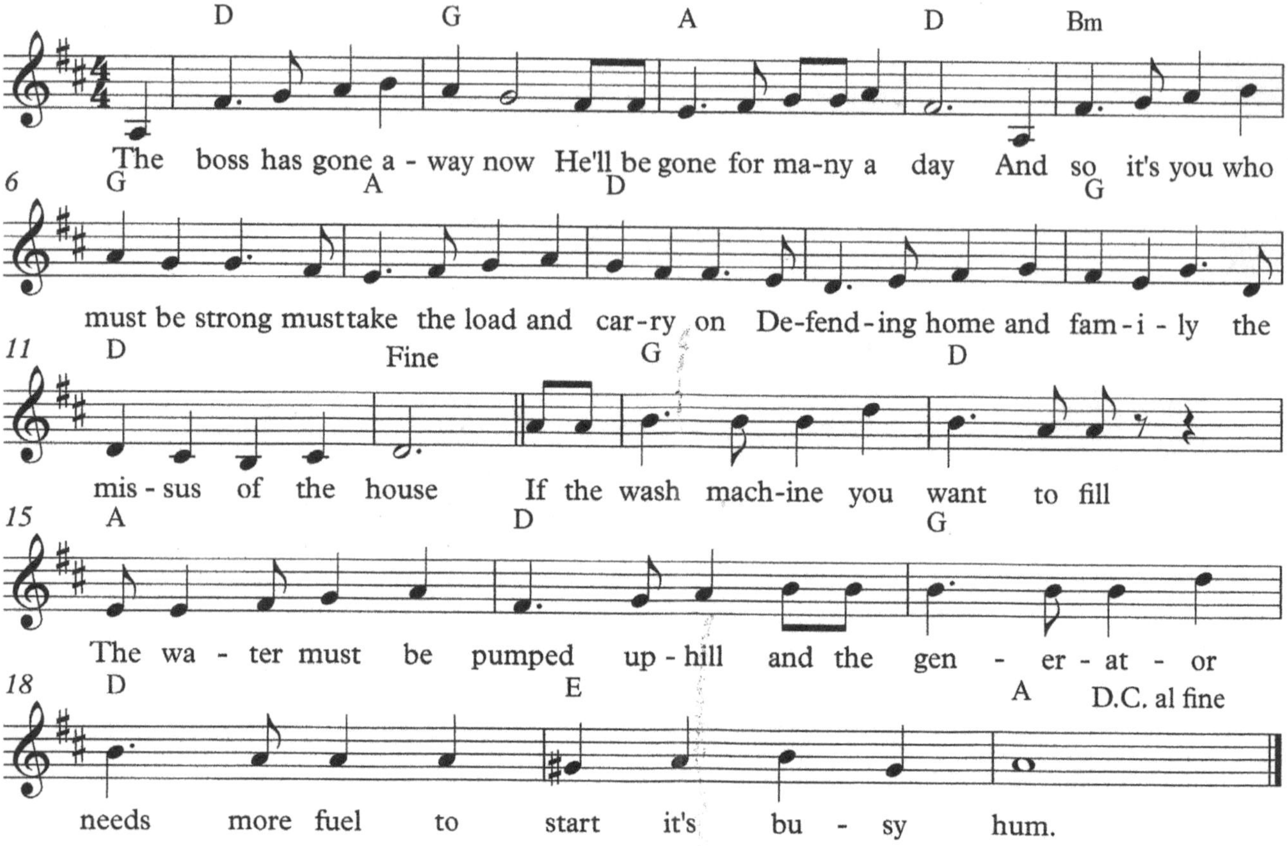
D G A D Bm
The boss has gone a - way now He'll be gone for ma-ny a day And so it's you who
G A D G
must be strong must take the load and car-ry on De-fend-ing home and fam-i-ly the
D Fine G D
mis - sus of the house If the wash mach-ine you want to fill
A D G
The wa - ter must be pumped up - hill and the gen - er - at - or
D E A D.C. al fine
needs more fuel to start it's bu - sy hum.

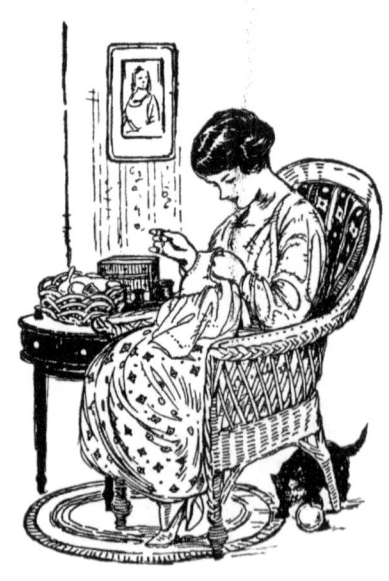

The boss has gone away now, he'll be gone for many a day
And so it's you who must be strong, must take the load and carry on
Defending home and family
The Missus of the house

There's a million things to do now, before the day is through
A fox has got into the pen, the horse has jumped the fence again
Tis you must catch and bring him home
The Missus of the house

If the wash machine you want to fill, the water must be pumped uphill
And the generator need more fuel to start its busy hum

Sometimes you think there's danger near and it is for the kids you fear
A snake has got into the pile and you don't like that stranger's smile
It's on your wits you must rely
The Missus of the house

You sit and sew alone now and wish your man was home
But you've cleared away the things from tea, the kids are sleeping peacefully
You know there's nothing you can't do,
The Missus of the house
Yes, you know your strength will see you through
The Missus of the house

Many women in the outback have to look after the house and family when their men are away droving, shearing, or other work that causes them to travel. In this case I was staying with a family on the West coast near Penong and the husband worked on the Eyre highway SA to WA border. I heard him discussing things to be done before he left for about three weeks away.

I'm a Flea

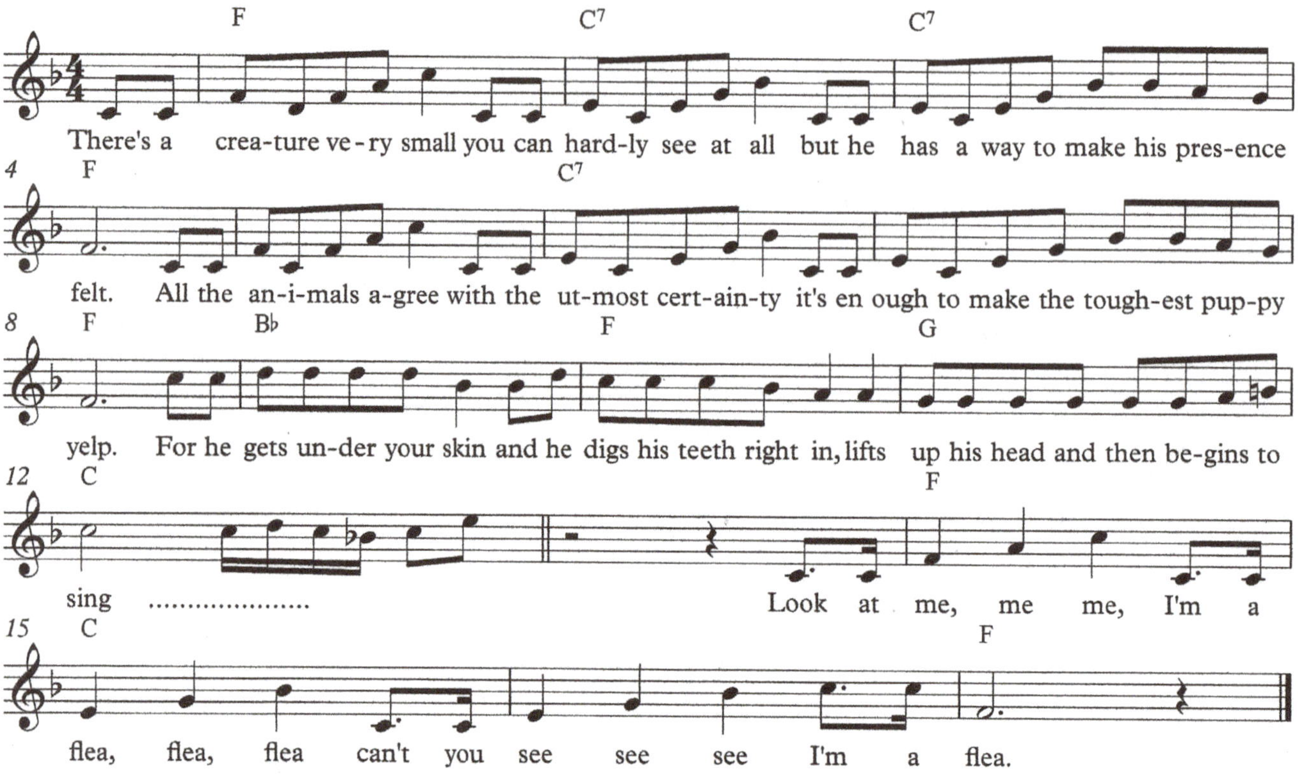
F C7 C7
There's a crea-ture ve-ry small you can hard-ly see at all but he has a way to make his pres-ence
4 F C7
felt. All the an-i-mals a-gree with the ut-most cert-ain-ty it's en ough to make the tough-est pup-py
8 F B♭ F G
yelp. For he gets un-der your skin and he digs his teeth right in, lifts up his head and then be-gins to
12 C F
sing .... Look at me, me me, I'm a
15 C F
flea, flea, flea can't you see see see I'm a flea.

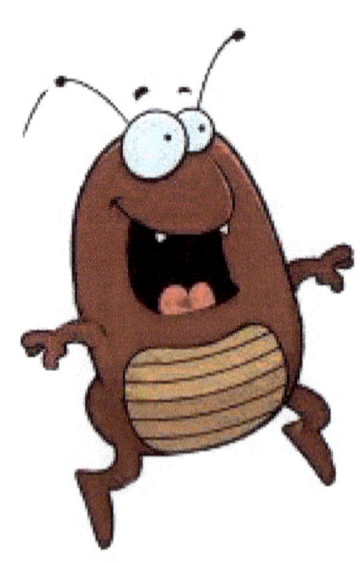

There's a creature very small you can hardly see at all
But he has a way to make his presence felt
All the animals agree with utmost certainty
It's enough to make the toughest puppy yelp
For he gets onto your skin and he digs his teeth right in
Lifts up his head and then begins to sing……

Chorus:
Look at me, me, me, I'm a flea, flea, flea
Can't you see, see, see. I'm a flea

Now it really isn't fair when you hardly know he's there
Until you feel your skin begin to itch
And he doesn't care at all whether you are big or small
I've even seen him make a camel twitch
For he gets onto your skin and he digs his teeth right in
Lifts up his head and then begins to sing…..

Chorus

So, it only goes to show what the flea already knows
There's a way to let the world know you exist
You can always have your say in an independent way
Without the need to raise an angry fist
You just get under their skin and you dig your heels right in
Lift up your head and then begin to sing…….

Chorus x 2

There's hope for us little people yet! Keep on making a nuisance of yourself.

Take My Breath Away

From 1984-7 I had been studying hard at Flinders and Adelaide Universities for a BA degree, as a mature age student. Hard work for a brain which hadn't looked at a text book for over twenty years.

This challenge was made more difficult when, during my second year, I had to have an operation in the Royal Adelaide Hospital followed by several weeks' recovery, bedridden at home, recovering from a poisoned foot after an accident with a lawnmower! Writing essays with a drip in my arm wasn't the easiest thing to do.

A good friend of mine, Viola, a language and outdoor education teacher, kindly helped me structure my essays and I learnt that, several years earlier, she had hiked in the Himalayas. So, in my last year of University, anticipating the successful end to my studies I asked her if she would come to Nepal with me the following year and act as my guide and she happily agreed. It would give me a well-earned trip outside Australia and see how well my foot had recovered.

Consequently, in March, 1988 we flew to Katmandu, spent a few days exploring that exciting city and getting trekking permits, then took a bus to our start point on the Everest trail.

I had no experience in high altitude walking, in fact, being a motorcyclist, hardly any experience in walking at all. A few months before we left my housemate, Kerry Holgate, had given me an old pair of her walking boots and also her red Karrimor rucksack. I did a few gentle walks in the Adelaide hills but didn't bother to try any fully laden. So much for preparation!

The bus journey from Katmandu to Lomosangu took all day, with many stops to pick up passengers. By the time we reached our destination the bus was jam packed, we even had people sitting on our laps and some were on the roof. My motion sickness was not helped by the fact that

barrels of spare fuel, exuding fumes, were kept in the inside aisle. By the time we reached our destination I was green and could hardly stagger to our accommodation. However, the next morning I had recovered and was ready to start.

Many people use the short cut to the walk, ie. they take a plane to Luckla to start. This is not a good idea, not only is it said to be the most dangerous airfield in the world because of it's short runway, close surrounding peaks and adverse weather conditions, but it is at an elevation of 9,334ft and therefore gives no time for acclimatisation. Though we were to use this airport on our return journey, we started our walk from Lomosangu which has an elevation of only 1,585ft.

For the first days walk Viola had organised a short walk so I could acclimatise and see what trekking was all about. Just as well; I couldn't believe how hard going it was to go up steep inclines with this pack. How on earth was I going to do this?

However, after a few days I began to toughen up and was lucky that both the boots and rucksack were comfortable. No blisters! I was thoroughly enjoying the scenery, the fresh air and the people we met on our way. Viola and I walked well together,

delighting in each other's company away from the stress of essays! We stayed at little tea houses overnight, eating dahl-baht and sleeping in our down sleeping bags on basic beds, some just platforms with other walkers lying alongside. While Viola had a couple of days break, due to a spot of flu, I visited the Thami monastery drinking Tibetan salt tea with yak milk, then, together, we walked through rhododendron woods and on precarious swinging plank bridges over raging rivers.

After about two weeks we reached Namche Bazaar, a small town busy with yaks in the street carrying expedition equipment and many shops with hiking gear. It transpired that one of these expeditions was the Australian one and we often crossed paths with the participants on the way. In Namche we hired down jackets to wear in the evenings as the nights became colder in the snow fields at the higher altitude. I was pleased that, not only was I much fitter, but I had lost several kilos in weight. So it was onwards and upwards.

It had never been our intention to go to the Everest Base Camp as we had been warned that it was crowded and full of rubbish so we took the fork off to Gokyo a couple of days hence. The snow made the going more difficult and finally, we just had a few more hundred yards to the summit. It seemed so near yet, in the rarified air, we could only manage two steps at a time, then a stop for a gasp of breath. Step by faltering step we inched our way upwards until finally we reached the summit and gazed, awe-struck, at the Everest peak and the glaciers of Tibet, way off in the distance. Everest stood proudly with its swath of cloud signally its challenge to more hardy climbers. We were just glad that our own successful expedition had taken us to 17,575 ft and we were still alive and kicking. No problem with my foot!

Certainly an effort to take your breath away.

I Smell a Rat (1989)

Horace was hungry, well not really hungry – he was always well fed – but just sort of peckish. The truth was, he just liked nibbling things that were around. His powerful teeth chewed through just about everything. The nice curly telephone wire, for example, that sometimes hung temptingly inside his cage. People were always complaining they couldn't phone through to the house. Then of course there was the foam inside the sofa. When Philip and Sally let him out at night to roam the lounge room, his very favourite spot was up inside it. He'd chewed right through both of the arms and could now run clean across the seat from one side to the other, disappearing at either end. The black vinyl was no problem and the foam padding was a cinch. Best of all was, they couldn't get you out once you were inside. He had hidden there for days at a time just making a quick dash out every now and then to find a morsel of food if his store was running low.

His favourite trick was on an unsuspecting house-sitter who had been asked to give him a run. He'd disappear in the sofa, keep quiet and make them think he'd escaped. That sister of Philips had searched the house high and low all night getting in quite a frenzy and phoning long distance the next day to apologise for losing him. That was a laugh. He'd been just happily having a chew inside all the time, keeping quiet while she was around. Shame when she spotted him sneaking back. Silly cow. Served her right for being so mean with the sweet corn.

But tonight the mob was around. They sat on the sofa and the floor playing those board games and smoking that stuff that made him feel a bit light-headed and silly and which led to all sorts of inspiration. Philip was droning on as usual. Sally was rocking back and forth on her heels in front of the fire, as was her wont, occasionally sticking her pert little bum in the air when she dived under the shelf to find another CD to play.

Andy, the South African was complaining about his Dad again and how he hated the catering industry so he was more content on the dole as long as he could cadge a joint now and then. Smiley, with his ever-present grin was telling them about his new job in the local hospital and how pretty the nurses were.

So, as the smoke thickened and the dog-ends filled the ash tray, Horace started some of his raiding trips from the sofa to the coffee table. Those bits of paper on the bottom shelf were an easy haul. Rush out, grab one and rush back to the nest. A few minutes good munching and they were shredded. Telephone bills, gas and electricity accounts, final demands of all sorts, not to mention a few valuable invoices or orders from Philip's business, were all fair game and it gave him a laugh listening to them hunt for them in the next few days. They knew he liked them – if they were so damned important why did they leave them there?

The hours went by, the giggling increased and Horace began to feel more and more emboldened running back and forth with all sorts of goodies, pens, pencils and rubbers while they played on, hardly noticing him. Then he noticed something small and mouth- sized wrapped in paper on the edge of the ash tray. It had been abandoned while they were arguing some point in the game. He twitched his whiskers, cast a beady eye on the distracted foursome and made a run for the ash tray. With the stub firmly in his mouth, he disappeared sleekly into the vinyl hole and put it with the chewed papers while he poked his nose back out to see if they'd noticed. No, the game was at its height, all busy in an argument over some rule or other and no-one had missed a thing.

After a while Sally started the ceremony of rolling another joint and after a few puffs their eyes had that droopy look that signalled it was almost time for bed. That meant they'd do a quick search for him, maybe enticing him back to his cage with some fresh sweetcorn, a trick he knew well but didn't mind cos it meant he could flirt for a bit with Sally and pretend they were good friends and all.

But suddenly Philip began to cough and choke. From the light haze of hash and tobacco smoke the room was now filled with thick toxic black fumes and everyone jumped up~ 'There's a fire!' shouted Philip. 'Everyone outside!'

Horace was a bit non-plussed; a strange turn of events indeed. He was increasingly aware of a sensation of heat and his whiskers began to frizzle.

Some-one shouted 'Call the fire brigade'.

Philip was running around with buckets of water shouting to the others to stay outside. 'The fumes will kill you'.

Horace felt a cold wash of water hit him as he made a dash away from the burning sofa. Talk about feeing like a 'drowned rat'.

'It's OK,' Philip spluttered after the third bucketful. 'It's out. You can open the doors now. Wait until the smoke goes before you come in, though.'

He was holding his hanky over his face, peering through the clearing smoke and looking puzzled. Soon his watering, bloodshot eyes settled on the cowering, bedraggled and slightly-singed Horace and he started to laugh.

A few weeks later the insurance assessor came to view the damage. The claim for a new sofa and carpet had to be approved. Accidental domestic fire.

Philip and Sally looked surreptitiously at Horace, safely tucked in his cage, then at each other.

'I wonder if he'll smell a rat,' Sally whispered and giggled.

Horace just hoped the new furniture would be to his taste.

Driving to Dunbar (1989)

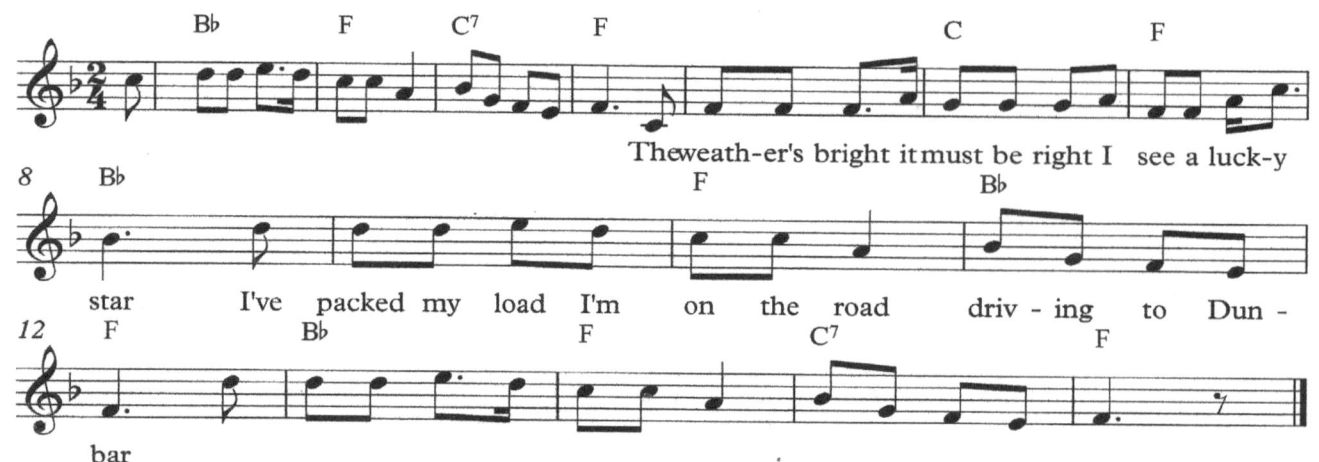

The weather's bright, it must be right
I see a lucky star...
I'm heading North, a steady course
Driving to Dunbar

Top up the oil and check the lights
And tool kit in my car
I've packed my load, I'm on the road
Driving to Dunbar

I leave behind the hum-drum life
There's better things by far
There's friends to meet and songs to sing
When I reach Dunbar

So come what may, I'm on my way
To drink whisky in the jar
With laughter bright, we'll fill the night
When I reach Dunbar

The weather's bright, it must be right
I see a lucky star...
I'm heading North, a steady course
Driving to Dunbar

While living in Burton on Trent in 1989 I began singing with a handsome Scot who invited me to meet him at a Folk Festival in Dunbar. My little 127 Fiat was only just able to make the journey there but I wrote this song on the way.

Affaire Chanson
(The Next Time I'm In Town) (1989)

She went to the Lichfield folk club fairly regularly nowadays, probably at least once a fortnight. Since her own local club had closed early for the summer she had transferred her allegiance, made a new circle of friends and felt accepted. It was only ten miles away anyway which even her battered, old, red Fiat could manage – most of the time.

The numbers at the club waxed and waned as usual and at times different faces were seen amongst the old faithfuls. She hardly noticed him until it was his turn to sing because he was quiet and unobtrusive, just sitting slightly apart with his glass of mild. She noted that his guitar was a Martin, one of the more expensive and respected makes. He introduced his song briefly but effectively and then began to sing with simple accompaniment. His accent was Scottish and it was then that she really listened. His voice was deep and honeyed with a timbre that struck a harmonic note within her. His delivery was sincere but not ostentatious. This man was obviously a regular performer and at ease with an audience.

'Who is he? I haven't seen him before,' she said to Ruth sitting beside her.

'That's Richard,' Ruth replied. 'He lives in Scotland but works away from home a lot and when he's here he calls in at the folk club. Must be hard on his family and a bit of a lonely existence for him. Good isn't he?'

Yes, he was and not bad looking either, though not the usual dark, bearded, folky type that she had last lived with. Richard was fair and clean cut. Though simply dressed in T-shirt and jeans he carried his slim body confidently and elegantly. She knew that he was obviously off limits but, as one singer to another, she spoke to him briefly at the end of the evening, asking him if he knew any of the Corries songs that she was familiar with and which were similar to his style. He said he did, hadn't sung them for years but liked and remembered them.

'I enjoyed your song,' she said.

'And I yours,' he replied. 'I really liked your harmonies.'

'Thanks,' she said. 'Goodnight'.

And that was it, she never gave him a second thought. Nice man, nice voice, married, hope to hear him again sometime.

During the next two months or so her life took a different turn as she was expecting to leave and work abroad and was training for the job. Away from her base a lot of the time, she didn't visit the folk clubs for quite a while, losing contact with her folkie friends. However, after a lot of trauma, the job did not eventuate. Feeling depressed and desperate for company one night, she headed out of the house to retry another club that she had not been to for a while but which had impressed her on a previous visit. It would at least give her a chance to sing and perhaps meet some new faces.

She entered the pub and walked to the bar to get a drink before going to the upstairs room where the club was held. A slim, fair-haired figure stood at the bar, a Martin guitar case on the floor beside him. He turned toward her as she ordered her drink.

'Haven't I seen you somewhere before?' he said.

For a minute she had to think, then she remembered, it was that man from the Lichfield club who sang so well. They re-introduced themselves.

'I thought you'd gone overseas somewhere,' he said.

'Yes,' she replied, 'I was supposed to go to China.'

'Oh, I heard it was somewhere exotic.'

'Anyway,' she said hastily, 'I didn't go.' She didn't want to have to go into details, so spent the next few minutes asking about his work.

He was an accountant for an international company, the head office of which was in Glasgow but at the moment he had been put in charge of a company in Birmingham so commuted every week, returning home at weekends. He went to the folk clubs around the area to fill in the evenings when he didn't have business meetings.

After a while they went upstairs together and joined the circle of singers. By contrast to the last time she had attended, the evening was peopled by some very interesting performers and her spirits lifted.

When it came to her turn to sing she turned to Richard and said, 'I'm going to do Irish Rover in B flat if you want to join in.'

He did and accompanied her as if they'd been playing together for years. When it ended she sat down flushed with the pleasure of being 'in tune' with another musician.

When he picked up his guitar for his turn he said, 'D'you know the Banks of the Roses?' and when she nodded eagerly, he added, 'Then join in on the chorus.'

Her natural soprano harmonies blended with his deep mellow voice perfectly and another 'first time' effort sounded practised. A musical bond was instantly established.

A Scottish couple, Jean and Neil, struck up a conversation with them, obviously thinking that she and Richard were 'together'. She liked them immediately and was happy to jot down their address for an invitation to a musical get-together sometime. She let the illusion of their partnership remain. When the folk club finished and people drifted away she walked out to the car park with him. She didn't want the evening to end. She had been inspired by their songs together and wanted to talk to him some more. Having established that he had to go almost right past where she was living to return to his accommodation, she invited him in for a coffee.

Her brother's house where she was staying was somewhat untidy and derelict but the lounge was respectable enough, so she made the coffee and they sat chatting about songs. He ran a folk club on Sunday nights in Glasgow when he was home, he told her.

'Well,' she said, 'Funnily enough I'm thinking of going up to Scotland at the end of this month to go on a sailing course, maybe I could pop into the club.'

'Do,' he said. 'This is my number in Glasgow,' and reached into his pocket for his card.

Suddenly she felt physically aware of him. It was the easy way they got on together and the feeling of being 'with' someone that had started at the club. It was something she missed badly since the breakup of her previous relationship.

Several times she thought he was going to leave. One time he rose to get his jacket and she jumped up expecting to see him out but it was just to find his notebook to give her a number she wanted. She began to feel uncomfortable. What does this man want of me? If he's married there can't be any sort of relationship, yet I find him attractive. Does he find me attractive? Does he have affairs? That's not my cup of tea.

Eventually she said, 'I think I have to go to sleep, I have a busy day tomorrow,' and she hurriedly saw him out. 'Maybe I'll be at the Lichfield Folk club tomorrow night,' she said.

'Thanks for the coffee.' He waved as he drove away in his expensive Renault 25.

Confused, she went to bed but switched her thoughts to other things. Some friends of hers from Australia had rung earlier to say that they were in the country and likely to visit next week and were there any clubs that she could take them to. She had been asking Richard if he knew any on a Tuesday night, when they were due. She was looking forward to seeing them. Ron she had sung with regularly in the past and he was a good friend. Although the last time she had seen him, other group members had been in difficult emotional times in Australia and she wanted to catch up on the news and share a song again.

Damn and blast! The next day the red Fiat threw a fit and the starter motor packed up. The early evening saw her, spanner in hand, trying to get it out, cursing that she would not be able to go anywhere that night, let alone Lichfield. But out of the blue, her Aussie mates arrived, deciding to call in on the way up North instead of on the way back. She was overwhelmed.

After establishing them in the spare room and sharing a meal, they took off somewhat belatedly in their hired car for Lichfield. Richard was there but she was so excited singing and playing with Ron and Co. that she hardly spoke to him, apart from introductions. It was like a strange flashback, singing these Australian songs that she had sung so often with the people she had been with but in a totally different environment and situation. Even after two years, Ron was just the same and she felt bereft when they left the following morning. Another fragment of her life lying shattered.

She turned to her red Fiat, battling again with the starter motor. Not only did she rely on it for work but there was a folk festival that she wanted to go to that weekend.

The last night, just before she left, Richard had asked her if she was going to the Abbotts Bromley Horn Dance on the following Monday. She had said, No, she hadn't thought of it as she was going to Whitchurch down south, but anyway her car was not working. But he'd said, 'Just in case you want to go on Monday, here is my work number. I can give you a lift. And I'll take your number too if you don't mind.'

Having found another starter motor at the breaker's yard, the car was fit for its trip to the festival that afternoon and enjoying the festival, she delayed the journey home until Monday.

On route back to Burton she gave a hitchhiker a lift. He was a young graduate from Melbourne, Australia, and she'd picked him up as he had a guitar case. They swapped stories and by the time she'd detoured to take him into Oxford it was getting late. Then she remembered the Horn Dance. Did it continue into the evening? She knew it started at dawn and went on all day but was it too late to get there now?

It wasn't 'til 8pm that she finally found the small village. The streets still thronged with tourists and Morris dancers. She found several of her friends in some of the pubs but felt restless in the smoky, crowded atmosphere and went to a less crowded pub at the other end of town to play her whistle with some fiddlers and accordionists. No sign of Richard. Feeling depressed at the thought of going back to Burton that night, she missed her turning and spent hours driving in the narrow lanes before reaching her lonely room.

Two nights later she sat again disconsolately wondering where to go or whether to start another job when the phone rang and a familiar Scottish voice said, 'Hallo, this is Richard from Glasgow. I was wondering if you'd like to come to a folk club in Stafford with me tonight.'

Forgetting she'd given him her number, it took a few seconds to realise who was speaking – and how pleased she was.

'Yes, that would be nice.'

'And if you haven't eaten,' he continued, 'would you like to have dinner first? Find a nice restaurant locally and we'll go there. See you in an hour.'

As she put the phone down her spirits lifted and she immediately began to think of what to wear. She hadn't been asked out by someone she liked for years. Of course it was only on friendly, singing terms but it was so nice to be asked! Running upstairs to the bath she dug out her only presentable dress and took a lot more care than usual with her hair and make-up.

The evening was very pleasant, even if the Chinese restaurant wasn't up to expectations. She chattered away merrily, amusing him with her many anecdotes and then, somewhat belatedly, they found the folk club, were invited to sing together and made a suitable impression on the audience.

He drove slowly back, saying he had in fact gone to Abbots Bromley, but they had obviously missed each other in different pubs. He dropped her off outside her house. It was way too late for coffee.

'Thanks for a lovely evening,' she said. 'I enjoyed it.'

'So did I,' he said. 'You're good company.'

She hopped out of the car, waved goodbye and hurried in to let sleep block out her feelings.

Inevitably, she looked forward the following night to their next meeting at the Lichfield folk club but the red Fiat decided to break down again and her wait of an hour or so for the AA man meant she arrived half an hour before it finished. Frustrated by the short time she was in his company, she invited him to a local restaurant for a coffee. As she talked about her forthcoming trip to Scotland for the sailing course, he mentioned that the date she gave coincided with a folk festival in Dunbar that he was going to attend. If she wanted to meet him there they could sing together on Friday and Saturday before she was due to join the boat on the Sunday evening.

'I'll show you where it is on the map,' he said, as they walked back toward her errant Fiat and, getting his AA book from the Renault, came in to sit beside her. She felt very conscious of the tattiness of her vehicle and even more conscious of his presence. This time as they said goodnight he leant over and gave her a quick, cool kiss on the lips.

'I'll give you a ring next week,' he said and was gone.

She sat there for a few minutes, finally admitting where this was leading. Unless she put a stop to it, it wasn't going to be 'just friends'. The thing was, she didn't want to put a stop to it, she wanted the feel of someone's arms around her and she found him more and more attractive.

By next week when he called she had found another club that was having an Irish night. It was closer to her place than where he was staying so he said he'd call for her and they decided to have a practice session before they left. He arrived around 7pm and they played around with a few Irish songs they both knew, discovering new harmonies and a greater delight in their music together. In fine spirits they left for Derby where their recently made Scottish friends were also attending. They had a great evening.

When he brought her back and had coffee they further discussed the coming weekend.

'I'll be at the Seaview Hotel in Dunbar tomorrow night around 7pm or so,' he told her. He was flying back to Glasgow and driving out from there.

She would have to leave early in the Fiat after packing for a week's sailing. As he left her he turned and they embraced. His kiss was warm and his body firmly against hers.

'I'll see you tomorrow night,' he said, his eyes full of promise.

'If I make it in the Fiat,' she joked. 'Have a good trip.'

This was all wrong, but oh, so exciting. A trip up to Scotland and someone there waiting for her. A whole weekend of singing and then off further north to learn to sail. She knew she was lost. This affair was going to happen.

She'd never had an affair before. All her relationships had been genuine, no complications, living together as partners until something happened. This was not going to be anything like that. It was not going to be equal or even fair but she was going to either stop right now or take the consequences. Was she strong enough for either alternative?

Next morning up at 5am she was packed and raring to go, had also written the beginnings of a song for the competition at Dunbar.

'The weather's bright, it must be right, I feel a lucky star. I've packed my load, I'm on the road, driving to Dunbar.'

But she had to take the Fiat for its MOT which would run out while she was away. There the trouble started. After waiting for half an hour or so for it to go on the ramp, the mechanics discovered a long list of problems but the most imminent one was a rear wheel bearing which was so bad that the wheel was just about to fall off.

'I wouldn't take this car more than five miles up the road,' the mechanic said. 'It's positively dangerous.'

Where to get it fixed quickly? She had to be away by lunchtime. She had a spare bearing in the back. She'd already tried to replace it herself but being rusted in, it had proved too difficult. Frantically she thought who might help, the thought of her whole week slipping away because of her wheel bearing was too much to bear. Finally she had an idea. Jim the welder. He did a bit of mechanic-ing. Would he be home? She drove up to his house. As luck would have it he was sitting down over a cup of tea, not at all busy and took the job in his stride. Because the old bearing had disintegrated and seized, it took an hour and a half of swearing and innovation but she was overjoyed when they finally succeeded.

They fixed a few other minor problems and Jim, in his gentle West Country accent said, 'Send me a postcard,' when she asked how much she owed him.

'Bless you Jim. You just don't know how much this means to me,' she said gratefully as she waved goodbye.

The sun was shining. It was a glorious autumn day and she felt free at last. Even at 60 – 70 mph she ate up the miles. Heading north was always a delight; away from the depressing Midlands and into the grandeur of the northern moors and dales; over the border into Scotland and finally out to the little fishing town of Dunbar; about a five-hour, two-Snickers-bars drive. As she drew up outside the hotel she was almost shaking with excitement. She was only dressed in jeans and a jumper and the weather had cooled but she was burning with anticipation. Two burly, bearded Scotsmen welcomed her as she walked to the bar and said she was looking for Richard Bowers. They automatically bought her a whisky.

'Oh, wee Ricky. He's away in his room reet now. We'll tell him you're here.'

A few minutes later he came into the bar and greeted her with a light kiss which she hadn't expected. She had another whisky and they went out to the campsite for her to pitch her tent. It was fairly exposed and blowy but protected by the sea wall. With that settled, she left her car and things there and drove back with him into town.

They did the rounds of the pubs singing in each as Richard had been booked to do and then ended up at one that was packed with musicians. Song after song, tune after tune was played on guitar, fiddle, banjo and bodhran. At about 1am the landlord threw everyone out except Richard and another Scottish woman singer. They had more double whiskies and the songs and mood was mellow. She was singing with her eyes closed. The 5am start and excitement of the day had taken its toll and she just wanted to sleep. At last at 4am they went out into the cold night air. The other girl drove off home.

She knew this was it, either she walked back to her tent, which was quite a way or she accepted his invitation of coffee in his room ... and whatever might go with it. You made the decision before you left, she told herself, or you wouldn't be here.

They went upstairs to his room, Richard not a little tipsy from all the whisky and she dead tired. As the pot boiled, he put his arms around her. 'I want you, stay here with me.'

Her head was swimming, her conscience pricking and her body yearning. To go back to a cold, lonely tent when she had a comfortable bed before her and the promise of his warm body was too much to bear. She capitulated, but they just slept comfortably in each other's arms, both too tired and drunk for anything else. A long lie in the next morning before they went and found breakfast and entered the song competitions which dragged out much too long as they both wanted to go back to bed.

The weather had turned bad so they went to the campsite to rescue her things. The tent had blown down and all her sleeping bag and mat were soaked through. The perfect excuse to de-camp and move to the hotel, she thought. The games we play with ourselves.

That afternoon she found out what it was like to be loved again. He was gentle and considerate, conscious of the mental battle which inhibited her. His own complete lack of self-consciousness made it natural for them to be together and at last she unwound. Curled snugly against his slim body, she slept to try and get enough energy for another night of song ahead.

That evening a real Scottish Ceileh was held in the town hall and she dragged him onto the floor for the set dances, laughing happily as they swirled in time to the lively music of the accordion, changing partners, then coming thankfully back to each other's arms. They took their turn on stage, singing the two part *Hunting Tower* – a romantic traditional Scottish song – and the raucous *Irish Rover* in which she used her lagerphone thus causing comment from some members of the audience who had not seen one before.

'You're on a roll,' Richard chuckled in her ear. 'First you've won me, now Dunbar.'

They went back to the hotel and led another music session in the bar there. She really let go, singing a lot of her own Australian songs. Whatever she sang, Richard was right there with her – they were so good together.

Sunday morning she knew would be painful. He would be going back to his family and she was driving up to Argyll. She must be away by 2pm to rendezvous with the boat at 6pm. The day was windy but clear. They walked arm in arm around the castle ruins and had a drink in one of the pubs before going back to the hotel to pack. She could hardly move because of the emotion which she had to hide. This could be all there was to it – she didn't know if he would contact her again. It could have been just a weekend fling for him.

They drove in tandem 'til they got to Edinburgh, then she took another road, concentrating her thoughts on the route and the week ahead. The five day course had her battling with stormy seas and seasickness but it served its purpose in putting the weekend and Richard out of her mind. Physically and mentally purged, she at last had to take the Southern road back to Burton. Despite all her resolutions, she stopped on the motorway near Leeds to make a call. His secretary said: 'Mr Bowers is not in his office today, we expect him tomorrow.'

She replaced the receiver with relief. Well, that saved me making a fool of myself again. But arriving back in Burton to her lonely room she stared at the telephone, willing it to ring. At approx. 6pm it did.

'I've just arrived in town, would you care to have a meal with me tonight?'

She was dizzy with relief. He hadn't just written her off as an easy lay then. He actually did want to see her again!

They arranged that he would pick her up, as her car was now illegal and it was an hour later when he arrived. Grinning from ear to ear she jumped in the car and he leant over to give her a light kiss, saying, 'It's good to see you again.'

They went out to dinner, saw a firework display in Walsall and then ended up back at his hotel.

'Do you want to stay for a while,' he said indicating the big double bed.

'Either you take me home right now or I stay all night,' she replied, not even wanting to contemplate what would happen in the morning. She stayed, having to borrow his jeans and T-shirt to not look conspicuous in her evening attire at breakfast. Not that it helped her feeling of being a scarlet woman. She felt everyone must be looking at her thinking that she was a right hussy.

Somehow, much to her amazement, the relationship continued. She knew from photos and his conversation that he had three children, the eldest of whom was 16 and the youngest 9. He and his wife had a good relationship, it was just that he was away from his family a lot. Working for the same firm for 16 years he had reached a high position and was given responsibility for several offices both in the UK and overseas, mainly France. He therefore flew abroad frequently. He and his family had lived for some time in the USA working for the firm and he could be sent away at any time. It was obvious that his life was dictated by his work. His family fitted in with that. He had a comfortable life and he enjoyed it. His hobby was his music and he was very good at it and loved performing at every opportunity.

Because of his travelling lifestyle he had not sung with anyone else for years. Usually to have a good singing partnership at the high performance standard that he wanted, entailed hours of practice and this could only be done with a regular routine. But with her and him, it was different. Although they needed to work on new songs together, they fitted in well musically, tone and timing blending so easily that it came out right, with little effort. It was a joy for both of them to sing together and the harmonies of song were matched by the harmonies of their bodies. His long tender fingers, so adept at caressing the strings of his guitar also played wonderful melodies with her body. She had never felt so physically in tune with anyone before.

It became a practice that he would call her on his car phone when he was on his way South, leaving a message on her answering machine if she wasn't there. Then they would arrange to meet at a pub in Lichfield. They decided to abandon the hotels he usually stayed in – which she hated anyway, and go to a Bed and Breakfast. A number of really nice places were around Lichfield, as it is a tourist town, and they tried them all in the first few weeks. It became a joke between them that they 'slept around', having tried so many beds in such a short time. Was it a record? she asked.

'Ah,' he said, 'but it doesn't count when you are with the same woman.'

The hardest thing for her was trying to come to terms with the situation, just taking it for what it was – an affair. Not only did it go against all her principles but she knew that it would end and that she would be left with nothing but a memory. Was that good enough? No, it wasn't. She was used to being in a loving, trusting relationship where the other person didn't drive away at the end of the week back to another life. She couldn't even work out what she felt; not jealous or resentful of his family. She probably saw more of him than they did at the moment and it was a different world. It was just the insecurity and the play-acting that was part of the excitement of the affair, especially for him, but which she felt she was most likely to be judged badly about.

Still, it was romantic, holding hands across the table over a candlelit dinner at different restaurants, staying in comfortable and even luxurious rooms and most of all the wonderful togetherness in singing and lying snug in his arms.

How long would it last? She didn't know. Every time he went away she didn't know when he would contact her again. She knew this affair was under his control. There was no-one else that even vaguely interested her; the rest of her life was very unsatisfactory and being with him was the most relaxing and happy way to spend a night, so when he called she always went to meet him.

There was no talk of love, no promises. He sometimes bought her some duty-free whisky from abroad. She bought him song books or tapes that she knew would interest him. She amused him when she talked about her travelling life that was totally different from his.

The regular B & Bs that they stayed in (after trying them all and deciding on a few they liked best), thought they were a delightful couple and they had to make sure their stories matched when they returned. At least it wasn't boring!

Gradually though, she could feel the passion dying, not the affection, on her side at least, she still delighted in his company. He was so different from her. She loved his elegance, his impeccable manners, his well-managed life. He never became flustered or ill tempered, though sometimes withdrawn. He appeared to have every situation under control and she felt totally secure when she was with him. But all the time she braced herself for the end and it eventually came.

Trouble at work had caused one of his colleagues to try and contact him one evening, believing him to be staying in the usual hotel. When he wasn't there the man had called his wife to check and she, of course, knew nothing of a change. So he was challenged about his whereabouts at home and the company insisted that he inform them of his accommodation in case of emergencies.

'So, we'll have to stop sleeping together for a while, until things 'cool off,' he told her when they met in the bar late one evening, 'but we can still go out together and sing.'

She had had a very strenuous day at work and a rather difficult meeting with some other people earlier in the evening so was shattered by his news and felt physically and emotionally exhausted. To go back home alone after their meeting was like a slap in the face. She was almost in tears and felt they must talk this out.

'Do you want us to stop this relationship altogether?' she tried to think logically while sitting beside him in his car in the carpark.

'It's up to you,' he said. 'Of course, I'd like us to still be friends.'

The next half hour's conversation was like something out of a Mills and Boon story. She felt she knew the script already. She knew the score... she shouldn't have got emotionally involved... it was only ever a superficial relationship ... etc...

At last she could stand no more and tears were totally inappropriate. Knowing herself to be the total loser, she got out of his car and drove away in hers.

After that they did sing together a few times but less frequently as his work took him away to France. Although she never really knew if the business trips were genuine or an excuse to stay away, she knew she had to turn her mind to other things and the plans she had been working on to leave the country were eventually completed. They spent one final night together to say goodbye.

She kept her emotions well in check as they packed their bags together in the morning. He was dressed elegantly in his business suit. She cast a final appraising glance over his slim, controlled body, remembering the joy it had given her.

'Send me a postcard,' he said in a tone that denoted the episode was now closed.

'Sure,' she countered lightly, 'and maybe I'll see you the next time I'm in town!'

'Now it's been something, seeing you again
And in the time we've had to spend
You've been so good to be around.
And I thank you for that special thrill-
Keeps me going on, until
The next time I'm in town'

Mark Knofler/Chet Atkins

Perish the Thought (1990)

Today was the day and she was running out of time. Yesterday she had been thwarted, in a very pleasant way. While she was looking at the ordinance survey map of the mountain on the hostel wall, a young Australian had started chatting to her about hiring climbing gear and together they had gone along to hire boots for both and wet-weather gear for him. He was a fresh-faced young lad, straight out of Melbourne Uni, and they had enough in common to enjoy a good chat – in between gasps of breath – while walking up the steep, primary track to the snowline.

The weather forecast had been bad for the summit so they didn't expect to get too far but enjoyed the bracing air and increasing views of the surrounding lochs and peaks. As they ascended the clouds rolled in, greying the day. On approaching the first hut, the wind to their backs, first sleet began and then heavy snow. All the mountain side above was completely hidden. Being well protected in her rubber boots, thermal wear and Gortex she felt warm and safe, enjoying the wildness of the weather and the battle with the elements.

In the shelter of the hut wall they shared a flask of hot tea and some biscuits before starting the descent across very boggy terrain which completely soaked the Aussies' leather boots. She was glad she'd opted for the rubber ones even though they were beginning to pinch and feel uncomfortable.

By the time they reached the road into Fort William the rain was pouring down and she was hobbling. They thankfully reached the pub and had a couple of pints of heavy before hitching a ride back to the youth hostel. Apart from the painful feet, it had been a great day.

That was yesterday. Today the young man was on his way and there were no more excuses. She waited until the other climbers had left so they would be well ahead. Climbing out of her bunk she packed her bags, checked out of the hostel and put all her gear, apart from her day pack, into the car. She would have to hire boots again, which was a bit of a problem, but the shop owner had said that if people were late getting back he didn't send out an alarm until late at night and it should be all over by then.

The day was glorious, couldn't be better for mountaineering. Yesterdays' blizzards had left a sparkling new dress of white on the mountain enhanced by the sun.

She was quite a while choosing her boots. She avoided yesterday's sore patches by wearing a different pair, leather this time, as the snow was fresh and she wouldn't be using that boggy return route.

The man in the hire shop was cheerful, 'Yes, it's a great day for the summit. Have a good climb!'

So it was after ten when she started, late for a day's climb unless you were a fast walker but OK for her purposes.

Taking the same ascent route as the day before she enjoyed the view which was even more spectacular because of the clear air. Valleys, lochs and even more distant peaks gradually unrolled under the wonderfully blue sky.

About half way to the summit turn she came up behind a very unfit looking fella walking very slowly and wearing jeans, (always the sign of a non-walker, she thought). But she was proven wrong. As she fell in beside his slow pace she learnt that he was a physical education teacher at an upper crust private school in the South of England, one that she was familiar with, it so happened, as it was in the region she had spent her childhood. With that to discuss and the fact that he was South African, she was able to relate her experiences in that area and the walk was slow and interesting. Yes, she had wasted yet more time to get to the summit and back before dark.

He looked up. 'Those are my pupils,' he said, pointing at an antline of figures crossing a much higher ridge. 'I'm just having a day off, a slow amble while the other teacher, an experienced mountaineer from this area, is leading them. In fact I shall turn back now. I don't want to get stuck on the mountain in the dark.'

'No,' she said, 'that would be a terrible thing. I shall have to hurry.'

They parted and she increased her pace toward the top. Another twenty minutes or so of walking and she started to meet other walkers returning. It was after 2pm and they said it was another hour to the top.

The snow was thicker and harder to walk in. Her feet crunched slowly but satisfactorily through it. She smiled and greeted more returning parties, eventually even the boys from the public school, led at a striking pace by their Scottish teacher.

She knew they must all think her foolhardy for going up when all sensible people were going down. Every experienced mountaineer knows you don't play games with the Ben, even on a clear day. The weather can change and, besides which, in the New Year darkness, comes early and swiftly. However, they could not know of her intention.

Eventually the trickle of downhill parties finished. People looked flushed with the thrill and triumph of a mountain climbed, especially on such a magnificent day as this. True, a few whispy clouds had drifted over but they were not threatening a change and just added to the kaleidoscope of colour.

As she reached the summit the full beauty of the vista spread out before her. Blues, greys, sparkling white and the crystals of huge icicles hanging down from the craggy peaks on which she was now standing. Looking over the side of the crevasse she shuddered at the thought of the fall. Momentarily she wished she'd brought a camera, then laughed at the absurdity of the thought.

The air was perfectly still. Gradually the colours were deepening as the sun began to go down. Yes, it would be a spectacular sunset and one that it would be thoroughly irresponsible to see unless you were very experienced and well-equipped with powerful torches for the dark descent.

Well, this was it. Time for the tablets. It was well below freezing now and after dark the temperature would drop much further. But one more thing ...

She reached into her bag to bring out the whistle pouch. As was her tradition every mountain she climbed must have *Si beg, Si Mor* (Big mountain, little mountain) played to it. Christ, it was cold! She hadn't felt it with the physical effort of walking uphill but now she was stationary she felt her body temperature dropping fast. She had to remove her mitts to play the tune. Her fingers seized with the cold almost immediately and it was an effort to finish the tune. It rang out across the peaks. Her last tribute to the mountain. What a spectacular place to bid farewell to the world she thought, as she tentatively reached for the small phial that she had been carrying for so long...

'That was a great wee tune!'

She spun around to see two heads popping up over the side of the ridge. Two guys dressed in army greens scrambled over the summit, complete with pick-axes. They had ascended the difficult face. They proceeded to open their packs, drank from their coffee flasks, handed her a piece of chocolate and chatted about the climb and the brilliant day.

'Ye're a wee bit late up here tho,' they commented. 'Do ye ha' a torch?'

'No,' she muttered, feeling silly.

'Well, ye'd better come wi' us but we ken the quick way doon.'

She hesitated, this wasn't the plan but what could she do?... Chicken.

'OK,' she said. 'Thanks'.

They took off at a great rate of knots, literally throwing themselves over the edge of the steep slopes and rolling down. She did her best to follow but couldn't match their pace. She struggled for about half an hour or so, not only with the terrain but with her conscience. Meanwhile the sun spread its last spectacular rays over the surrounding countryside and settled on the horizon in a ball of crimson, sinking quickly away and leaving a twilight which deepened the shadows and made it increasingly difficult for her to pick out the disappearing figures ahead.

As she caught up with the waiting men she knew they had begun to be worried.

'Ye shoulna left it sae late if ye didna' ha' a torch,' they said.

She knew that she was not only holding them up but putting them in a life-threatening situation. They <u>had</u> to get down quickly to beat the dark.

'It's OK,' she said, 'if we are now back on the path I can manage. Go on, I'll be alright.'

'We canna do that.'

She was aware she had created an ethical problem.

'Look!', one of them pointed back and above. 'There are some lights on the mountain. Some others are behind us. We can leave ye safely. They'll catch up and help ye doon.'

'Thanks very much,' she said, overcome with embarrassment, but relief for their sakes. They took off at a great pace and she prayed that she hadn't held them up to the extent that they would miss their footing in the dark. She knew they felt her irresponsible.

In the last grey moments of visibility, she carried on, beginning to stumble now as her feet were aching and her limbs were tired. Eventually the lights caught up and a Yorkshire accent said, 'Are ye reet lass? If you have no torch you can walk with us.'

'I'm a bit slow and I don't want to hold you up' she muttered, and, as they stopped to re-organise their load she carried on as fast as possible. At last she had to stop. The complete blackness surrounding her made it totally impossible to see the track.

The cold, even at this lower level beneath the snowline, was bitter. This is where I should turn off the path, she thought. This is what you came for. But again her courage failed her. And now more people knew she was around and might worry. She looked back for the lights and could see none. Conversely the panic now started that she was indeed alone on the mountain, that she had turned off the track and there now wasn't anyone following. It was pitch dark, very, very cold and she felt oh, so alone and frightened.

But here they came, welcome footsteps crunching on the loose rock. As they approached she said, 'Yes, if you don't mind I would like to come with you cos I can't see a thing.'

' No problems', they said. With one of their own torches failing they chatted on about the dangers of being unprepared on mountains. They spoke of all the mountains they had climbed and she compared experiences of the Himalayas, Mt Kenya and others, enjoying their easy companionship. In fact, despite her aching legs and sore feet the walk down was good fun and she was able to give them a lift in her car to where they had theirs parked.

'What about a drink?' they said. 'We'll meet you in the pub in the main street in about half an hour when we've got changed.'

Having booked out of the youth hostel she found another hostel the other side of the glen. She changed and hurried back to the pub, anxious to be in their warm company. A great evening followed, swapping yarns and anecdotes. She bought them a pint and a sausage sandwich for 'saving' her. They remembered some French red wine they had in the back of their car so carried on the party back in the hostel. She inwardly contemplated the irony of the situation. It was evenings like this, with kindred spirits, that made life worth living.

That night she lay warm and wine-drowsy in her bunk.

Alive – perish the thought.

Ben Nevis

Photo by: Leo Hoogendijk

A Great Result

He was barely twenty when the war began
A young man in his prime
They were short on pilots – so they took him
But gave little training time

He left his childhood love behind
Not knowing if he would return
As he braved the skies she faced the Blitz
Watched her neighborhood bombed and burn

To Canada on bombers to train
Then to Egypt's desert sands
There where his fighting squadron stayed
For forays on enemy land

One moonlit night he flew alone
Shadows fleeting on snow below
When out of the sky a Meschersmitt dived
There was nowhere for him to go

He pulled the joy stick back at once
To dodge the enemy's lethal aim
But the engine stalled, the plane was hit
His manoeuvers were in vain

With bullets raining all around
An emergency landing he made
Though wounded he crawled out from the plane
And thanked God his life was saved

The partisans found his broken craft
And him lying, in pain, close by
On a kitchen table his back they set
And smuggled him to Italian allies

At length he returned to Blighty's shore
Although posted 'missing, believed dead'
He married his childhood love at last
No more flying – but produced me instead!

Arthur Royle Bootherstone
1920–1973

The true story of my father's time in the RAF in WW2.

Flying with Angels (1993)

Old Tom pulled his thin, red cardigan around his boney shoulders and stared into the blue flames of the gas fire that was bravely battling the cold December weather. His small flat, part of a sheltered accommodation complex in Croydon, was adequate for his meager needs: he could spend the last years of his life in relative comfort.

'Me little castle,' he'd chuckle to his fellow pensioners in the common room. Here they'd sit playing dominoes while the telly blasted in the background, loud, you understand, for the deafer members of the community.

His little castle was showing signs of the festive season. The Lions ladies had been round last week to run an activity with the pensioners, encouraging them to make their own paper chains. Tom had laughed good-humouredly at their well intentioned, though somewhat bossy, efforts showing the old folk how to stick the chains together.

'I may be eighty three, love,' he'd said with a naughty wink, to one of the ladies, 'but I still know how to lick!'

'Get away with you, you rascal,' she'd laughed back and come into his flat with another woman to help hang the chain and tinsel around the pelmet.

'Brought Elsie as me chaperone,' she'd declared.

Now Tom took a sip of beer from a battered pewter mug and rubbed his thumb over the inscription. 'Welcome back Tom – from your mates in 213 squadron – January 1944'

His eyes glanced away from the mug and up to the mantel piece where several Christmas cards were displayed. From his daughters, grandchildren and great grandchildren mainly but there was one on the end that had a foreign greeting and his mind started to wander back, as it often did these days, and recall vivid memories.

Yes, it had been just before Christmas '43, the boys in the Squadron were looking forward to a spot of Christmas cheer, a break in the recce flights from their base in Italy across Yugoslavia. Night flights mainly, watching for enemy movement in that large theatre of war.

His dreamy eyes turned to the small Christmas tree his granddaughter had brought in for him. Sprayed with artificial snow, and he smiled. 'Bloody snow!'

He remembered how the moonlight reflected off the white blanket covering thousands of 'Christmas trees' in the forests of Yugoslavia. The sight had been enchanting, almost religious, 'an angels' eye view' he remembered thinking as he was on his way back to attend a party in the mess.

By the light of the almost full moon the shape of his aircraft cast a moving shadow on the snow below, flitting over the contours of the land.

But just then his eye caught another shadow converging on his and, looking up through the cockpit, he saw above him the Fokker. Fucking Fokker! There was no fight, he'd been taken by surprise and had no time to manoeuver. A burst from the Fokker's guns and his engines were hit, black clouds of oily smoke streaming behind him as he threw the plane into a glide and prayed for a clear patch of land and that he could escape the fire. He was too low to use the parachute. His luck was in, there was a clearing. He struggled to flare out and dropped the damaged craft onto an icy hard field. The undercarriage broke and the sound of tearing metal was like a death scream as the plane flopped on its belly.

Tom was thrown against the instrument panel, knocking his breath away and crushing his chest. Gasping with pain he threw the cockpit open and struggled out, only then realising, as the bright red blood dripped onto the white snow, that the straffing bullets had put a hole in his leg.

Fear lent him the strength to limp away to the shelter of some trees just before the petrol tanks exploded colouring the countryside and alerting the locals to his whereabouts. Fortunately, he was found by a group of partisans headed by a man named Stanic who carried him back to his farmhouse, cleaned and set his shattered leg and bandaged his broken ribs, laughing, distributing Slivovitch to both patient and 'doctor' (himself) and helpers, as anesthetic, medicine and Christmas cheer.

Despite the language barrier Stanic became became Tom's firm friend during the days he stayed hidden in the house while the resistance movement arranged his escape over the mountains to the hospital in Italy and finally back to his Squadron.

Stanic was long dead but his granddaughter kept the connection with Christmas cards.

Tom's mind was brought back to the present by the sound of giggling and shuffling feet outside the front door. Childish voices broke into song..... 'God rest ye merry gentlemen'.

'Yes,' thought Tom, 'I'm tired now, I'd like a rest.' His eyes closed as he heard the sweet refrain of 'Silent Night'.

'Little Angels,' he thought as he drifted back into recollections of his past and faraway friends.

The Meals on Wheels lady found him still there in his armchair the following day.

On the wings of memory Tom had flown to meet the angels.

Interview with Mr Rick Burgess, an Old-Time Motorcyclist

A young man, smart but casually dressed, found his way through the estate in Brixton to a small unit. He knocked on the door and, after a short while, it was opened by an elderly man, short and wiry in build with sparse, greying hair but with a lively twinkle in his eye.

'Good morning, you are Mr Burgess?' the young man enquired.

'Yes,' the occupant replied. 'What can I do for ya?'

'Mr Burgess, I am Harry White from the Brixton Times. I understand our editor told you we were coming to interview you. May I come in?'

Rick: 'Come in, come in lad, mind the step. Sit down and make yourself comfy. Now, what was it I can help you with? I'm a little hard of hearing these days.'

Harry: 'Mr Burgess, we are doing a series of features on our senior citizens in this area and have been told you have had a very interesting life and we would like to hear more about it. We understand you have travelled a lot and had an interest in motorcycling. Can you tell me more about it? I have a little recording device here. Is it ok if I set it up?'

Rick: 'Yes, that's ok. Marvellous what they 'ave these days. Just put it on the table.'

Harry looked around the sparsely furnished flat and put the recorder on a coffee table between two rather tatty armchairs.

Harry: 'If you just sit here Mr Burgess I'll sit opposite you. Don't take any notice of this little device. Just tell me about your adventures.'

They both sat down.

Rick: 'Ah yes, I've had a few adventures in me time. Call me Rick. Can't stand on ceremony you know. Gawd what an exciting life it's been. Can't get around much anymore 'cos of me arfritus but I sit 'ere wiv me memories and tell them wot's interested 'bout wot I got up to in the good ol days when I was on the road.'

Harry: 'Rick, please call me Harry. Can you tell us where you were born and brought up? Are you an original Londoner?'

Rick: 'I was brought up in Battersea near the old power station. Could see those old smoky towers for miles. Not much of a house, one of the terraced kind and there were a few of us kids sharing beds and the weekly barf in the old tin tub but it were 'ome. Me dad was a lorry driver and me mum took in washing. Didn't think much 'o school, got out as soon as I could and just took whatever job was going.'

Harry: 'Can you tell us how you became involved with motorbikes?'

87

Rick: 'In those days all of us lads had motorbikes to get around on; the old British ones, yer know BSA, Triumph, AJS, Matchless, Norton. I hadn't much money so I just had a 175 BSA Bantam to start off with but I saved some money a finally got a 500cc Velocette Venom, second hand 'o course, but was I proud!'

Harry: 'We understand that back in those days, the early 1960s, there were rural gangs 'mods' on scooters and 'rockers' on motorbikes. They had some clashes at Brighton, I believe, which made the news. Were you involved with this?'

Rick: 'Nah! I joined a local motorcycle club, the *Saltbox MCC* in Biggin Hill, Kent. The lads and lassies there were great. Did all sorts; road-racing, scrambles, trials and touring. Held in a caff, it were run by Bernie and his wife Joyce. Frothy coffee, big mug of tea, juke box, football tables, lots of friendly arguments over who had the best bike. Was mine o' course! If we swore or talked about sex or politics Bernie would fine us and we'd put a tanner in a pot which went for parcels for the old age pensioners at Christmas.

We had a committee, a Club magazine and organised club runs, take us hours to get anywhere as, with about 20 bikes, they was always breaking down!

I remember one time we went to Stonehenge, about 70 miles, it took us 10 hours to get there!

When we got there we tried to sacrifice one of the girls on the alter, young Linda, but she wouldn't 'ave it! You could walk all over them stones back in the sixties - can't do it now.

The bikes was unreliable in them days but it meant we all knew how to fix them. Anyway no-one could afford a mechanic. Most of the lads were apprentices on five quid a week.

Them 'as could, used to go rallying - that meant visiting a campsite in another part of the country, run by a different bike club. We'd have a bonfire and a sing-song on the Saturday night or go down the local pub if it were pissing wiv rain, which, 'o course, were usual.'

Harry: 'Was this just in Britain or elsewhere?'

Rick: 'We'd go 'on the Continent' too. One of the first foreign rallies I went to was the Chamois Rally in the Alps in France. Bloody loverly, lots of snow-topped mountains, but blue skies, no blooming rain. Then we went to the Stella Alpino rally in Italy. The local priest blessed the bikes on Sunday morning .Tasted me first proper Itie pizza, not a bit like *Pizza Hut*! Them rallies were in the summer but in the winter our favourite rally was the *Elephant Rally* held in the Eifel mountains In January. We'd go sliding along the frozen autobahn to get there having been up the previous night on the ferry across to Belgium.

Bloody freezing! But them Krauts! How they could drink! Schnapps! Eins, zwei, drei, suffa! Down it and get another. Great times wiv 'em fellas, just don't mention the war! He, he.'

Harry: 'So do you speak any other languages, Rick?'

Rick: 'Naw, just use sign language. Can't do that foreign lingo but I get along fine.'

Harry: 'Was there any special country you went to then?'

Rick: 'In 1967 I saw a mention of the FIM rally (*Federation of International Motorcyclists*) to be held that year in Moscow. Was behind the bloody Iron Curtain then, old Khrushchev in power. That looked interesting but you had to have special permission to go, an official invite, a visa and get an extra travel allowance. At that time you could only take fifty quid out of the country at one time.

We got to take eighty as it was such a long way – 1,800 miles. Three of us went from the *Saltbox* club. Me on me Velo, Linda on her 500 Triumph and Dave on his 305 Honda. Them Jap bikes were a novelty then, only one in the club– that were Dave's, and we used to give him packets of rice for fuel, he he. Bit of a different story now!

Had to go in convoy when we reached the Russian border, joining with the riders from other countries. An Intourist guide accompanied us in a car. The bastards made us drive at night! Bloody dangerous!

Our bikes were impounded when we got to Gorky Park and we had to go in Moscow central on public buses. The locals were a bit wary of talking to us. One bloke spoke English 'cos he'd been with the Brits in the war. He started singing, 'It's a long way to Tipparary' and the police came and dragged him off. Had to queue for everything in the big Gum store. Lots of dealing on the black market– we lived like kings.

There was vodka and caviar at the posh official opening of the bike rally in a grand hotel. There was only a couple of women riders and they got prizes. Our Linda was one of them.

We were taken on a tour of the Moscow underground, luverly mosaics and got to see the Moscow circus. Them clowns were a laugh.'

Harry: 'And did you have any breakdowns on this long ride?'

Rick: 'On the way back me petrol tank split in Czechoslovakia. A local guy nearly blew us up welding it back together! He put me and the others up in his house and fed us. More sign language. I think the battery on Linda's Triumph went kaput too somewhere but we just bought another one.'

Harry: 'And was that the longest journey you did?'

Rick: 'Nah, in 1968 I thought I'd go for a bit of a ride to Australia, check out the *Kangaroo Rally* there. So I got aboard me trusty Velo and off I went. Only took eight weeks. In those days you could go through Afghanistan and over the Kyber Pass into Pakistan. It were a bit dodgy, lots of bandits they said but I didn't see none.

Had to catch a boat from Madras in India to Penang in Malaysia and ride down to Singapore for another boat to West Australia. Then I went up to Shark Bay to dig salt. Now there's a job; you have to eat half the bloody stuff to keep yerself alive in that heat! Earnt a bit 'o money, enough to keep going around Oz to see what their bike scene was like there.

Got to the *Kangaroo Rally* in Ballarat and the *Southern Cross* in Adelaide. Aussie pubs were a bit rough. No sheilas allowed in the public bars. Not like at home where half the girls thrash you at darts in them there.

Sailed back to Blighty after a year or so and had a bit of a stint as a dispatch rider in London. Gawd, that were hard work weaving in and out of that traffic and dodging the black cabs. Hard on the bike too, I were always changing chains and cables.'

Harry: 'When was the last time you went on a long journey by bike?'

Rick: 'Me last long trip on the bike was up the Alaskan highway in the '80s. Those Yanks are a funny crowd but hospitable too. Then I came back home and got a job on the buses. Crikey! You get some strange members of the public. I'm only a little bloke and some of them were pretty rough.

Well, that's about it. Retired now and don't ride anymore. As I said, I have trouble wiv me old bones, me fingers pain me somfink cronic specially in the winter.'
Harry: 'Just one last thing, Rick, have you ever been married?'
Rick: 'Naw, never been one for the birds but I did have a girlfriend later on in life and we did a few bus trips and overseas visits together but she weren't too well and has passed on now– Gawd bless 'er.'
Harry: 'Well. Thank you very much, Rick, it has been so interesting talking to you and I think we have enough for an article now. We will let you know when it will be printed.'
Rick: 'No problem, nice to fink back on those good ol' days. 'Ere, want a cuppa before you go?'
Harry: 'No thanks, must be on my way back to the office. Thanks again, Rick, a wonderful story, I think the boss will be very happy with this.'
And picking up his recorder Harry left, leaving Rick to reminisce alone.

A Scotsman felt chilled round his knees
As his kilt lifted up in the breeze
He started to frown
Could not pull it down
Cos his pipe he was having to squeeze

Some people do live in glass houses
With all their children and spouses
And their neighbours can see
When they finish their tea
That they slacken the belt on their trousers

Ann Davison

There once was a lady, her life had been shattered
She lost all she had to the deep rolling sea
Though deep in despair with spirit unbroken
She thought of a way she could once more be free

So she found a wee boat and she made it her own place
With charts and provisions she sailed far away
Leaving behind her the Straights of Gibraltar
She faced the Atlantic alone and afraid

But Ann Davison won her own fight with the ocean
And landed at last on Dominica's shore
First woman to sail that great sea singlehanded
She made a new life, came to England no more

Now forty years later another brave woman
Will again make that passage in Ann's memory
For Julia Bartlett will face the Atlantic
Another small ship on that deep rolling sea

Ann Davison wrote three books: 'My Ship So Small', 'Last Voyage' and 'Home was an Island'.
See 'Sacrifices for the Sea' on the following page.

Sacrifices for the Sea

Not all yachties are law-abiding. It seems that some would rather face the storms of nature than those of a man-made legal kind. The no man's land of the ocean offers an escape route from land-tied obligations.

Two strong, adventurous women bear out this theory and have many experiences in common.

In 1952 a 37-year-old Englishwoman, Ann Davison, was the first woman to cross the Atlantic single-handed, from Plymouth to Antigua. Her vessel was a tiny 23' yacht, the *Felicity Ann*, built in Cornwall by the Mashford brothers.

Ann's successful voyage, with no self-steering or GPS, was the result of hard work and determination, following a previous disastrous attempt to leave the UK for America three years earlier.

A remarkable woman, she grew up in the West Country and at an early age learnt to fly. She met her husband to be, Frank Davison, whilst working for a flight company for which she was an aviator, delivering mail all around the UK.

Ann and Frank bought their own airfield but sold it shortly after WW2 and took up farming on one Scottish island, later moving to another. Both locations were remote and entailed self sufficiency on a gruesome scale. Scottish weather is not conducive to pushing the boat out to get to a village to buy provisions and collect mail.

Finally the couple decided to leave Blighty and head for America, the land of opportunity. To this end they purchased a 70' ketch and moored it in Lancashire while they began the re-fit. To equip a ship so large, to be manned by just two, needed much planning and physical work. Frank, being a perfectionist, would not compromise and the debts for mooring fees and materials kept mounting. Finally, in desperation, without full equipment but with a re-possession note about to be pinned on their mast, Frank and Ann weighed anchor and their home *Reliance*, slipped quietly out of harbour after dark.

Unfortunately, the time of year was wrong for safely navigating the unpredictable Irish Sea and they were blown off course. The ship was wrecked on the treacherous rocks of Portland Bill. In the middle of a violent storm Frank was washed overboard, totally lost, and Ann found herself, deposited by the cruel sea, alone on the beach with only the clothes she stood up in. Soaked by the icy cold waters and in shock she crawled up the cliffs and found a local cottage where she was taken in and revived.

That was in 1949. Ann was devastated at the loss of her partner and her way of life but found a job in a boatyard and with courage and determination saved enough money to realise the dream she and Frank had had three years earlier. She bought *Felicity Ann* and set off once more to America.

This time she was successful. She stayed in America, never returning to the UK. During several years touring the inland waterways on other craft she met her second husband, Bert, who shared her love of sailing. They settled in Florida. Ann wrote several books of her experiences and finally passed away in 1992.

In 1990 another female English sailor, Julia Bartlett, was inspired by Ann's story and decided to follow in her footsteps forty years on. Julia had a skippers' licence and a 28' Morgan Giles sloop which she had moored in Malta. She sailed around the Mediterranean during her holidays from her demanding job as a Senior Probation Officer, which entailed working in high security prisons such as Brixton and Dartmoor.

Unlike Ann, who had no offspring, Julia was a fifty-year-old grandmother. Although divorced, she kept in touch with her children and also had a very active private life. Her slim body and blond good looks attracted several suitors and her quick mind and practical abilities meant that she was seldom a lone sailor. However, Julia decided that, to make this solo attempt, she would choose a female crew to prepare the boat and sail it as far as the Canaries from whence she would go on alone.

Of course rules had changed since Ann's voyage in 1952 and prices had also risen. In order to fund the enterprise Julia set up a company *The Mermaid Initiative* literally taking on board two other women to help with the publicity and fundraising in the UK before crewing abroad.

Ann, in America, was contacted in the hope that they could meet up when Julia arrived in the States and everything was set to go.

Julia and the crew worked on the little ship *Forlanda* in the boatyard in Valetta, Malta and set sail in the summer of 1991. Unfortunately one of the crew, though having helped in the fitting and publicity, could not overcome her seasickness and had to leave the boat in the Aeolian Islands from whence she made other arrangements to travel to Gibraltar and meet up with the yacht there.

The Mediterranean leg was uneventful and after re-fitting and another crew change in Gibraltar, Julia left for the Canaries. From there she continued alone, facing the Atlantic in her tiny craft, just like Ann, forty years before, and also without self steering as funding did not suffice.

Her Gibraltar contacts heard nothing for weeks and then came the news that, only about 300kms from the American coast, *Forlanda* became embroiled in a huge storm. Julia sent out an SOS and a passing freighter lifted her to safety. *Forlanda* was abandoned and her bedraggled captain taken to America.

And what was the cost and result of this voyage?

Julia had not been able to keep up the mortgage payments on her house in the UK so it was repossessed. Her solicitors, also lacking payments, issued a summons, which being out of the country, she ignored. The fees for salvage could not be collected as it was discovered that the little boat *Forlanda* was not actually in Julia's name and it had no insurance.

Calculating all these risks beforehand and knowing she was out of money before she even left Gibraltar, Julia was prepared to, and did, lose property and some credibility from her old life but went on to forge a new, successful and happy one in the States. Soon after her arrival there she re-met another sailing acquaintance and they set up home together on his yacht. Now in her 80s she writes for sailing journals and is involved with yachting brokers in the Caribbean area.

Unfortunately, she did not meet Ann, who died just before Julia reached her part of the world. I think maybe that was Julia's one regret in the whole experience.

Both women were remarkable for their tenacity and positive thinking in the face of both natural and man-made, even self-made, obstacles.

They both defied law and convention to follow their dreams and go to sea. Sometimes one has to sacrifice one life to find another.

A Mountain Scorned

The weather was hot and sticky in Catania, Sicily. The *Forlanda* was moored alongside the old docks which had no facilities but it was too expensive to dock at the new marina. Julia, the captain, wanted to stay and play with the errant Loran navigation instrument on board *Forlanda*, so Linda and Mel set off for town together to find the bus station that would take them to Mt Etna. They were told that the bus would leave in about half an hour. The presence of other Northern European faces in the queue confirmed that it was the right one and eventually the bus did show and they climbed aboard. Linda chatted to the Yugoslav couple who were also heading for the mountain and the hour's journey, broken by only one coffee stop, passed pleasantly enough.

Climbing away from the town limits and gaining height the countryside changed to gorse-covered greenery and the air grew cooler. Linda realised, with a sense of self-annoyance, that, having been dressing only in the minimum attire for hot conditions on the boat at sea level, she had completely forgotten about the effect of altitude. Her shorts and T-shirt were still adequate for this height but she had brought no extra clothing for the climb. Silly person.

Mel was quiet on the bus trip, saying she didn't feel too well and her recent leg injury, sustained in the boat yard, was not completely healed. Linda wondered at her insistence in coming to climb a mountain.

The bus eventually pulled up at the base area where the souvenir shops abounded and tickets were available for the cable car which saved a good two hours' walk but still stopped some way from the summit. The cost was exhorbitant. They decided that if they walked briskly, they should have enough time to make the return trip by foot and still catch the afternoon bus back to town.

Unsure of the way, they took a while to locate the beginning of the uphill track. The loose volcanic debris was difficult to walk on and their feet slipped on its strange texture. The mountain was just like a dirty grey slag heap, no vegetation or beauty here above the snow line. As they climbed, it became obvious that this sort of terrain needed full physical strength to walk over and that Mel, with her knee injury, was in trouble trying to keep up. The other couple were polite in waiting for her and obviously Linda felt obliged to keep going back to make sure she was OK. Her frustration increased.

'Go back, Mel, this is not for you,' she urged. 'Wait at the bottom.'

'No, I'll just go as far as I can,' the injured girl replied but her slow pace held up the whole party and by the time they reached the cable car stop, it was obvious Mel would have to descend by mechanical means.

They had lost over an hour of climbing time and now it would be impossible to get to the top and back in time. However, Linda and the Yugoslav boy strode out to gain some extra height for another half hour's walk before they would turn back to meet his girlfriend for the descent. The mountain had changed its face. Now early afternoon, the clouds had rolled over and the sky looked threatening. The higher altitude added to the considerable drop in temperature. Shorts, T-shirt and canvas shoes were no attire in which to continue but neither of them had any choice. The trip further up caused more frustration. The summit was in sight but was unobtainable timewise. Linda had never yet left a peak unconquered. To turn back without reaching the top was very annoying, especially when this was probably her only chance at this mountain. Muttering unkind thoughts about people not being fit to climb mountains, making it impossible for others who were, she reluctantly turned back down. It was now really cold.

Just as they left the shelter of the cable-car coffee shop the heavens opened and the hail began. The cold was now bitter and the stones pummelled the skin, stinging and numbing her limbs. Thoughts of exposure, the foolhardiness of coming without proper protective clothing, and how in extreme conditions people even lost their lives over such a stupid mistake, all flashed through her mind. Some other people had stopped a little further down, under a rocky overhang but its narrow roof was not adequate for all of them and Linda became anxious as she noticed the Yugoslav boy turning blue with cold and shaking uncontrollably.

'We must keep going,' she said. 'Run as fast as you can. Keep moving to keep up your body temperature.'

As they headed back out into the streaming rain and hail, her canvas shoes began to disintegrate and her fingers became numb with cold. She slapped her hands on her thighs as she ran.

'Could you get frost bite in these conditions?' she wondered. In some ways it was quite exhilarating and if she hadn't been so cold, it would even have been enjoyable.

The rain and hail ceased as they lost altitude, the storm clouds remaining above them. When they reached the base camp area, the sun was out and some warmth returned to her limbs, bringing with it a painful, tingling sensation. What an experience! Linda felt stupid at not having been prepared. Mountains always have to be respected, and she'd climbed enough to know. Then another thought hit her. There was an important procedure that she had omitted and this had obviously invoked the wrath of the mountain gods. In her frustration and anger at not reaching the summit she had neglected to play *Si Beg Si Mor* on her whistle when reaching her highest point.

No wonder there had been a storm!

She'd not forget to do that again. Hell hath no fury like a mountain scorned.

The Wee Magic Stane (1990)

She sat at the cafe table, sipping her iced coffee and gazing out on the idyllic scene: clear blue skies, a sheltered bay with whitewashed houses, splashed with Mediterranean-blue paintwork, sun-bronzed, beautiful people lazing on beach and boat, gentle waters lapping against the jetty and the smattering of yachts and powerboats anchored out within rowing distance of the shore with its trendy restaurants and souvenir shops. This was Lipari in the Aeolian Islands, the Italian millionaires' playground.

She had walked the small town from end to end not daring to look too closely at the overpriced souvenirs, instead just buying a few post cards, receipt of which would incite a few envious comments she knew. Just goes to show, she thought. Even paradise can have its problems. And she drew her mind back to her own. Her eyes focused once more on *Forlanda* bobbing up and down at anchor a few hundred yards out. That was the problem – *Forlanda* bobbed. All boats bob in the water. They are built to, but she wasn't and that was the final unalterable fact.

She had never had a relationship with a ship before. Other land vehicles – yes. She'd grown fond of a few of them in her time, working on them and riding or driving them through all sorts of countries and conditions until she felt attached to them and often found it hard to sell them. But boats? No. For years she'd known, that even though she admired their lines and concept, motion sickness was a problem, so she'd never become intimate with one – until *Forlanda*. In becoming involved with her owner, Julia's trans-Atlantic project, she'd desperately wanted to try and overcome the problem, hopefully with the help of the new anti-emetic drugs.

She'd seen photos and videos of *Forlanda* and read her specifications on paper in all the promo literature they had circulated for sponsorship, but it had been a year until she actually clapped eyes on her in Malta after driving overland from the UK. Yes, she was a pretty boat, 30 foot long, deep-keeled, narrow and dainty. Julia had decorated the interior tastefully and her weeks of hard work on the deck and exterior woodwork, not to mention rebuilding the rudder and repositioning the bilge pumps, gradually endeared *Forlanda* to her.

The trip from Malta to Lipari had taken two weeks and had been a real endurance test. Though they had seldom encountered more than force four to five winds there had not been one single day when she hadn't vomited. She had tried Stugeron, wrist bands, ear patches and even suppositories, one after the other – or even together! To no avail. She was sick, sick, sick – and sunburnt – and thoroughly fed up. She had spent two hours swaying around town this morning feeling sick on dry land because the motion stayed with her from just being at anchorage when the power boats created a swell.

It was now or never. If she sailed on the next leg of the journey it would take several days of open sea and then they'd touch even more remote islands from which there could be no return. The next possible retreat wouldn't be until Sardinia and that would make it very expensive if not impossible to get back to Malta where her trusty BMW motorcycle lay in storage. Her eyes blurred with tears. It wasn't fair. She'd so much wanted to become a sailor. She loved the life and the people she met, the exotic places and the camaraderie, the salty tales and gin and tonic. But she *couldn't* go on.

The very thought of setting foot on that bobbing deck made her stomach turn again.

What were the options? None really. Useless to the other crew members she must leave now and take connecting ferries back to Malta. Then what? This needed discussion. Too much of her mental and physical effort had gone into this project to abandon it completely and *Forlanda* was more than just a boat. It had become a home base. Now where would she go to find another?

Julia had arranged to meet her here on shore at midday. From the café, Linda watched as she lowered the dingy over the side, got in and rowed ashore, her lithe sun-tanned body dressed in the familiar red T-shirt and bikini.

'Hi, Linda', Julia called. They exchanged greetings and then ordered iced coffee.

'Julia, I have something to tell you,' she blurted, the words hanging dramatically on the hot still air.

As they sipped their drink she haltingly and unhappily told Julia of her decision. They sat for more than half an hour discussing the pros and cons of what her departure would mean to the rest of the team; how she could continue to be useful, how they could keep in touch; the possibility of a return to the UK for publicity purposes, depending on flight costs, or coming down to Gibraltar by road to continue with the shore-based activities before Julia's final departure for the Canary Islands and then America.

Somewhat comforted by the thought that there might be an alternative plan of action, she remained on shore while Julia rowed back to inform the other crew member of the discussion and decisions made. She made a few more enquiries in town as to ferry times and costs, visited the port office to have her name taken off the crew list and took a last look around the island before heading back to the shore for her pick up. She would have to endure another two days on

Julia Barlett, Linda Bick and Sally Read

the boat before the ferry to the mainland departed.

As her feet shuffled in the pebbles and shells she noticed many ceramic tiles, broken and worn smooth by the action of the sea and deposited in a colourful collection. Some of the pieces were plain white ceramic on their terracotta background. Her initial thought was that they could be painted on, perhaps tiny pictures of *Forlanda* as a souvenir of Julia's crossing. She began collecting them, intending to mention the idea as soon as she got aboard. Amongst the plain tiles there were one or two that had patterns on them and one in particular caught her eye. Roughly triangular in shape, about 2" long, it had a central pattern like a five petalled flower and was toned orange and brown which blended well with its terracotta base. Along with some others she popped it into her bag. For some reason it had attracted her.

Once again aboard *Forlanda*, discussions continued and preparations were made for her departure. Two days later she left the ship, Julia rowing her across the bay in the still, translucent dawn light to where the ferry terminal hummed with people carrying their holiday souvenirs back to the mainland. She was laden with a huge sail bag, tent, sleeping bag, clothes, cameras and tapes ; all her possessions that had been tucked away on *Forlanda* over the past few months on land and sea. It was indeed a struggle to get them transferred from one ferry to another and back to Malta. And then what? Should she continue, or maybe make a home-base here? The Maltese people were friendly and helpful and there was a possibility of a teaching job. But then what of the project? She was still tied to *Forlanda*...

After two weeks she re-packed her bike and took to the road once more. She spent a week travelling and camping, first taking a ferry to Marseilles and then travelling through Spain to Gibraltar where she intended to await the arrival of *Forlanda*. Her tent was once more her home for the duration of the trip. After helping in Gibraltar with the refit and provisioning of *Forlanda*, her usefulness was at an end and the problem again arose of where to 'settle'.

She had been camped for some time just over the Gibraltarian border in Spain in a campsite that surrounded and sheltered her with familiar Australian eucalypts. She had become friendly with the inhabitants, many of whom worked in Gibraltar and commuted back to this patch of greenery amongst the Spanish hills each night. It was a haven from the concrete jungle and hassle of that small city spread around a barren rock.

As the autumn drew on the rains began and it was obvious that a decision had to be made. To spend the winter months anywhere in a tent is uncomfortable and impractical. With no reason to stay in Spain, her thoughts flew back to Malta, the friends she had made there and the possibility of returning and finding work and a home there.

She checked ferry times, made phone calls and had farewell drinks. She allowed three days to ride to catch the cargo boat from Marseilles and braced herself for an early morning start. 6.30 am. Time to get packing but already the rain fell, dampening the ground and her spirits. She just didn't want to go. She was tired of travelling and being rootless. There was but one alternative; a friendly English woman on the camp-site, Cath, had a tiny caravan for sale, cheap. If she could negotiate a reasonable price for land rent then perhaps it would provide suitable shelter for the winter where she could do her writing and find some work in Gibraltar to keep her going. Within minutes she was running over to Cath's caravan and stated her intention to a somewhat bewildered husband who was just leaving for work.

A few hours later, with key in hand, she entered her new possession and looked around. The van was basic and newly cleaned and Cath had thrown some freshly laundered curtains over the bare foam of the seats to provide some sort of cover and a more homely feel. The place had potential. The size, layout and utilisation of space reminded her of the interior of a boat. It was with a sense of relief that she packed the tent and transferred her few belongings into the van. The first place that she had called her own for several years, it gave her a feeling of belonging somewhere. As she moved around, straightening the makeshift seat covers, the pattern on them caught her eye. It had a sense of familiarity about it; the tones of orange and terracotta brown. Unpacking continued and going through all her possessions to find a nook and cranny for each one she eventually tackled the pockets of her rucksack, holder of everything of worth. In one of the small pockets her hand fell upon the smooth texture of ceramic and she drew out the weathered stone that she had found on the beach at Lipari, the only one that she had kept, having passed on the rest to Julia. With dawning realisation, she looked at the pattern and colouring of the stone, then at the pattern on the seat covers. There was the floral shape, the brown and white colouring… almost identical.

She felt a buzz of destiny, a link lay between the losing of one home and the finding of another.

The wee magic stane.

My new home in the south of Spain.
I lived in this caravan for about a year.

Women On The Rock (Gibraltar 1992)

'Motorcycling is a sexually transmitted disease,' laughed Nicole Corby when I asked how she became involved.

Having met her husband-to-be at age 13, she immediately shared his interests and, by the time she was 16, she was more than ready to get her own bike - a Honda 400/4. Now at age 26 Nicole is mother of three young boys and admits - much as she loves her family and nursing job - if she did not have the bike as a means of unwinding and escape from their demands, she does not know how she would cope.

'Women who do not ride bikes do not know what they are missing,' she said with great feeling.

In Gibraltarian society Nicole is unusual. She emphasises that without her husband's support it is unlikely that she would have combated the cultural pressure against Gibraltarian women riding. Even now (1992) the Gibraltarian motorcycle club is for men only and only about eight Gibraltarian women ride proper motorcycles.

Last year Nicole initiated the organisation of a charity run for all women bikers that she hopes will bring them together in a society which is a hotch-potch of mixed races, mainly Spanish and British, and a meeting point for travellers and tourists from all over the world.

The British-owned Rock of Gibraltar itself offers very little attraction for motorcyclists, the whole area covering two and a half square miles and the town jam-packed with traffic. However, the surrounding countryside in Spain has magnificent vistas, well-sealed winding roads in mountains and along a sparkling seafront and plenty of interesting Spanish villages to explore - not to mention the availability of cheap wine.

What the Rock does offer for British bikers especially is a year-round riding climate (average 12C in winter and 24C in summer) and an English-speaking community in which it is permissible to work. These factors have combined to attract quite a number of expatriate motorcyclists and a growing percentage of these are women. Some rode their own bikes from the UK either with their partners, as in the case of Hilary Simkins (29, EN 450 Kawasaki) and Kim Bonner (23, CB 250 Honda) or alone like diminutive 20-year-old Megan Davis who rode her CB200 Honda all the way from the Isle of Wight with no wet weather gear and only two spark plugs as spares and a lot of faith!

Other women bought their bikes in Gibraltar some having a previous interest in motorcycling and others more recently encouraged by husbands, boyfriends or other women riders like Liz Acris who rides a Yamaha 250 Virago.

Many use their bikes for commuting from their cheaper accommodation in Spain to work in Gibraltar and find a bike is the most sensible form of transport to use to get through the queue across the Spanish/Gibraltar border, but now, having shared experiences and skills, they also meet in the many bars along the waterfront and in the town centre and arrange other activities.

The *Manana Motorcycle Club* (headquarters Rodolfo's Bar) was recently formed to cater for British motorcyclists, both men and women and Sharon Hassall is secretary. This club organises social events, charity runs and bike shows as well as camping weekends in Spain. MAG (*Motorcycle Action Group*) and FEM (*Federation of International Motorcyclists*) are promoted in the club by

Hilary Simkins, the Gibraltar rep. Hilary lives on a 30'boat in the Marina, but plans to dismantle her bike and take it with her when she and her boyfriend sail away – stowing it in the forepeak. For some, like Hilary, Gibraltar is the first break away from the UK and for others another stop on the way around the world.

Obtaining motorcycle insurance in Gibraltar is not cheap or easy. Many companies simply will not insure bikes or anyone under the age of 27. The company most people insure through is Generali, an Italian company which will only insure Gibraltar-registered bike and only on a 3rd party basis.

It is understandable that the majority of two-wheeled vehicles are 50cc mopeds which do not attract the same high rates.

Petrol in Gibraltar, which uses Sterling, is 37p per litre and oil £1.60p.

Despite registration and insurance difficulties and delays in shipment of spare parts, motorcycling in Gibraltar continues to flourish. With their *Women for Somalia* charity ride in October the women on the Rock, both Gibraltarian and British, intend to take part in the promotion and enjoyment of the international world of motorcycling.

NOTE
The womens' ride for Somalia was a huge success with about 20 women riders taking part and collecting quite a large amount of money for the cause.

In 2001 the *Women's International Motorcycle Association* (WIMA) held its annual international rally in Castellar, Spain (where I was living) and as part of the week long festivities I organised a ride for the women across the runway at Gibraltar airport. This has never been done before or since. There were about 80 women riders from Gibraltar, England, Spain, Australia, Japan, Germany, France, Holland, Sweden and Australia who were led on two passes of the runway (which dissects the road in that was closed to traffic) by one of the RAF officers who was on his Harley Davison and grinning from ear to ear!

Birthdays I Will Always Remember (47th)

My 47th in 1992, saw me living in a small caravan in Spain on a campsite, La Casita.

I had the good fortune to meet musician Michael 'Beans' Gardner and his artist girlfriend, Kelli Snivelly. They were from Michigan, USA and touring Europe for a year in a station wagon they had bought in the UK. They were out of money and looking for work so stopped to enquire at La Casita to see if they could find employment there; Beans as a musician in the restaurant and Kelli behind the bar.

The owner, Pepe, agreed and so they stayed and we became friends, me introducing myself with my whistle as another musician.

On the night before my birthday, I rode back from Gibraltar late and came into the bar to sing with Beans. Kelli knew it was the eve of my birthday and kept plying me with Margaritas. The last thing I remember was talking to her, nursing probably my third or fourth glass and then... 'twas morning, my birthday. I was lying on my back in my caravan, fully dressed and with blood all over my face. When I was able to sit up and look in the mirror a horrible sight stared back. Bloodshot eyes and ripped nose and lips. I couldn't remember what on earth had happened. Was this a flash back to my 7th birthday – a 40 year time warp?

I sheepishly asked my neighbours but they said they'd left the bar before me and didn't know anything. Who had I been fighting with? Eventually I found Kelli and Beans who said that I had been so legless that they'd driven me home but on getting out of the car I'd fallen flat on my face on the gravel path. They'd just been able to lift me inside the caravan where they'd left me out cold. My face took weeks to mend. Funnily enough though, I still like Margaritas.

A Sort of Sortie

As another way of making money, I suggested to Beans that we write an historical show and present it to the Gibraltar schools. I had already done a show like this in South Australia so was familiar with the format and Beans was an excellent musician and performer.

So, with a little research in the Gibraltar library and a lot of creative script and songwriting, *A Sort of Sortie* was born.

It was very well received in all the schools in Gibraltar and even a few in Spain. We made some money for Bean and Kelli's onward travel and even produced a song cassette. Kelli had a successful art exhibition in Gibraltar.

Michael 'Beans' Gardner now sails his yacht around the Virgin Islands performing musical shows at marinas. Kelli's art is sold from galleries around USA.

Michael 'Beans' Gardner and Linda in Gibraltar, 1992

Is it a Mountain?

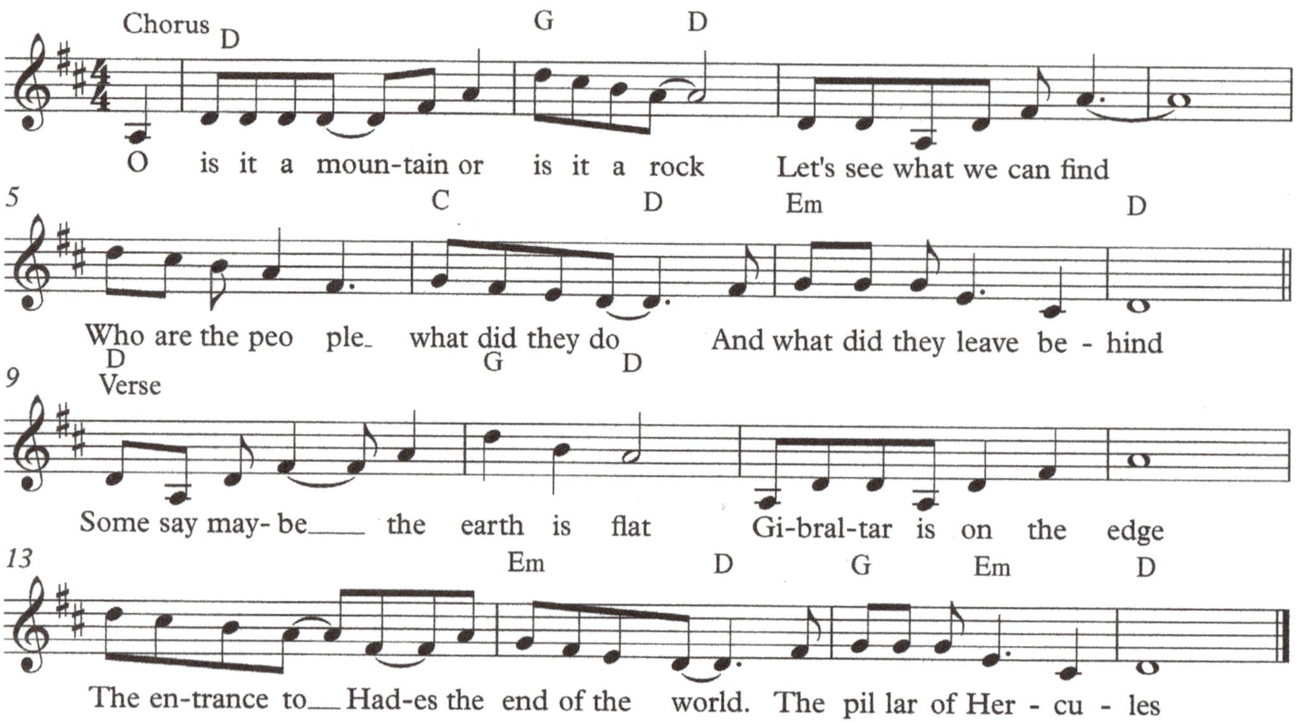
Chorus
D G D
O is it a moun-tain or is it a rock Let's see what we can find
C D Em D
Who are the peo ple what did they do And what did they leave be - hind
Verse
D G D
Some say may- be the earth is flat Gi-bral-tar is on the edge
Em D G Em D
The en-trance to Had-es the end of the world. The pil lar of Her - cu - les

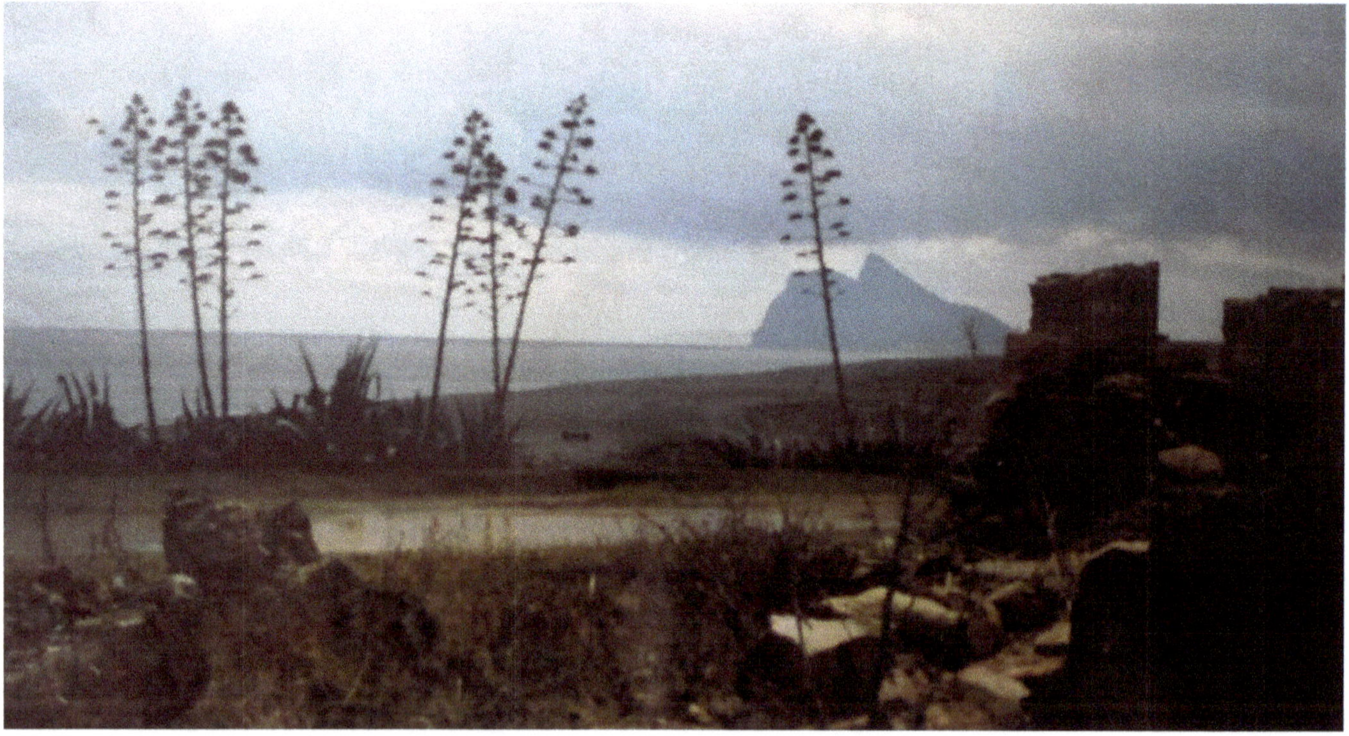

Chorus:
Is it a mountain or is it a rock
Let's see what we can find
Who are the people what did they do
And what did they leave behind

There's some say maybe the earth is flat
Gibraltar is on the edge
The entrance to Hades, the end of the world
The pillar of Hercules

Chorus

Phoenicians and Romans and Visigoths too
They all had their own way
The Moors and the Spanish, the red, white and blue
Came sailing in the bay

Chorus

The sieges were many then Rook took the rock
The British were here to stay
But life wasn't easy, they still had to fight
To have what they have today

Chorus

So this is Gibraltar a time and a place
They've called it in history
A den full of smugglers, a basket of rogues
But a wonderful place to be

Gibraltar has been fought over by many nations and there is still conflict over it's ownership between Spain and Great Britain. The song describes some of the nations involved and also mentions the fact that many duty free items are smuggled over the border.

The Seige Song

Oh we had to shoot the hor-ses and stop flour-ing our wigs When the meat ran out we were forced to live on rice We got small pox we got scur-vy and we dreamed of legs of lamb and on the whole it was-n't ver-y nice. Oh we sent them beef from Bar-ba-ry it was fire ship in dis-guise and we near-ly sank that wret-ched Brit-ish fleet. But then they turned the boats ar-ound and sent them back our way. And we had to beat a ve-ry swift re-treat

Gibraltar:
Well we had to shoot the horses and stop flouring our wigs
And when the meat ran out we were forced to live on rice
We got smallpox, we got scurvy but we dreamed of legs of lamb
And on the whole it wasn't very nice

Spain:
Oh we sent them beef from Barbary, it was fire-ships in disguise
And we nearly sank that wretched British fleet
But then they turned the boats round and sent them back our way
And we had to beat a very swift retreat

Gibraltar:
So then we dug the tunnels and turned the rock into a gun
To try and shoot the gunboats sent at night
They bombarded us with cannon but rested after lunch
So we had time to load our guns up for the fight

Spain:
We tried very hard to starve them but their ships came right on through
However much we tried they got away
At first Rodney and then Derby came and gave them some relief
So they lived on to fight another day

Gibraltar:
Now the French and Spanish got together and made a clever plan
To build some boats they thought we could not sink
But we stoked the grates and fires up and gave them red hot shot
And when the boats caught fire they landed in the drink

Spain:
Then one night when we were sleeping they crept out on the Rock
And spiked our guns before we had a chance
So the Grand Assault was over, the Siege was at an end
We went back to Spain and the French went back to France
Yes, the Grand Assault was over, the Siege was at an end
We went back to Spain and the French went back to France

The Siege of Gibraltar by the Spanish and French was 1779-1783. Spain has been trying to get Gibraltar back ever since!! This siege was so well known that in 1782 Mozart composed music in its honour.

A Whistling Gypsy Rover (1992)

I'm a freeborn man of the travelling people,
Got no fixed abode-with nomads I am numbered.
Country lanes and byways were always my ways.
I never fancied being lumbered.

'Travelling People' Ewan McColl

If you walk along Gibraltar's Main Street any day except Sunday, between 10am and 3 pm, you will hear the strains of a tin whistle piping out a Celtic tune. Following the sound to its source you will find an elfin-like, dark-haired woman playing the instrument accompanied by a pixy-ish, fair-haired child adroitly juggling 'devil sticks'.

Sun-bronzed and happy in their work, this is Ross Asquith with one of her brood of four travelling children, making their way by earning a living on the streets of Gibraltar and indeed the road of life. Their home at the moment is a tent in a nearby campsite in Spain and, as busking has proved so successful, Ross and her kids intend to stay for the rest of the summer before moving on to the Canaries to spend the winter months.

For 42-year-old Ross, mother of 10 (although only the youngest four are with her now), life has been interesting and full of new experiences. Since becoming travellers four years ago, she and her youngest children have learnt to take the rough with the smooth and make the best of opportunities presented, especially learning new skills and using them to their advantage.

Ross wasn't born a traveller, in fact she came from a select and secluded society in Buckinghamshire, but at an early age she rebelled against that lifestyle, feeling more for the type of community spirit that she recognised in the TV program *Coronation Street* than for her own background. Marrying at sixteen, she 'escaped' to Yorkshire and started a family, living for many years what most people think of as a conventional life on a council estate.

By 1989 Ross was living sans spouse with six of her 10 children in a council house in Halifax, the other four having grown up and left home. By way of a change she decided to take them on a short holiday to the Canaries. The planned three-week trip turned into three months and four of the children stayed there, with her finding a new world in the sun and meeting many international people who inspired her with their travelling tales. She couldn't face going back to 'normal' life in Yorkshire so returned instead to Wales where she took jobs cleaning and washing up whilst living in rooms in winter but preferring to camp out in the summer months.

It was in Wales that Ross met up with many travellers, attended the Bala festival and decided on the idea of having her own transport in the form of a small van, supplemented by a small tent to accommodate them all at night. However, when the English winter again brought its problems, she rented a cottage for a while. The spring saw her putting together a horse and cart for a travelling life around Wales. On the whole, Ross and her band were well treated as travellers and, apart from the occasional hassle and taunts, found life free and happy. Two of the most memorable places that she visited at this time, both for their beauty and hospitality, were the villages of Berriew near Welshpool and Dinas Mawddwy.

As the children were not receiving formal education in school, Ross set aside time every day to teach them from course books that they carried with them and the children were learning many things about survival off the land, becoming more self-sufficient and more capable than many others of their age group and used to looking out for each other. The family never considered themselves to be 'New Age Travellers', not liking to travel in large groups and, though mixing with others in similar circumstances, preferred their own family support system.

They had another hankering for the sun in Feb '93 and took a short holiday to the Canary Isles. A friend looked after the horse and cart but on their return the horse (which it turned out had been badly gelded) proved to have become too difficult to handle and after another three weeks' travelling, made uncomfortable by the horses' bad temper and the damp English climate, Ross decided to sell the horse and cart and with the ensuing money buy tickets for all five of them to travel to Spain to try their luck there.

Now after two months, she and her merry band have become well known on the Gibraltar scene. Never having busked before, Ross took her limited knowledge of whistle playing to the streets where it was improved by constant practice. The children also learnt to play so that they could accompany her, plus they can show off their recently acquired skills on the 'devil sticks', an art learnt from other Gib. buskers. Conventional work in Gibraltar is difficult to come by and not well paid. Ross can provide far better for her children by busking than by being, for example, a bar maid or waitress and the children are learning the discipline of working too.

As concerned as any mother would be for the welfare of her children, Ross has often wondered if she is doing the right thing but feels that the children are better off than many of their counterparts 'back home' in the UK. They are living in a decent climate and have escaped the rat race and negative aspects of life on social security. They have the opportunity of meeting many different people, learning another language and are very aware of the variety of challenges in life.

Lisa 12, Samantha and Wayne 11, all play whistle and 'devil sticks', Gemma 9 is learning about being in charge of their pet dog Pip and the white rabbit. Sam accompanies her mother in Gibraltar nearly every day and the others take turns, otherwise their days are spent at the campsite which has a swimming pool and bar/restaurant where they help out for tips. They are all satisfied with life and look forward to learning new skills – perhaps the guitar and harmonica– and are hopeful that the future will bring other adventures.

Ross's other children, some married with offspring of their own, are living in the UK, somewhat aghast at her activities, but she has learnt that whatever others might think, as long as one is self-supporting and happy, that is all that matters in life.

Keep on playing Ross.

South Wind

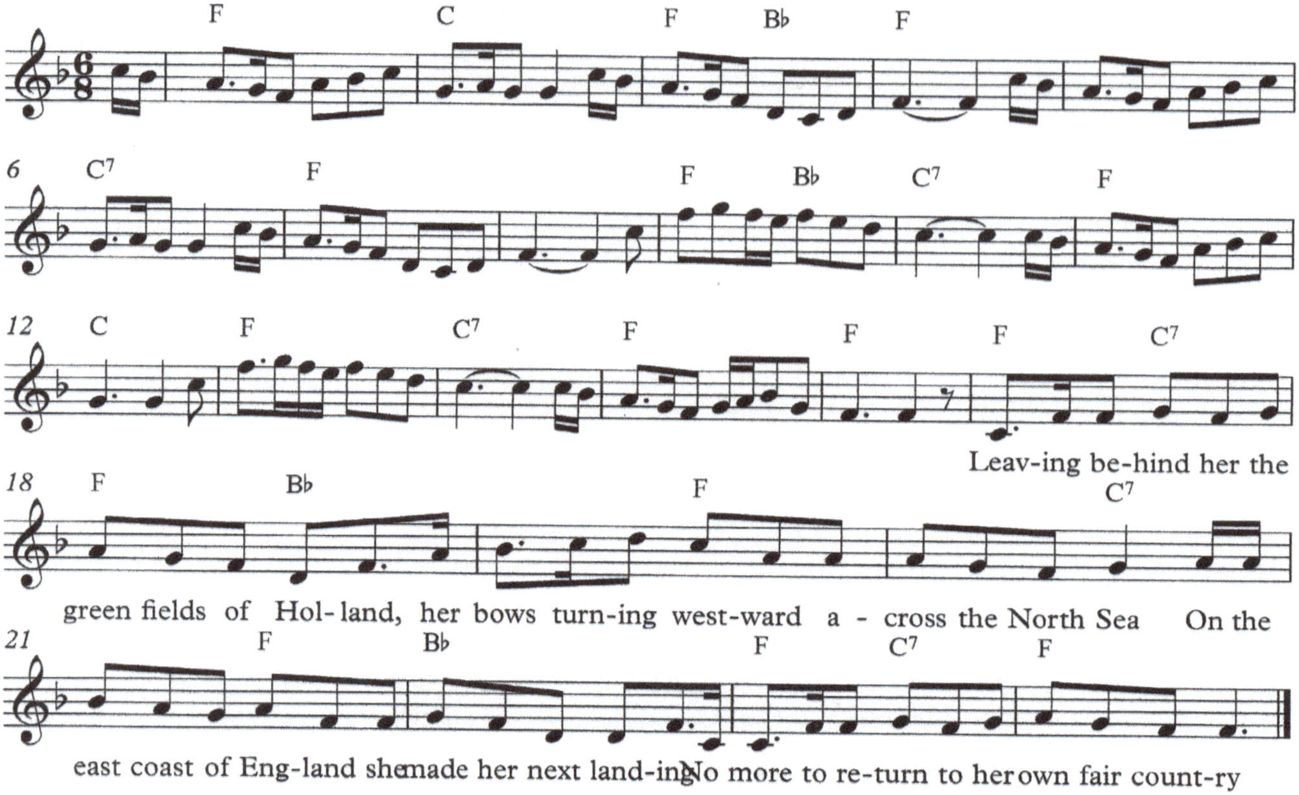
Leav-ing be-hind her the
green fields of Hol-land, her bows turn-ing west-ward a - cross the North Sea On the
east coast of Eng-land she made her next land-ing No more to re-turn to her own fair count-ry

DOLPHIN SAFARI
Ipswich

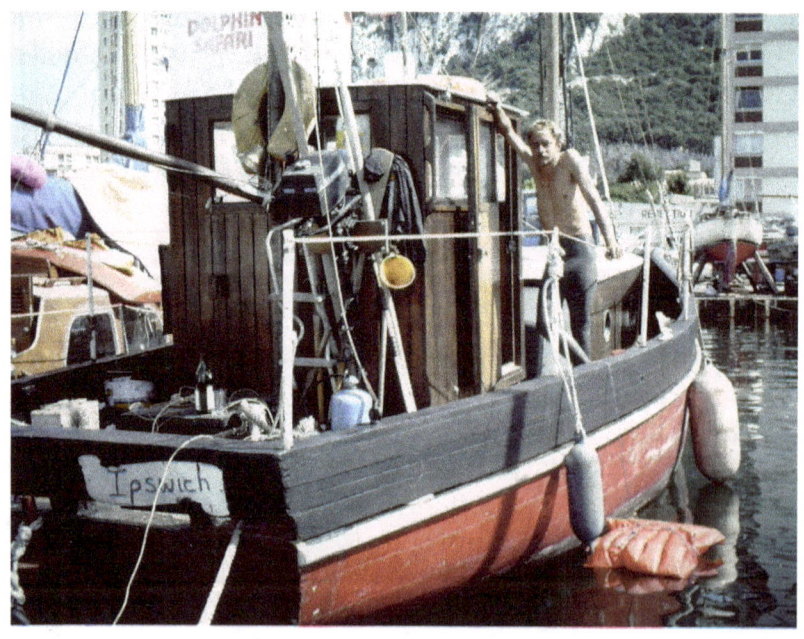

Leaving behind her the windmills of Holland
Her bow turning westward across the North Sea
On the east coast of England she made her first landing
No more to return to her own fair country

Her pitch pine and oak saw fair and foul weather
Her crew came and went as time passed away
And over the years their feet wore her deck smooth
As they cast their nets wide for the catch of the day

For eighty-six years her seas were well charted
She knew every port, every eddy and tide
Til the winds of change blew to carry her southward
From sea-scape familiar to waters untried

Through France and through Spain she made the long passage
Through canals and through locks each opening the door
To the Mediterranean's blue sky and blue water
Til she landed at last on Gibraltar's far shore

Now South Wind holds secrets of men and of money
Under cover of dark she roams far and wide
A pied piper for some and to those who dare follow
Freedom or riches come in on the tide

When I first arrived in Gibraltar, about 1991, I was searching for work and, since there is a large marina with many boats I hit on the idea of asking the owners if they would like to pay me to write a song about their beloved ship. One man took me up on the offer and told me the story of his boat *South Wind* which he now used, as you may guess, for smuggling people (from Morocco) or cigarettes (to Spain)

Puff the Magic Dragon (1993)

'Puff, the magic dragon lives by the sea', so the song says and this dragon actually lives in the sea though it was born half-way up a mountain and isn't averse to sleeping on beaches.

True to form Puff is green, not actually in colour but by way of the fact that she is made out of recycled material and, as far as possible, uses natural energy to get around. Puff is a boat, a Chinese junk with a dragon sculpted on its bow and sides. Its creator, Ken Upton, started his career as an engineer but worked in show business and the tourist industry. His practical skills and fun-loving personality have combined to create a boat that is jam-packed with character and innovative ideas. A keen member and contributor of the *Amateur Yacht Research Society*, Ken has spent a lifetime building and designing boats, from toy models when a boy to full scale mono-hulls, catamarans, trimarans and his latest creation, Puff.

Not just a dragon, Puff is also a guinea pig for Ken's experiments with structural materials and aerodynamics. Ken took three winters to build her on his property in Spain. He literally had so much junk lying around that one of his friends laughingly suggested that he build a boat. Ken liked the idea and collected old swimming pools to use in the fibreglass and persiana sandwich hull, used plastic window shutters for the core material and packing cases for the woodwork. Renault bumpers, prized for their high-density composite material, were used for many jobs. The sails, which are wing type, are made from polyethanol with composite battens and the freestanding masts are made from fibreglass and composite core.

Just over 9½ metres in the water but with the front overhangs and rear castle making her eleven metres overall, Puff draws 70cm at the stern and 20cm at the bow. Her flat bottom and long keel make her beachable and she has a steel shoe (part of an old railway tower) on the bottom for such occasions. Not a few landlubbers and other more conventional boat owners have been somewhat alarmed at the sight of a dragon charging up the beach and sitting squarely at rest.

The cockpit is designed so that it can be fully closed in bad weather or fully open on sunny days so there is no lack of comfort when sailing the boat. And sail she does, most of the time being able to make as much as 12 knots, another mind -blowing spectacle to other yachtsmen.

The boat is cat-ketch rigged for Mediterranean conditions and the sails are raised or lowered by pulleys situated in the cockpit so there is no need to go out on deck. Needless to say solar panels power the electrics and Ken only uses the little 10hp Yanmar diesel engine for manoeuvring in and out of port, preferring to go where the wind takes him, so long as it is approximately in the right direction. So far the boat has been to France, the Balearics, the Atlantic, Portugal - approximately 10,000 sea miles in five years in Ken's sailing season of April to November.

As creatively planned inside as out, the boat's interior gives the impression of being enormous. As Ken explained, the decks are actually overhanging the boat so there is much more space to utilise constructively for living quarters. The forepeak has a large double bunk and the saloon lounge furniture can be re-arranged to berth another five.

Ken is an excellent cook so the galley is well-equipped and includes a full-size gimballed gas cooker with oven, two sinks, a double drainer and a fridge. The dining table is adjustable for both height and position. Decorated with vegetable matting on the floor and walls, the oriental effect is continued with Chinese pictures. A stained glass window panel between the saloon and cockpit adds a touch of class.

The whole boat has an Alice in Wonderland feel about it, perhaps because with it Ken has created a world where fact and fantasy meet. His practicality and imagination have joined to create a dream boat with a little cash and a lot of work. He has already been offered a considerable amount of money for it and will be selling when he has built his next boat.

The inimitable Mr Upton has perfected another innovative idea in sailing using his 'KKwing' sails. They are being thoroughly tested and undergoing more trials by AYRS members using them on fast dinghies and large trimarans. His design has already been cited as among the five most advanced rigs in the world and is now ready for commercial marketing. The design gives 25–40% more power for each square metre and Ken describes it as being 'low tech with high tech results'.

His next boat will be very different from Puff, more like a flying saucer with wings (MKKwings- multi Ken Kite Wings). It is expected to take about 3 months for him to build and will cost about the same as Puff.

For the time being, Ken is still 'Jackie Paper' to Puff. In the words of the song 'without his lifelong friend Puff could not be brave, so that mighty dragon quietly crept into his cave.'

Hopefully Puff's next owner will also have the same sense of fun and purpose as Ken and Puff will continue to roar around the oceans.

Out of Africa – In an Allegro (1993)

Farewell to the tent and the old caravan,
To the tinker, the gypsy, the travelling man.
And farewell to the thirty-foot trailer

'Thirty-foot trailer'
Ewan McColl

In the case of Peter and Karen Whitney, originally from Yorkshire, the thirty-foot trailer is still very much part of their life. For the last four years it has been both their home and their means of making a living in that most interesting North African country, Morocco. Their impressive Allegro 30' campervan can be seen on sites all around that country, from Marrakesh near the High Atlas mountains, to Chefchaoen, in the Rif, to the coastal towns of Agadir, Kenitra and Tangiers.

Though not born into gypsy families, Pete and Karen discovered an affiliation with their travelling way of life back in the 1960s. They made their living following gypsy fairs, pop festivals and traction-engine rallies, buying and selling leather goods and handicrafts. With Pete's keen eye for a bargain and his natural trading instincts, they made a good living and had a comfortable home base in Thunderbridge which, by 1989, had considerably increased in value. This enabled them to sell up, buy a smaller property which their grown-up son could look after and invest the rest in their Allegro. This has a comfortable bedroom, kitchen and living room area and the 6.2 Diesel Chevrolet engine keeps them moving along, doing between 12 - 18 mpg depending on road conditions.

When the pair decided to make the break from the well-known English circuit and try their luck trading between Morocco and Europe they really had no definite plans but thought that they'd take a three month trip to Morocco to check out the ethnic goods. In so doing they would also satisfy their curiosity about the country which has a basic Arab Islamic culture with Berber remnants and, of course, the influence of Southern Europe, especially Spain. That was in 1990. Now, three years later they are finally thinking of leaving to try something new but both are loath to leave the laidback atmosphere of the African continent and the interesting life that they have which has kept them entertained as well as comfortably off for the duration.

During the first three months of their trip, while staying in the campsite in Marrakesh, they were approached by the local film company to hire out their comfortable mobile home as a location dressing room for visiting film stars This proved to be a lucrative deal for at a hiring fee of approx. £500 per week they could afford to spend the time in a very reasonable hotel plus even get work as extras on the film. Karen has been a Berber woman and Pete a warrior. Two of the more well-known films they have been involved in are, *Being Human* made by Pinewood Studios London, directed by David Putman and starring Robin Williams and *Blood and Sand,* an English/French-produced TV mini-series which starred Brian Blessed. They were also involved in some lesser Italian films which needed a desert setting. All were interesting and provided funds to continue their travelling life.

Neither of them speak French or Arabic, the country's two main languages, but this has not proved constrictive in their dealings with the local tradesmen. What they have needed is patience and understanding of the African ways of wheeling and dealing which have somewhat different rules to the British ones. For example, a deal can take a month to negotiate and involve many visits to tiny back-street dwellings in the maze-like medinas. Here they must partake of many cups of ultra-sweet mint tea while negotiations proceed. They buy and sell Moroccan artefacts such as carpets, scarves, traditional tea pots, jewellery and other unusual items that have a trading value in different parts of the country. For example in coastal towns they set up a stall next to their van on the beach, selling objects from the mountain regions.

On leaving Morocco this year they are loading up with things to sell at the *Bastille Day Festival* in Avignon, France in July and after that is the *Green Festival* in Frankfurt.

Future plans are to sell the Allegro in the UK and fly to America to buy another van and tour that continent, keeping an eye open for trading opportunities while seeing the land and visiting friends they have made along the way. They would also like to visit India and Nepal.

One thing they will not be able to bring back to the UK with them is their spaniel Captain who unfortunately died while they were in Marrakesh and who was ceremoniously buried at the campsite. Although Captain remains in Morocco forever his place has been taken by 'Bungle' an Arab cat found on the same campsite and who now travels with them.

So life for Pete and Karen, now in their early forties, rolls on with the wheels of their mobile home and though their house in the UK remains as security, they cannot envisage staying there for any length of time while they are still fit and able to continue their travelling lifestyle.

> A cook once making stews
> Didn't know which ingredients to choose
> She put in some meat,
> Potatoes and beet
> But was unsure of the herbs she should use

> There was an old man of Peru
> Who wanted to go to the loo
> He looked all around
> For a hole in the ground
> And some paper to help with it too

Birthdays I Will Always Remember (49th)

My 49th was a quiet but very touching affair, with a bit of a surprise. I was in Morocco, returning to Spain after a great trip with Georgia, the Canadian harpist. As I had left her in Agadir to continue her journey south I was travelling alone but went to stay with my Moroccan 'family' in Kenitra. When they discovered it was my birthday, Fatima, the Granny, took me to the local market where she asked me to choose a brass plate which she had gift wrapped and gave to me over dinner of a specially prepared fish tarjine. Hinde, her granddaughter, gave me a silver Moroccan teapot and Zohre, another daughter gave me a ceramic cat.

Then, sitting around chatting they came up with what they really wanted to ask me.

Hinde's brother, Ahmed, was 19 years old and the main job he had was to go out fishing sometimes with the local fishermen. He had had little schooling and was unlikely to get any other work. Would I please marry him and take him to Europe where he could get employment?

Well, this was the surprise! They showed me all his papers and said they were prepared to pay me – I don't remember the amount but they had been saving money for such an occurrence.

It took me the rest of the evening to explain to them – in my very basic French – that, much as I would love to help them (and what 49-year-old would turn down an attractive 19-year-old) it was not as easy as that. Not only do the authorities look very closely into international marriages but I actually wasn't really legally living in Spain myself and there was NO WAY that this would be believed there. The best I could do was take copies of his papers and talk to my Moroccan friend in Chefchaouen who had relatives in Europe and see if he could go over to work for them. Many French had houseboys from Morocco.

Finally they understood and I did talk to my friend, Brahim, and asked him to write to the family in Kenitra and tell them if he had any luck.

Of course, being practising Muslims, they couldn't offer me alcohol to finish the negotiations and the birthday celebration but the next day, having waived a fond farewell to the family and ridden north to Chefchaouen, I pulled out my supply of Moroccan moonshine (distilled fig juice bought further inland) and had another, rather less stressful celebration with some fellow travellers.

Left to Right: Standing Grandpa, family friend, Fatima, Zohre.
Front: Linda next to Hinde.
My Morocccan family.

Rose of Moses

A young Morrocan girl told me that they call the Oleanda the 'Rose of Moses'

Morocco (1995)

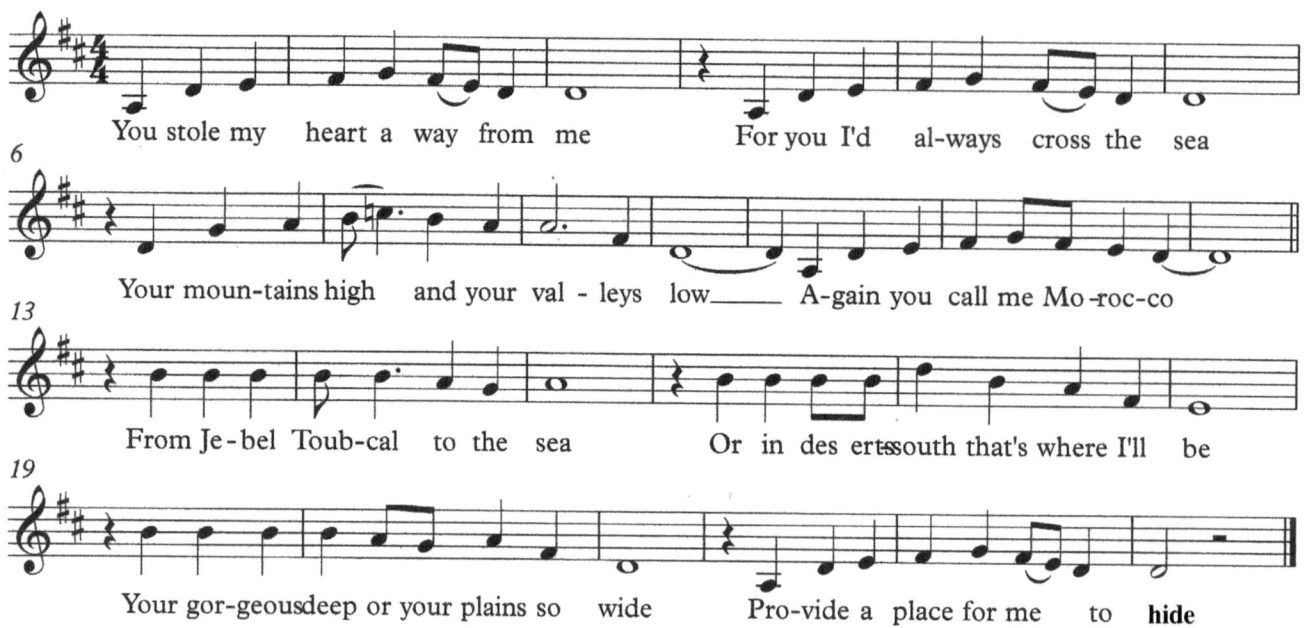

You stole my heart away from me
For you I'd always cross the sea
Your mountains high and your valleys low
Again you call me, Morocco

As birds fly south, then so will I
Their beating wings across the sky
For they all know the place to go
I'll meet them there in Morocco

From Jebel Toubkal to the sea
Or in desert south that's where I'll be
Your gorges deep and your plains so wide
Provide a place for me to hide

Cascading waters thundering down
Or mud brick houses red and brown
Palms silhouette in sunset's glow
Your timeless beauty, Morocco

Brown sparkling eyes, ça va bien?
Small outstretched hands for un dirham
Cous-cous and tarjine and nana tea
A welcome's always there for me

You stole my heart away it's true
And now I'm never far from you
Your mountains high and your valleys low
Again you call me, Morocco,
Again you call me, Morocco.

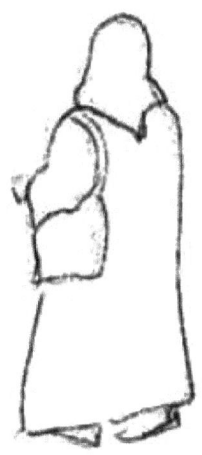

Probably my favourite country. I went there many times when I lived in Spain.

Riding On... An Odessa Odyssey
(Andalucia - Ukraine, July 1995)

Preparation

Faxes flying, forms a-filling
Visas chased and spanners turned
Planning, packing, maps consulted
Money changed and dates discerned

Departure

Gibraltar fades into the west
As Spanish deserts breathe their heat
Roman ruins and tourist centres
Recede with Barcelona's streets

Riding on...

North to where lush French vinyards
Refresh the eye as wine does the tongue
Then Italian traffic leads to tempting toll-roads
Timely taken around Turin

Riding on...

Past snow-topped mountains to relaxing lakes
Friendly faces and a well-earned rest
Mandello del Lario, Moto Guzzi Mecca
Means a welcome pause on the east-bound quest

Riding on...

Where Tyrolean towns with inspiring spires
Grandly lie in valley's green
While awesome alps bedecked with rainbows
Complete the picture postcard scene

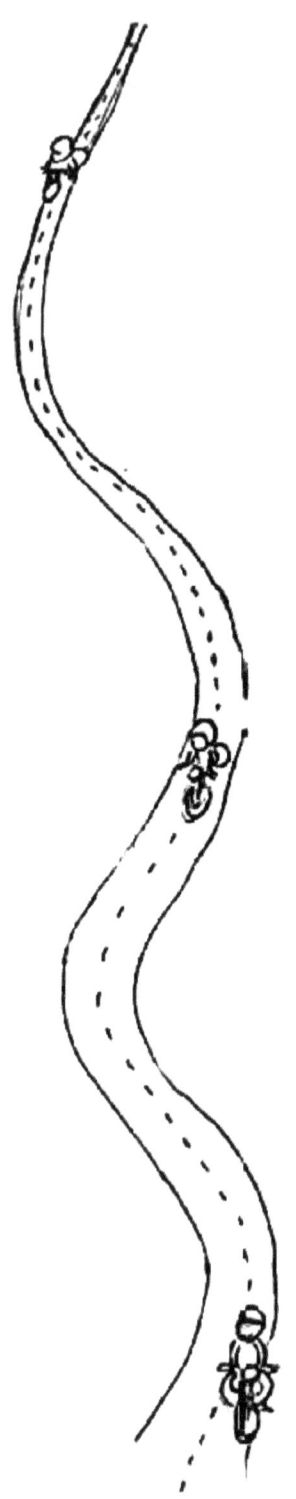

Riding on...

Into Austrian order, milch cows grazing
In flower-strewn meadows, green and lush
Ethnic chapels and ruined forts
Rise from midst surrounding bush

Riding on... humming

Hungarian rhapsody in the rain
Glistening tram-lines weave the city lace
Danube divine with many bridges
Eastward flows at waltz-time pace

Bumping along...

Lace-lined streets with working women
Heads bent, intent on weaving cane
Then Transylvanian torrents...
Where the horrors lie, not in Dracula's castle
But in Romanian roads and rain

Riding on... remarking

Maldovian mud houses with exterior patterns
Covered wells and flocks of geese
While CZ riders with BM stickers
Are all agog and keen to please

Stopped at...

Ukrainian border, with stern officials
Withholding passport to create delay
An anxious wait beside the BM
Nonchalantly whistling the time away

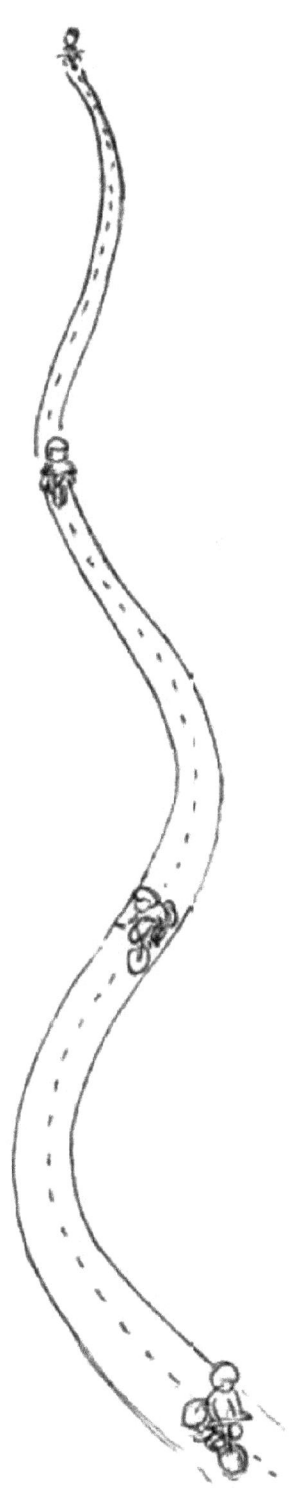

Riding on...

Free to fly the final distance
Past honey pots amongst the trees
Fishing villages and hopeful signpost, 'ODECCA'
To that gracious city beside the Black Sea

Riding on...

Through tree-lined boulevards that lead the traveller
To sun-drenched beaches where tourists play
Or where stately buildings in Pushkin Strasse
House museums to steal your time away

Arrival...

From many countries the 'Strangers' meet
And thus become no more
Talk and laughter fill the campground
Here and on the Crimean shore
Vodka, beer and wine flows free
Language barriers are broken with friendship
And tales of each, their own...
                    Odessa Odyssey

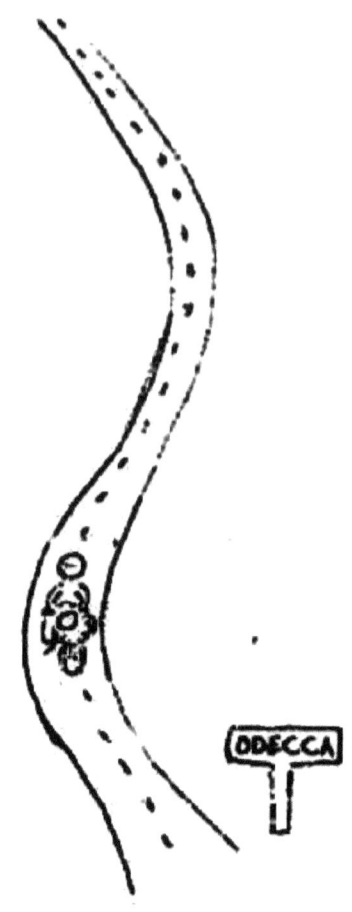

5,000 plus kilometres in 2 1/2 weeks to the 'Strangers' rally in Odessa. Poem completed in Andy Chernel's home in Czech Republic and typed for transmission in Michael Bidmon's home in Germany.

Odessa

By the sea Odessa, home to me
Though I sail away, I'll come back to you
Someday
La la la la, la la la la la,
La, la

My black sea pearl I find you're always on my mind
Though I sail away, I'll come back to you
some day
La la la la la, la la la la la
La la

No other lady fair could unto you compare
Though I sail away, I'll come back to you
Some day
La la la la la, la la la la la
La la

By the sea Odessa, home to me Odessa
Though I sail away, I'll come back to you
Someday
La la la la la, la la la la la
La la.

I bought a small balalaika in an Odessa market. This song was written when playing it .

Birthdays I Will Always Remember (50th)

And so to a bigger and better birthday. Whilst in Morocco with Debby, my American friend, she asked how I was going to celebrate my demi-century. I replied that I hadn't a clue, I didn't know where I would be.

'Well', she said, 'I think we should spend it together in New Orleans'.

Somehow that idea really appealed. After she returned to her home in Louisiana, I experienced some pretty traumatic changes in my situation in Spain and my mother died. I was in the UK for the funeral in May and things seemed to be spinning, I hadn't heard from Debby as the summer's end approached. Georgia (my harpist friend) was back in Canada and I'd promised her I'd move hell and high water to see her for Xmas. Eventually, in late October, I heard from Debby and I phoned her.

'Do you still want me there for my birthday?' I asked.

'Sure,' she replied, 'you know you're welcome anytime.'

The next couple of weeks was another whirlwind and I struggled madly to get out of Spain and into the USA via the UK.

A few days before I left Castellar I had a birthday celebration in Mara's bar in the castle. An international crowd of locals, mainly Dutch, English and German, came to wish me well giving me many presents and buying me drinks. I was even given some ganga! A great night was had by all.

And so, to the USA.

My actual birthday was spent at Debby's house in the Mississippi Delta, looking out over the Aymite River, watching the white heron land on her boat deck and admiring the hanging moss in the trees that were changing all colours of red and gold. We drank gin and tonic as I opened all my presents, which included a silk scarf and a *Riverdance* video. We made plans for the coming Friday night when we'd hit the town with Debby's Portuguese exchange student, Rui, and her sister, Janet.

Come Friday we were dressed up and raring to go. Straight to the French Quarter and Bourbon St. We cruised up and down, watching the tap-dancing buskers, the stripey hot dog vendors, taking in a few beers at one bar, then off to the famous piano bar *Pat O'Brien's* for a couple of Hurricanes (very large cocktails). After that, a jazz bar where they wouldn't let me play my whistle but told us of an Irish pub up the road. After the jazz session where they at least played my request of *Midnight in Moscow* (as a reminder of a Muscovite I rather fancied in Odessa that summer) we headed off to *O'Flaherty's*. The courtyard sported some kilted pipers who played 'Dark Island' for me and then we went inside to drink Guinness and hear the Irish singer sing all the songs I knew and could raucously join in with. Before I had a chance to jump up on stage Debby pulled me away as we were all starving and she knew she'd never get a bite to eat if I started playing. We finished the night with a meal in the *House of Blues* (opened by the Blues Bros) and then just managed to stagger back to Janet's car where I fell asleep before we even left the car park. Older, yes but very content.

WARNING: While I was in Bourbon St, New Orleans, I took the opportunity to go into a voodoo shop and buy a voodoo doll. I had been having a lot of trouble with a couple of men in Castellar, one of whom had attacked me, so I named them while sticking two pins into the dolls.

A few months later there was a result. One man died (a drug overdose) and the other was sent to prison for trafficking. So, beware, don't upset me, I think I still have the doll.

A Castle in Spain
or 'She Fell Among Thieves' (1992)

Castillo de Castellar de la Frontera was built as a fort by the Moors in the 13th century, when their empire stretched across Andalucía. With cities in Granada and Cordoba, and outposts along the chain of mountains within striking distance of the coast, the Moors battled against the Spanish Christians. For two centuries the castle fort was regularly under siege, first in control of one then the other warring side. But in 1504 the Spanish eventually gained control and have held it ever since. The Moors were either integrated or expelled.

Built as a garrison and not for peacetime settlement, the walled town and its environs were unsuitable for a growing population. The Moors had put down two water cisterns inside the castle to service the troops, but this soon became insufficient and women faced a 3km walk to the Guadacorte river in the valley below to collect water and carry it back up the rocky hill.

Andalucía as a whole was slow to develop and electricity did not reach Castellar (and then only part of it) until the 1950s. Small one-roomed cottages without sanitation had sprung up on the hillside surrounding the castle and a few fincas (small farms) were in the valley below.

In 1966 the Guadacorte dam was completed, flooding the valley and the fincas, and the government offered the ageing population of Castellar a new town built some 8kms away on the plains - with sanitation, health services, schooling and easy access to Gibraltar & Algeciras. By 1970 the population had almost deserted its spectacular surroundings, now enhanced by the dam. But this was the hippy age and Northern Europeans were travelling south in their combi vans looking for escapism in drugs and flower power. Many found Castellar and moved in, especially the Germans and Dutch. The only way they could finance their lifestyle was to join the drug and contraband smuggling gangs dealing with Morocco and Gibraltar. Castellar became known as the 'Hippie Town' and had a serious drug problem, many junkies never returning from their last 'trip'.

In the last few years the Andalusian government has had a clean-up session both with the drug problem and also by starting a YTS scheme for local youth to help renovate the castle itself and remove rubbish from the surrounding area. A few reformed hippies and other 'straight' people are opening bars, craft shops and art galleries and there is a mixture of nationalities and lifestyles.

The setting is amazing. The lake shines blue in the surrounding hills, now very dry with the scorching summer sun. A bush fire started by squatters nearly annihilated the town this year, but killed off the tick plague and the regrowth will be spectacular when spring flowers heavy with perfume, burst forth again after the winter rains.

The winding road, 8km from the flat plains is enjoyable for motorbikes and cyclists and an ancient cobbled pathway leads 2km over the rocky ridge to give many picturesque views over the hills where Andalucian white towns twinkle in the distance and eagles fly.

The house in which I live, 2km from the top of the hill, belongs to a German smuggler who is banned from Spain (for one of his many misdemeanors) and lives on his boat in Gibraltar. There are no facilities except a well which gathers water from a spring in the hills behind. One has to keep a cat to chase away the rats, and the ants need regular spraying. My neighbour is at this moment battling with termites which are eating her bedstead away from under her and she can hear the munching sounds at night!

Gas lamps provide lighting, and after two years cooking on my Trangia methylated spirit stove, I now have a gas cylinder and a 2-ring cooking plate. A wood stove will have to be mastered in winter and I may even find a porta potty before then to save the 50metre walk into the bush for the daily constitution.

There is no post or telephone, except one phone in a bar that opens when the Spanish proprietor feels like it. You can get hash, ecstasy, crack etc. etc. at another bar or illegal fags smuggled from Gib. There is also a respectable tourist bar run by a German/Dutch couple which is my main hang out and the 2km walk is appreciated by the Shilpit (my dog). It is better to walk or get a lift to the castle bar than ride the bike around the hairpin bends, especially after a few glasses of strong Spanish beer, the effects of which tend to creep up on you.

Life here is not boring. The Costa del Sol and Gibraltar are renowned for their high percentage of rogues; Great Train Robbers, con men, drug dealers, IRA gunmen etc. etc. There are many interesting incidents to discuss. Or a short ride to the Gib/Spain border where the seafront can provide nightly entertainment watching the Guardia Civil try to catch the Gib smugglers' power boats.

So, if anyone is considering a trip this way and wants to experience an alternative lifestyle, there is plenty of crashing room. For a holiday with a difference, come to Castellar and see a castle in Spain.

This was written when I had not long come to live in Castellar in the early 1990s. Things have changed a lot since then, the old castle is now a very up-market hotel, the streets within the walls are now filled with recently renovated houses and a gift shop and there are many plants to brighten the walls. Tourist buses bring people from all over the world to see this very attractive Moorish castle with its spectacular views over the dam.

Grazalema

Gra - za - le - ma___ de mi cor-a - zon___ Es - can - di -
do___ en las si - err - as Gra - za le - ma___ de mi cor-a -
zon___ Rec - uer - do bien___ su tran-quil - i - dad
Break Voy ar - ri - ba en las si - er - ras___ A - ver las
a - ves___ y los ar - bo - les A - ver a - ba - jo___
sus tech-as ro - jas y es - cu cha las___ cam - pan - as

Grazalema, de me corazon
Escondido in las sierras
Grazalema, de me corazon
Recuerdo bien su tranquilidad

La naturelza y el serendismo
Alrededor sus casas blancas
Grazalema, de mi corazon
Recuerdo bien su tranquilidad

Voy arriba en las montanas
A ver los aves y las arboles
A ver abajo sus techas rocas y escucha las campanas

Aun el mundo cambiado
En sus calles hay amistad
Grazalema de me corazon
Recuerdo bien su tranquilidad

While living in Castellar, Andalucia, I used to take a weekend off every now and then a go into the mountains to this village, Grazalema, where there were walks in the surrounding forest and views down to the village with its red roofs and bell tower. There was a nice hotel to stay where I sat and drank red wine by the fire and played my guitar. This song came from those peaceful, friendly moments. My only song written in Spanish!

Castellar

Vultures flying, dam drying
A silver strip on the valley floor
Dust is blowing, cattle lowing
On new-found land, appeared once more

Road winds steeply to the fortress
Homes are hewn among the rocks
Bars serve and save the dreamless people
On a street where time's turned back the clock

International intonations
As cultures mix or turn away
A Moorish seed that others harvest
Castle queens all for a day

Does your future lie in footsteps
Brought to walk the cobbled streets?
For new attractions caught in commerce
Where the past and present meet

Will progress wake a sleeping demon
Or light you like a bright new star?
Let's hope, like drought and storm, you'll weather
What lies ahead now, Castellar

Castellar, Spain, October 1995 (Drought year)

Cork harvesting at Castellar

Pole Polka

My dog Pole (pronounced Polee) was named for Pole Pole, which is Swahili for 'slowly'. I had to get to know him slowly as he been abused by previous owners, used as a fighting or hunting dog.

Andalus Lullaby

I lived in Andalucia for about 16 years. Visitors were always amazed that it wasn't sunshine all year round. I had to disappoint them and say that we did get a lot of rain in the winter and sometimes it even dislodged rocks and roads were closed. Yes, the rain did fall down!

Summer has passed, all the vine leaves are dead
Now all I see are the clouds overhead
And the rain falls down, the rain falls down
Winter is here

What has become of the sun
Those sleepy siestas and midnight fiestas
The loud castanets and the gay dancer's dress
And the strum of flamenco guitars?

Our castle in Spain has faded away
Shrouded by mist as blue turns to grey
And the rain falls down, the rain falls down
Winter is here

Where is the sparkling sea
The beaches so white under full moon at night
The bodies so tanned and the sound of a band
As we sip our sangrias and sing?

Bring in the wood and stoke up the fire
Soon we'll be wading through inches of mire
As the rain falls down, the rain falls down
Winter is here

When will we see them again
The gay daisies bobbing, the sunflower heads nodding
The mauve bougainvillea in Andalucia
Alive with its colours so bright?

Thunder will crash and lightning strikes bright
Torrents of water flow through the night
As the rain falls down, the rain falls down
Winter is here

Though the rain falls down, the rain falls down
Springtime will come

The Angel Of Lagos (1995)

Touching earth briefly in Gibraltar for the next two weeks is Georgia March, dubbed *The Angel of Lagos* by her Portuguese admirers.

Georgia, from London, Ontario, is a trained vocalist and for many years toured a theatre company in Canada and the United States. She is currently travelling the world with her close companion – a celtic harp.

Last year, after experiencing a personal tragedy, she suddenly felt a great need to learn to play the harp and, on approaching a harp maker in London (Ontario) was disappointed to hear that it would take many months to have one personally built. However, the very next day an offer of the loan of a harp was made for her to practise on while hers was being built.

Three months later, in June 1994, and two days before her departure from Canada, the instrument was ready and Georgia set off the see the world, confident that her harp playing would enable her to survive.

She had planned on staying in France for a year but this country proved to be too expensive and an American traveller, met on a bus, suggested she try her luck in Portugal.

En route to Lagos in the Algarve, Georgia decided she would start writing a book about her life and travelling adventures and, to this end, she stayed with a Portuguese family, writing in the mornings and spending the afternoons practising the harp, exploring her new found locality and learning Portuguese

After a month she felt confident to play in public and compose her own music. She changed her style of playing and took her music and voice to the streets of Lagos to play for the people there. Public reaction was immediately rewarding: toddlers stood in awe before her, crying when busy mothers tried to drag them away. A French woman cried tears of compassion and Georgia had to stop playing to put her arms around her. A dog put his head in her lap at the debut of one of her songs and people of all nationalities showered her with gifts and invitations.

Georgia's music has been described as 20th century and has a feel and weight of its own, flowing through her person and reaching out to help, heal and bring peace to people.

Her next goal is to travel through Africa and she is leaving for Morocco on the 10th October. In Africa, as in other countries she hopes to share her music with other musicians, learn different styles whilst interacting with a variety of cultures. She wants to 'get back to the beginning of time, sleep in the jungle and desert and learn from the tribespeople'.

As well as being a writer and musician, Georgia is also an artist, using watercolour as her main medium but sketching scenes in pencil while travelling.

She has completed the first draught of her book *Shadow Dancing with Angels* and hopes to find a publisher on her travels, which are, at the moment aimed at arriving in Cape Town—sometime.

Since leaving Canada last June she has thoroughly enjoyed her travels which she feels have been made possible and interesting by people she has met along the way who have offered hospitality and shared their life with her.

Gibraltar she finds friendly, interesting and with an atmosphere that she describes as being 'exotic and homely at the same time'.

Watching Georgia perform, her amazing soprano voice carrying the length of Main Street, it is clear that her interaction with the public is immediate and sincere. Her dress and approachability make it clear why she was fondly called *The Angel of Lagos*.

NOTE:
I took Georgia to Morocco as pillion, with her harp, on my BMW motorcycle. I took her as far as Agadir in the south and we did a concert together in Casablanca en route. The full details of this journey can be read in my book *Where Angels Fear to Tread*. See page 246 for details.

I last saw Georgia in Canada in 2010 where she has her own house in Ontario, has written several books and uses her harp playing for healing and self-awareness workshops. We keep in touch by email at Christmas.

A Friday Night Deluge in Castellar (1996)

Footsteps falter, intentions alter
Ideas, like streams, diverted by water

Mara's bar seems a million miles away
When flooded tracks deter the car
Running rocks and swollen streams
Makes three kilometers seem very far

Gutters stream on overflow
Splishing, splashing through the door
And where else can the water go
Than run from rafters to the floor

In a place not built for rain and flood
It's hard to keep a cozy home
But my rustic life will charm once more
When sun reappears and flowers bloom

When I lived in Castellar, Andalucía, Friday nights were a regular time to go up to the Moorish castle at the top of the hill in which there was a bar run by a Dutch woman called Mara.

Castillejos Rant

Castillejos means 'far from the castle'. My house, pictured above, was in the hamlet of Castillejos, which comprised six houses, and was three kilometres south of the castle of Castallar de la Frontera.

Flamenco (1995)

During the time I lived in Castellar de la Frontera an annual event was begun which was to become very popular and draw many tourists. It is the *Full Moon Flamenco Festival* in August held in the grounds of the 13th Century Moorish castle, a very picturesque and historic venue. This festival was instigated by the *Pena Flamenco* of Castellar and aided by the local council. It has now been going for over 20 years.

Pena Flamencos are in most Andalucian towns. They are clubs which promote Flamenco and have been in existence for many years. Members provide money to bring in singers and guitarists and encourage new singers rather than new songs.

There have been many ideas brought forward as to where Flamenco originated. They are usually linked to gypsies and, of course, these people came from many different countries and ideologies, Arabs, Jews and even Indian religions.

The genre began with just singing; people gathered in blacksmiths shops to sing with wine and friends. The first rhythms were beat out with the hammer on the anvil - la Tona. So first it was just voice then came guitars dancing and dress.

The first singers of note in the 1800s were El Planeto and El Fillo who brought Flamenco to public recognition. In 1840-50 came Silvio Franconeti, with an Italian father and Andaluce mother, he sang 'sequiriya por cava' a style which provided a change of chords and melody. A more contemporary idol is Cameron de la Isla from San Fernando, who had a very good voice and interpretation. There was also Paco de Lucia and Tomatito who is still playing today.

Flamenco rhythm (or compas) uses 12, 4 or 3 beats which is very distinctive compared with other music and makes it exciting. The dance itself involves a mime language. Both men and women display a form of arrogance, insolence and sensuality but generally the women move more naturally and sensitively. Guitarists and dancers interact with the music and are aware of each other throughout. It is a captivating display of a type of mating technique.

Flamenco guitars, though nylon strung

and similar to classical guitars have a faster action and feel lighter. They are constructed to give a more immediate sound or 'punch' which allows the guitar to cut through other sounds when in accompaniment with Flamenco song and dance.

Pure Flamenco songs are sung to places or to other people and they describe emotions such as love, sadness and hate. Soleas are sad, suffering songs with deep meaning. (some I find a bit hard on the ear!)

Cadiz, Jerez, Seville and Malaga all formed their own style of singing and music. There were more European gypsies in Cadiz province while more Arabs in Granada. So, depending on the province different styles were formed. Castanets have been introduced for percussion but they are viewed as more folkloric instruments and there is a distinction between Folkloric and Flamenco. Flamenco is seen as an art form to be listened to and Folkloric is something that can be joined in with, thus certain dance steps introduced for public dancing and, as far as the dance and dress are concerned this again depends on the region. In the area I lived (near Algerciras, Cadiz, Sevillana style was the most popular. The dress is flouncy and there are certain steps and body movements. However, in the villages and mountains, especially toward Granada, the dress and dance steps change as the Moorish influence is stronger.

Flamenco festivals start in May and run to September. They are commercial festivals which attract people from all over Spain and abroad who can see the best artists. The festivals are managed by promotors and town halls but the purist Flamenco is found in the more intimate Penas.

Whatever style, Flamenco is seen as relating to Spain and many tourists come to see it and a good many to study it in special schools in Jerez. Whatever its many origins are you could say that they were the ingredients but Flamenco was baked in Andalucia.

The Song Of The Sea (1996)

Once upon a time there was a beautiful mermaid called Marilyn who lived just offshore in an underground cave but who spent most of her time sitting in the sun on a rock watching the world go by. She had a lovely face, a neat little tanned body and a shiny gold/green tail. She wore two shells over her tiny bosom and a string of smooth, cream pearls, a present from some oysters, around her neck. She stared with her big blue eyes into the mother-of-pearl mirror of a clam shell as she brushed her long, blonde, wavy hair.

The crabby crabs, who ran sideways across the beach, saw her sitting on her rock and said spitefully, 'That mermaid is stuck up and vain. Just watch! she's always looking at herself in the mirror and combing her hair. Whatever use is she to anyone? She can't even sing!'

That was true, but if they looked closer at Marilyn, instead of just criticizing her from the beach, they would have seen that while she sat and brushed her hair she sighed and a large tear would gather in those big blue eyes and run down her cheek. It was a great disappointment to her that she couldn't sing. All the other mermaids could, indeed they were well known for their singing. Sometimes the sailors would listen to their singing and forget to watch where they were going and bump into the rocks. Then their ships would sink and the naughty mermaids would laugh. But Marilyn didn't want to sink any sailors. She just wanted to be able to sing to her friends the seagulls and the dolphins. After all it's nice to be able to sing isn't it?

One night there was a terrible storm; lots of thunder and lightning, high waves and a strong, shrieking wind. Marilyn stayed huddled in her cave beneath the sea. The seagulls hid in the rocks in the cliff, the dolphins dived into the depths where it was calmer and the crabby crabs burrowed deep down into the sand. The local fishermen were tossed about in their boats. They quickly steered towards the ports but it was feared that some big ships further out may have been damaged for there was a dangerous reef nearby.

When the storm was over and the sea calm again Marilyn went back to sit on her rock and she found two things that had been washed up on it. One was a bottle of shampoo and the other was a pair of scissors.

'Oh, what luck,' she cried, 'I can try out a new hairstyle!'

She busied herself with her mirror and the scissors snipping here and there and shaping her beautiful, blonde hair. She cut off all the split ends that had happened because of the salt water. Then she gave it a good wash with the shampoo so that it became so bright that you had to wear your sunglasses to look at her. She was delighted.

'There she goes again,' sneered the crabby crabs. 'Silly girl, not a brain in her head, totally useless.'

Later in the day a group of sea horses came snorting and panting up to the rock. They were in great distress. 'Marilyn,' they whinnied, 'We've come to tell you that the seagulls are in a terrible mess and they need your help!'

'Whatever can be the matter?', asked Marilyn. 'It's a lovely day, the storm has passed but I must say I haven't heard the seagulls calling out to me like they usually do'.

'No', replied the sea horses, 'that's because they are trapped out at sea. Last night during the storm a big oil tanker hit a rock and the tank burst. The oil came out onto the sea and the seagulls didn't see it. When they dived into the water to catch the fish they got covered with oil and now they can't fly because their feathers are stuck together. It's too far for them to paddle all the way to shore with their tiny feet. They will die if we can't rescue them!'

'Show me the way!' cried Marilyn and she followed the sea horses to where a large pool of black oil lay on top of the water. The seagulls looked miserable bobbing up and down, covered in the slimy black oil and unable to lift their wings.

Taking a deep breath, Marilyn swam underneath the oil slick until she saw the gulls' skinny legs and then surfaced near a group. Of course her lovely, long hair was now matted with oil too but that didn't stop her from swimming. She had an idea how she could use her hair to help the seagulls. She divided it up into strands and told some of the seagulls to hold a strand each with their beaks while she swam back to her rock. In this way she pulled them out of the oil slick and back to safety.

She had to go back again and again to get all the other seagulls and by the time she had done this she was very tired and filthy. But she didn't rest. Once she was back on the rock with all the oily seagulls she began washing them with the shampoo. It was a big job but when she had finished their wings were free of oil and they could fly again.

'Thank you, Marilyn,' they screamed as they flew back to their rock nests, dive-bombing the crabby crabs as they went. Marilyn washed herself down also with the shampoo and then fell into an exhausted sleep.

The next day, hardly had she sat herself on the rock and begun to rearrange her hair when the seagulls came winging towards her. She smiled and waved, glad to see them flying again but Jonathon, the head seagull, flew down to her in a state of great agitation.

'Marilyn,' he squawked, 'Yesterday you rescued us but today some more of your friends are in trouble. Please can you help again? Last night some foreign fishing boats came too close into the shore and they caught their nets on the rocks. Instead of pulling them all in they left them and now two of the young dolphins have become tangled in the nets and can't get away.'

'Show me,' said Marilyn and immediately swam in the direction that the seagulls flew. She took her scissors with her and, after she'd quietened down the young dolphins who were very frightened, she cut them free. She had to be careful not to get tangled in the terrible net herself.

'Thank you, thank you Marilyn,' cried the dolphins and they swam home quickly to their worried mums who had been wondering why they were late home for tea.

'Well, another job well done,' thought Marilyn as she swam back to her rock. 'I'm lucky I found the shampoo and the scissors.'

The next day Marilyn was just getting comfortable on her rock again and was starting to comb out her hair when, in the distance, she saw the spout of a whale. It was a great spray of water and she watched with interest as it came nearer. Then she saw the water churning with activity. The dolphins came leaping toward her, a big crowd of them. The sea horses were arriving too and the gulls were screeching overhead. Then, to her amazement, she saw that behind the sea horses was a giant sea turtle covered with sea anemones and clams and with some octopus hitching a ride. A big stingray and an electric eel swam beside it and on it was... Neptune, the king of the sea. In his hand he held his trident and through his long straggly hair and beard she saw his craggy, wrinkled face smiling broadly at her.

The turtle drew up alongside her rock and King Neptune stepped off. His clothes were made of sea weed of deep green and blue and he wore wellington boots covered in fish scales because it's very wet down at the bottom of the sea where he lives. He spoke in a voice that sounded like the waves crashing on the shore, a booming yet gentle noise.

'Marilyn,' he said. 'Yesterday one of the big stingrays came down to my palace in the deep and told me that he had heard from the seahorses, the dolphins and the gulls that you had been very brave and kind and saved some of my creatures from man's pollution. I have therefore come especially all the way from the depths of the sea to reward you. I shall grant you one wish – whatever you want shall be yours. Think carefully now and don't waste your wish.'

Marilyn looked at him in amazement. 'Your highness, I was only helping my friends, I don't expect any reward, but there is one thing I want more than anything else in this world and if you could grant it to me I would be so happy.'

King Neptune nodded his great head. 'Just tell me what it is,' he said gravely, 'and it shall be yours.'

What do you think Marilyn wanted?

'I want to be able to sing!' she cried 'Could I, oh could I?'

King Neptune threw back his great head and laughed

'You mean to tell me you are a mermaid who can't sing! I've never heard of such a thing.'

'No,' said Marilyn, embarrassed, 'and I want to, SO much.'

'You want to be naughty and sink the sailors,' said Neptune, his eyes twinkling.

'No, oh no, ' Marilyn protested, 'I want to sing to the birds and the fishes and all the sea creatures.'

'OK then,' said Neptune. He waved his trident in the air and said, 'Oh great spirits of the sea, listen very well to me as we form this magic ring. Let our Marilyn mermaid sing.'

All the sea creatures swam around the rock holding fins and tentacles and chanting those words.

And then Marilyn opened her mouth and began to sing. Notes as pure as crystal flowed from her. 'La, la, la, la, la ...'

There was thunderous applause. Even the crabby crabs watching from the beach joined in. King Neptune smiled benignly, stepped back onto his turtle carriage and turned toward the deep, waving his trident in farewell. The whales followed, spouting happily.

'Marilyn,' the other creatures said, 'It's marvelous, what a lovely voice you have. We will come every night to listen to you.'

Then they went off home, happy and chattering excitedly about the visit from the great King of the Sea. Tears once again flowed down Marilyn's pretty face but this time they were tears of joy. She opened her mouth again and this is the song that she sang...

Song of the Sea

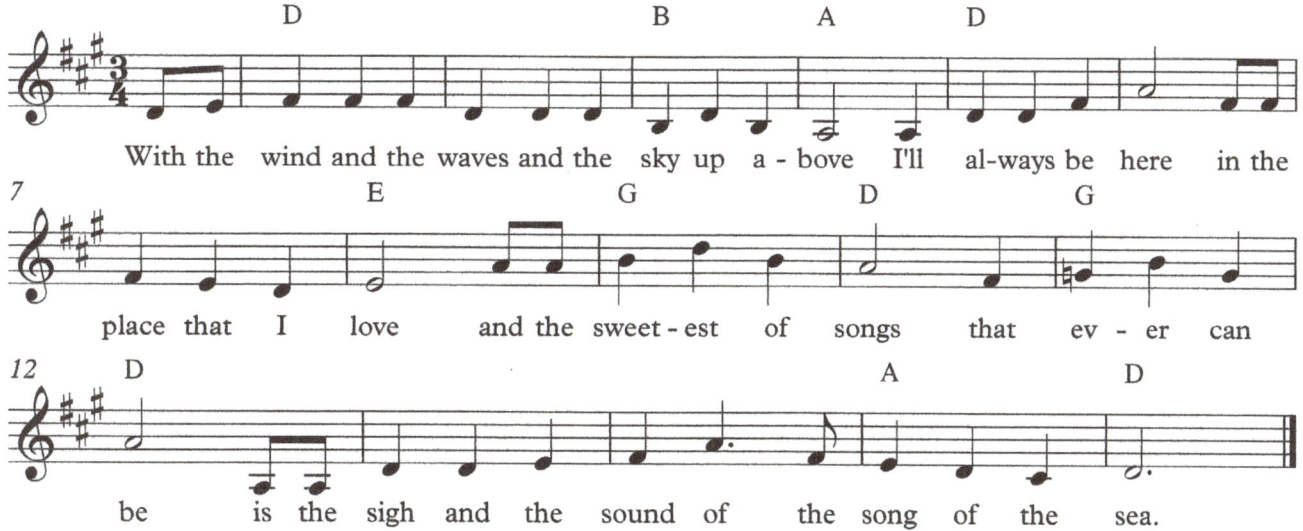

With the wind and the waves and the sky up above
I'll always be here in the place that I love
And the sweetest of songs that ever can be
Is the sigh and sound of the song of the sea

The whales and the dolphins play out on the waves
The eels and the octopus hide in their caves
And the sweetest of songs that ever can be
Is the sigh and the sound of the song of the sea

King Neptune he rules from his throne in the deep
And all the sea creatures are safe in his keep
And the sweetest of songs that ever can be
Is the sigh and the sound of the song of the sea

The sailors all know that their work and their lives
Depend on the wind, the weather and tides
And the sweetest of songs that ever can be
Is the sigh and the sound of the song of the sea

Repeat first verse

This was written and performed in a primary school in Andalucía about 1996.

After The Sun Goes Down (1990s)

It's Halloween on ---------------night.
All the witches are coming to town.
They mean to give you such a fright
After the sun goes down.

Chorus:
They dance around with ghouls and ghosts
To see who they can frighten most.
They're eating snacks of worms on toast.
After the sun goes down.

They fly around all dressed in black,
Those witches who come into town
On broomsticks brought from the outback.
After the sun went down.

Chorus

So come along and join the fun
With the witches who've come into town.
The party now has just begun.
No need to wear a frown.
You can dance around with ghouls and ghosts
To see who you can frighten most
And enjoy the snacks of worms on toast.
After the sun goes down.

I wrote this for the English class in the Escuela de Idiomas in San Roque, Andalucia.

Druid Chant (A Round)

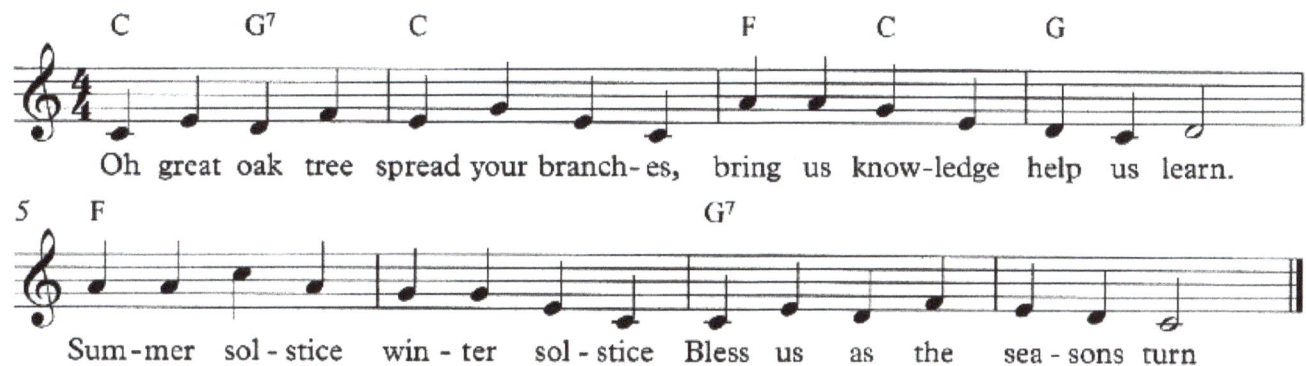

This was written for a show about English history for Spanish schools in Andalucia.

Oak trees were sacred to the Druids.

Gretna Green

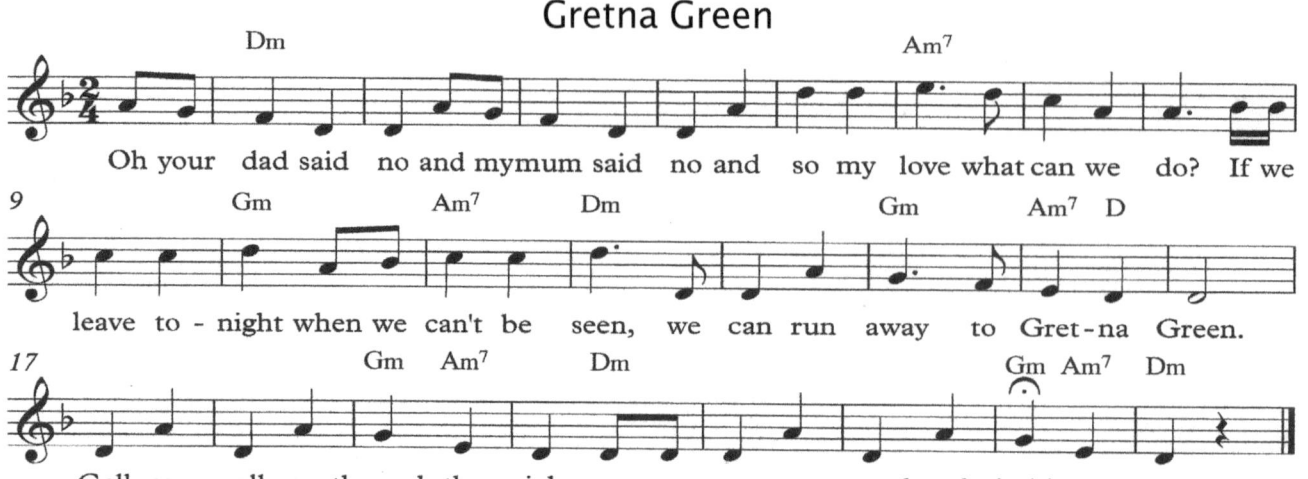

Your Dad says no and my Mum says no
So, my love what can we do
If we leave at night when we can't be seen
We'll run away to Gretna Green
Chorus:
Gallop, gallop through the night
Put your arms around and hold me tight
So pack your bag and make it small
Make sure you bring your woollen shawl
Upon Shap Fell it's cold and bleak
And we have no time to stop and sleep
Chorus
We'll find the blacksmith in his shop
And make him witness to our plot
To wed before we are delayed
Or by our family betrayed
Chorus
You'll have no gown or garter blue
No waiting maids or satin shoes
But all my love I promise thee
And my wedded wife you soon shall be
Chorus
So come my love let us away
To celebrate our wedding day
If we leave tonight when we can't be seen
We'll run away to Gretna Green
Chorus x 2

Gretna Green (1997)

In the 1700s in the northern English town of Manchester lived a young couple, Tom and Felicity who were very much in love but were not allowed to marry.

Tom, 18, was good-looking with dark hair and soft brown eyes. He was the son of the local Lord, privately educated and with a love of horses. His father owned a stable of race-horses. Felicity, 17, with auburn curls and dimples was the daughter of the local clog-maker and helped him with his trade. Neither of their parents approved the match and as they were under 21 could not marry without parental permission.

The lovers would meet secretly in the park after church on Sundays, both frustrated at the inability to legalise their love.

Then one day Tom said, 'There's nothing else for it, Felicity, we have to elope and go to Gretna Green to marry secretly.'

Just over the border, in Scotland, the law there allowed marriage under 21 and the official ceremony was done by the local blacksmith, or anvil priest, as they were known.

'Yes, yes, Tom,' Felicity agreed. 'Much as I hate to go against my parents I love you so much and I want to be your wife as soon as possible'.

So it was arranged that the next Friday night, under cover of darkness, Tom would take one of his father's horses and ride to Felicity's house at midnight where she must be ready to climb out of her bedroom window and join him on the long ride north. It was about a hundred miles, over the high country of *Shap Fell* to the Scottish border and it would be cold and exhausting. But they felt it was the only way to achieve their aim.

'Felicity, make sure you bring warm clothing and pack in the utmost secrecy, no-one must know of our plans,' Tom warned.

So the next Friday, after dinner Felicity went to her room and started to ready herself for the journey but the problem was that she shared her room with Lucy, her 10-year-old sister who had already retired. Quiet though she was, Lucy heard her moving around and awoke to see her sister with a packed bag in hand.

'What are you doing, where are you going?'

'Shhh', said Felicity,' I am going away to marry Tom but it is a big secret, you must tell no-one' and she crept over to the window when she heard the sound of approaching hooves, slipped over the sill and mounted behind Tom as they moved away.

They went quietly through the city streets but once on the highway north Tom expertly moved the horse into a gallop and they sped off northward into the night.

Now Lucy loved her sister very much and she didn't want her to go away and leave her. When Felicity left she started to cry and she cried so loudly that her mother heard her and she came in to see what the problem was.

'What ever is the matter, Lucy, and where is Felicity?'

'She's gone away with Tom' sobbed Lucy.

When Felicity's father heard the news he went straightaway to Tom's parents' house, and, waking his father cried, 'Your son has taken my daughter and they are on the way to Scotland. Give me a horse immediately and I will follow.'

Tom's father gave him a horse from his stable. He was too fat and unfit to ride himself and was only too glad to let Felicity's father make the ride.

Meanwhile Tom and Felicity were galloping through the night and next morning, only stopping briefly to give the horse a break. And have some food. They were tired and cold, especially over *Shap Fell* but they knew they had to get to Gretna Green as fast as possible.

Finally late that day they arrived in that small hamlet and went directly to the blacksmith's shop.

The strong man stood next to his forge in his leather apron and immediately knew the score. He had seen many young couples come for his services in this manner.

'Marry us quickly,' they pleaded and they moved inside his small dwelling to write down their names.

However, just then they heard the sound of galloping hooves outside. Tom looked out the window.

'It's your father,' he said, turning to Felicity with an expression of dismay.

But the blacksmith, already prepared for such a confrontation said, 'Quick through here, close the door behind you and jump into that bed.'

So they did.

As Felicity's father came storming through the door crying, 'Where is my daughter? I can't allow this marriage!' the blacksmith said calmly, 'It's too late,' and he opened the door to his bedroom where Tom and Felicity lay under the cover clutching each other in fear.

'Tom! You and your family will pay dearly for this,' cried Felicity's father and stormed out of the house, mounting the horse and galloping off.

Tom and Felicity crept out of bed.

'Now we can continue,' smiled the blacksmith. With the paperwork completed and the man well-paid for his services, he took them over to his anvil and with a strike of his hammer pronounced them man and wife.

This story and song were written for a show *Scotland the Brave* I wrote and performed in language schools in Andalucía.

It is based on fact. Apparently in such circumstances the blacksmith had a bed handy and made it look as if the marriage had already been consummated.

Travels with Sammy the Seven-Year-Old (1998)

When I first arrived to live in Spain it was on my BMW motorcycle but it soon became apparent that, with rebuilding a house, I needed a car to transport materials. Second-hand cars in England were cheap and, though not entirely legal to drive one for more than a few months on UK plates, over the years I bought a few cars in England to drive down to Spain. The second one was a little silver Renault 5 called Tinkerbell. My drive back to Spain co-incided with school holidays in the UK so I suggested that Sammy, my niece, could come with me and fly back later. Her mother, my sister Janet, was only too happy to have some time without her so this is the story of our journey.

Saturday 7th February in Tinkerbell, the Rambling Renault, we left Purley at 2pm and drove to Farnborough, arriving mid-afternoon to see some friends en route.

At their house en route, Sammy played with the rabbits and dogs and their computer games. Hot potatoes and sausages ably cooked by our friend helped us on our way to Portsmouth. We hunted for the old ships but as darkness was upon us, they were all closed.

Sammy was very excited about her first 'fairy' trip. The two-hour wait for the boat proved hard work even with the aid of children's books, one offering what proved to be a vain attempt at familiarisation with French words using coloured stickers. At last we could board and Sammy ran, exploring, all over the boat until 1.30 am by which time I had given up hope of any sleep on the uncomfortable reclining chair. A fitful night followed and I was glad to be off the ship and in the car, on the road at Cherbourg at 7am, French time.

It was dark and misty. I realised that my lights were pointed in the wrong direction and hoped the sun would soon rise so that I could extinguish them. When it did, the mist remained and I had to keep them on.

We took a road I had not intended but it probably didn't make much difference. It is not an easy drive from Cherbourg as there are no main through-roads and I frequently needed to consult the map. We continued slowly through mist and sleepy French villages (it was Sunday) with our dodgy lights on almost all day. Eventually stopping for lunch in a town on the Loire, Sammy was given a novelty biro when we bought coffee and hot chocolate and I then took almost an hour finding the right road out of town!

'Stop swearing,' said Sammy. 'My Dad is bad enough. How can I give it up when you do it too?'

All afternoon I wondered whether it was worth trying to get to the Bayonne area in one day or find a pension. The weather was bad and at least the car was warm and Sammy was sleeping and quiet for a change so I carried on, using the stickers from Sammy's French book to block the errant headlamp beams. By 9pm we were within striking distance of Salies-de-Bearn but it took another three quarters of an hour of driving through misty country lanes before we finally arrived at Roger's abode. His new house was centrally heated and, though not quite finished, provided the comfort of a bedroom and, even more important, scotch and ice which I desperately needed.

Monday saw us exploring Salies-de-Bearn and catching up with friends there. It is a charming medieval town, based on the finding of salt in the local water which initiated a salt industry. Every September a salt festival commemorates the once thriving business. Now its salty waters attract visitors who use them as therapeutic baths. In a prosperous area which hosts cultural events, especially during the summer months, picturesque Salies attracts many artists of which Roger was one. He lived and ran classes there.

Sammy was invited to go swimming in the baths with a few local children two days hence and also to a birthday party. A bright sunny Tuesday morning saw us walking up the Pain de Sucre, a small hill overlooking the village. The main attraction for Sammy was a small herd of deer which she fed enthusiastically with clumps of grass. That evening we fed ourselves at a restaurant with Roger where I indulged in my favourite dessert, creme broule.

Wednesday, while Sammy was busy with her social affairs, I took a trip to the 'decharge' (the town tip) and came away with two wooden chairs and a birdcage. Tinkerbell was repacked to accommodate these treasures and on our departure on Thursday morning we had to squeeze Roger in too as he needed a lift to Ortez, ten miles away to pick up his errant Winnebago campervan. The brakes had failed the day before and he was due to catch the ferry from Bilbao to the UK that night! We left him in the car park preparing to drive brakeless to the local garage. As the sun rose we continued in the frosty morning to Biarritz where we stopped for a coffee and I showed Sammy the ritzy town and its famous beaches.

We followed the coast road out and drove into bright sunshine as we crossed the border into Spain. The heater, which was jammed on, had been great during our driving in the UK and France, but now was a bit too warm and we were soon stripped off down to tee shirts in the car.

Tinkerbell was running very badly, gutless and pinking, but when we eventually re-fueled, the performance improved. I had my suspicions that the pump attendant, when we refilled in the dark at Salies-de-Bearn, had mistakenly put in unleaded. It had not helped in negotiating the high Pyrenees mountains which straddle the border. Tinkerbell was not as fast as Hekel, the flying Fiat, my previous car which I had driven down two and a half years earlier. It was frustrating driving as I had no power to overtake. However, we made my normal half-way point at Candelario, a mountain village near Bejar, and as there was snow on the peak behind us, I refrained from camping and treated us both to a lovely 'casa rural' room where, after a two hour wait (this is Spain) for hot water we indulged in a bath!

'This is the life, Lindy!' said Sammy, who had got in first and smothered herself with suds. I was filthy and very tired and was screaming at her to get out so I could submerge my tired bones, scrub off the miles and *sleep*!

As I lay luxuriating in the bath Sammy was slamming cupboard doors, apparently looking for a hair dryer.

'Go down to reception and ask them,' I said, knowing that Sammy didn't speak Spanish and the staff were unlikely to speak English.

'Just mime it,' I said, so off she went. A few minutes later she reappeared, standing with her hands on her hips, looking exasperated.

'They haven't got one! What kind of a hotel is this, Lindy?'

I had to laugh. This was the only hotel she had ever been in and, with her family circumstances, I doubted if she would go to any other.

From Bejar to Aracena in Andalucía was uneventful. The countryside is mainly flat and open on this stretch, apart from the final few miles through a green hilly area, at this time of year sporting sparkling streams and clumps of yellow soursobs. Arriving in the small town, we parked outside a bar in the main square and I phoned Dave the Bee to come and find us. As his 3km track is four-wheel drive only, we left Tinkerbell in a side street and, armed with sleeping bags, jumped into his Toyota Landcruiser for the short drive to his property.

Dave, his wife Anna and three-year-old Lucy, had recently moved onto six hectares of land in a lovely valley. He had chestnut trees, cork oaks and olives. Two bore holes, two natural springs and a river meant that he always had water and there was plenty of land for growing vegetables and rearing pigs as the area is famous for its bacon.

As his nick-name suggests, Dave is also a bee-keeper and is following the business of honey production and queen breeding. However, the family at that time lived in a hovel, as bad weather during the winter had held up building, mainly because the local trucks with materials couldn't negotiate the track. Another year though and the house was a lot more comfortable. Dave's past house renovations testify to his industrious nature. He takes after his bees!

Sammy spent the next day chasing the four dogs and six cats while Dave, Anna and I caught up on our news. We all made a trip into town to the market and local caves which are spectacular. As a show cave enthusiast who has visited many in various parts of the world, I can honestly say these are among the best I have seen.

We made the final **run** to Castellar via Seville and Sammy had a chance to stretch her legs when we stopped at a rocky outcrop near Los Barrios. She showed an enthusiasm and ability for rock climbing so we spent half an hour or so scrambling in the area.

Fortunately we drove up my track before dark as the first job was finding a saw in the shed to cut our way into the kitchen. The wooden door had swollen with the heavy rains and before we could have a cup of tea, it was necessary to saw off the excess and free the lock. Just as I succeeded in making entry my Spanish neighbor invited us for coffee!!

Home at last!!

In Search of Earthly Treasures in Spain (1999)

At last the summer heat had cooled, the scent of autumn blew in the wind and I realised that it was the perfect time to travel inland to explore a fascinating area deemed useful to society for over 5000 years. It lies in the province of Huelva, Andalucía and is where the Rio Tinto mines are situated. As you may guess Rio Tinto means tinted river and, sure enough, the rich, ruby colour of the water that flows beside the mine workings indicates the presence of many minerals. There is a lot to see and the BMW and I were ready to explore.

The location is about a five-hour ride north-west of my home in Southern Spain and the journey entailed passing through a variety of scenery. The summer had left some areas brown and parched, with stark rocks breaking through sparse soil but in other parts a now kinder sun illuminated the golden gleam of harvested fields and reflected off the white walls of houses perched on the steep slopes of old castle towns such as Arcos de la Frontera, a strategic position in the Moorish/Christian wars.

My route took me through the stately city of Seville and just before reaching the ring road I pulled over to dislodge a buzzing insect from my helmet. On slowing down, I discovered I had no clutch. Panic! I pushed the laden bike off the highway and investigated. No, not a broken cable as I first suspected but just a slipped locating pin on the clutch pushrod arm. Phew!

I proceeded merrily on over the huge suspension bridge crossing the Guadalquiver River, Seville's lifeline, and into the next province where the road climbs into the Sierras of Aracena.

The small town of Rio Tinto nestles in a hilly, previously-wooded area and is the hub of activity for the mine personnel and now those in the tourist trade. I parked the bike next to the old pump tower outside the museum and entered on my fact finding mission.

Remains from Roman times, 500BC - 100AD prove that minerals found locally were used for decoration and for making household goods and instruments of war.

The Moors, following in the 7th century, also located supplies of copper, silver, gold and iron for their own cultural requirements. However, the mines lay dormant from the 14th to the 18th century and not until the 19th century did they regain their importance.

After the Napoleonic Wars, the establishment of the Republic of Spain necessitated an urgent redevelopment of the country and in 1873 the area was sold to an English mining group headed by a man named Matheson. This gentleman formed the *Rio Tinto Mining Company*, bringing out British experts and accommodating them in Victorian-style houses in a purpose-built village, complete with a Protestant church. The Spanish labourers who poured into the area from all over Spain and nearby Portugal lived in shacks and hovels that they hurriedly erected.

Thus began the golden age of mining in Huelva province. The Rio Tinto Company revolutionised the mining systems of the time. The first great open cut *Atalaya Mine* was started in 1907, extracting copper ore rapidly and at low cost and providing work for many people.

In order to transport the raw materials to the grinders and foundries and finally to the coast for export to world markets, the British built a railway system which ran due south for 84kms to the port of Huelva where a new wharf was especially erected. Starting in 1890, the line was initially only for the mine but by 1903 was also carrying passengers and opened up a new world for the previously isolated people of the area. New towns were created near the mining works and an expanding railway network linked them.

After World War 2 and the Spanish Civil War, Franco came into power and the mines were bought by the recently created Compania Espanola de Rio Tinto. Little by little, the reserves of copper decreased and the price of the ore fell. It became unviable to mine the line of copper and the economy of the region reverted to other rural resources. However, with new extraction techniques, the old slag heaps are now being reworked to reclaim the copper and also traces of gold and silver. Sulphur is also found for making acid. Though not as rich as in earlier times, Rio Tinto is once more a mining town.

The industrious feel about Rio Tinto is endorsed by the entry road passing through a landscape ruptured by huge diggings. The exposed earth shows its kaleidoscope of colours; red ochres, sulphur yellow, white, grey, green and brown.

The well laid out museum has an audio visual display and a comprehensive collection of mining artefacts from over the ages and even includes a railway carriage, *The Maharajah*, specially imported for a visit by Queen Victoria.

A full tourist ticket includes a tour around the museum in the form of a bus ride to see the huge *Atalaya Mine* where work finally stopped in 1986. The huge hole is almost 1 km wide and 335 metres deep. In the afternoon, to complete the tour, a small train travels along the old track following the Rio Tinto, direction Huelva port. When it reaches the first station, passengers can alight and marvel at the red colour of the water splashing over white rocks with a background of pine and eucalyptus trees scenting the air. Steam enthusiasts are in their element on the last Sunday of each month when one of the original British locomotives is used.

Having taken the train on a previous visit, I now wanted to try my luck with the BMW on the small track that ran close to the railway line, deviating at times through the old workings. There had been a little rain so I took it slowly through the mud puddles and finally gave up the ride when the track broke up on a steep descent. As I am unable to pick up the bike alone, I decided that discretion was the better part of valour and backtracked.

After over-nighting with friends in the area, I headed home. The return trip was just as interesting as, on re-crossing the bridge to re-enter Seville, I noticed a nasty wet feeling on my left leg and looked down to see that the oil filler cap had vibrated loose and my trousers and the left side of the bike were covered in warm, black liquid. There followed a quick clean and top-up job at the next garage before I continued my soggy way home, the final stop being the car wash.

Ah well, I was looking for minerals and I found them.

Johnny Won't You Come Along Now - Linda Bick & Cornish Traditional

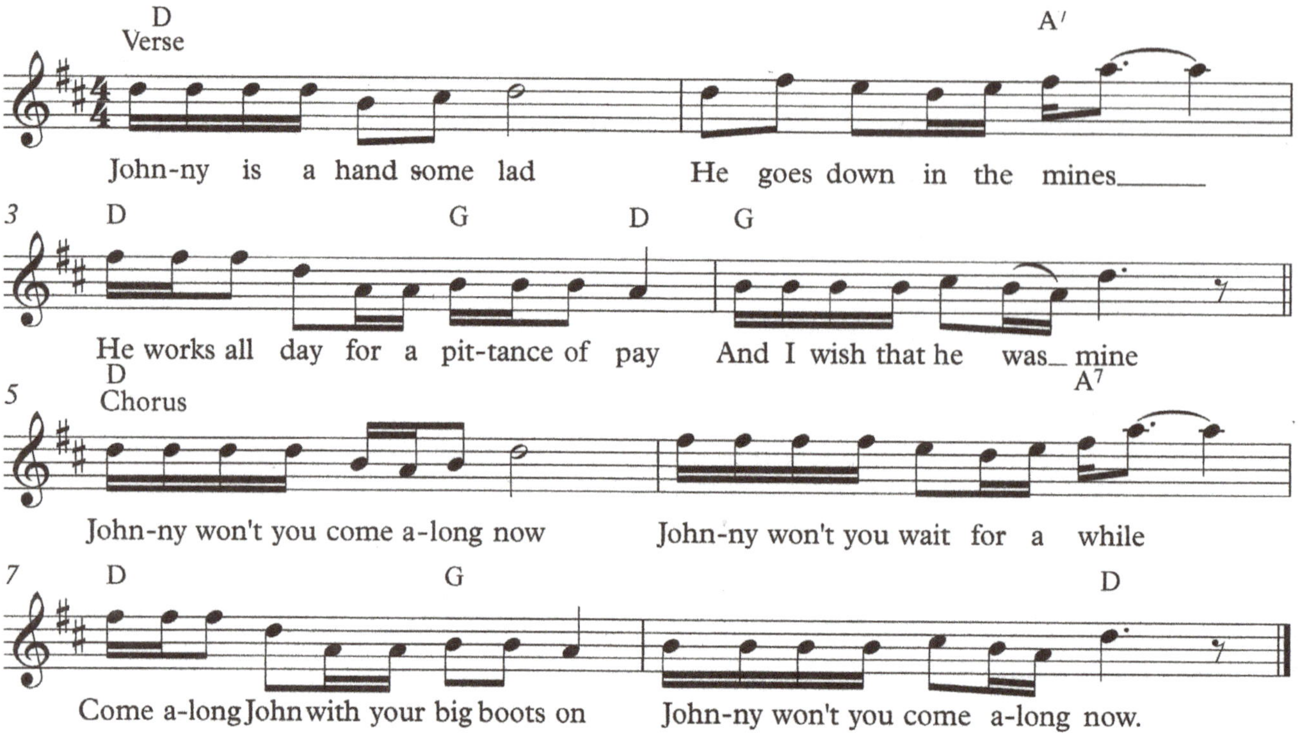
Verse
John-ny is a hand some lad He goes down in the mines
He works all day for a pit-tance of pay And I wish that he was mine
Chorus
John-ny won't you come a-long now John-ny won't you wait for a while
Come a-long John with your big boots on John-ny won't you come a-long now.

Proper
'ansum!

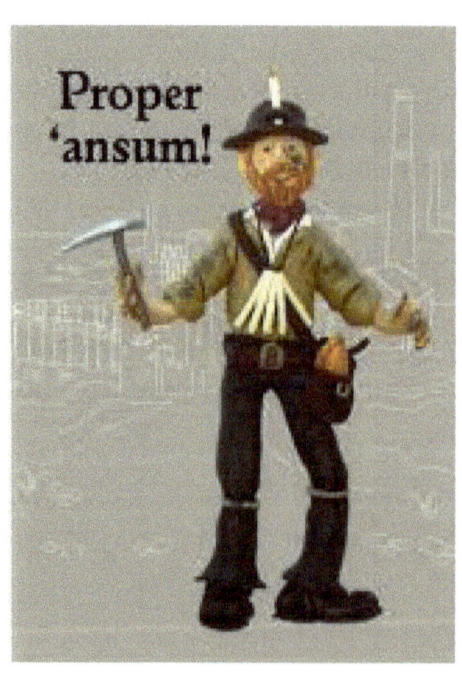

Chorus
Johnny won't you come along now
Johnny won't you wait for a while
Come along John with your big boots on
Johnny won't you wait for a while

Johnny is a handsome lad
He goes down in the mines
He works all day for a pittance of pay
And I wish that he was mine

Chorus

I'll show my petticoat white
Blow a kiss as he comes by
Wear my bonnet of blue and my pinafore new
To try and catch his eye

Chorus

I'll wash his dirty clothes
And clean his pit boots too
His oggie I'll make for his midday break
And at night his mutton stew

Chorus

Hey, hey, I dream all day
I'm right there in his arms
I swoon with joy for that darling boy
If he'd only see my charms

Chorus x 2

Playing Music Way Out at Boghill (1999)

There's jigs and there's reels in between meals
At a table where you eat your fill
And laughter and jokes with all kind of folks
Playing music way out at Boghill

There's peat out to dry 'neath a blue summer sky
Or burnt on the fire when it's chill
There's a big pot of tea for whoever may be
Playing music way out at Boghill

You can get on your bike or go for a hike
Or just read a book and be still
If you're looking for fun there's a lot to be done
Playing music way out at Boghill

There's tunes from Clare or any old where
Being played at a pace that would kill
In the sessions at night where you go for a pint
Playing music way out at Boghill

There's fiddles and flutes and banjos and lutes
And whistles that play with a trill
There's cellos and drums and melodeons
Playing music way out at Boghill

Sure, it's grand to be there in the county of Clare
Where the Burren and cliffs cast their spell
There's plenty of craic and you know you'll be back
Playing music way out at Boghill

In 1999, while living in Spain, I went for a week to Ireland, County Clare to attend a fiddle workshop. It was great fun with people from all around Europe coming to learn to play traditional tunes by ear. We learnt to drink lots of Guinness too!

Out Of The Frying Pan (1999)

'I suppose I've always been into hot things, so this is a natural progression,' mused Lizzie, the fire-eater.

Initially a professional chef, then a candle-maker, now, in her mid-thirties, she is the initiator and solo performer of the *Sacred Flame Fire Theatre*. Having always had an interest in drama and the performing arts, Lizzie jumped 'out of the frying pan and into the fire' five years ago and decided to go on the road with a show that incorporates storytelling with pyrotechnics. She learnt the basic skills of juggling and fire eating and now uses innovative movements and effects to keep audiences spellbound during her 20 minute performances that show off her talents.

Getting started on the festival circuit entailed months of hard work becoming known at local fairs and private events. Gradually, over the years, her reputation and popularity grew and now she has bookings nearly every weekend in the summer months at battle re-enactments, historical villages and alternative and folk festivals. Her Celtic and Medieval themes fit in well at such events.

Depending on the venue Lizzie has an appropriate story to tell in which there is quite often a dragon involved, and her performance includes juggling flaming 'devil sticks', club and scale swinging, fire eating and wielding a flaming sword – to kill the fiery dragon.

Her tools of trade are paraffin with sawdust, methylated spirits, and bought or homemade pyrotechnic special effects such as coloured smoke or flares.

As her show has become more spectacular and more involved, Lizzie has needed help with the setting up and practical side of things and for the past two years she has had Siobhan as her assistant. Siobhan has the important task of lighting the fires on cue with the background music that creates mood and timing for Lizzies dialogue and display.

Lizzie likes being her own boss and the life of a travelling performer is always interesting. She has a car and a small caravan to make her weekend stopovers at show locations easier to organise and more comfortable, and to give her a greater degree of independence and flexibility. But she says that for her keeping a vehicle in running order is more hassle than eating fire.

Future plans? Though normally a solo performer Lizzie is hoping to put together a larger show with the theme of a celebration of witches. This will include other female fire workers and musicians. She already has two other performers in mind and will probably spend this winter writing and organizing the show.

Lizzies' partner is also in show business – he is part of a clown troupe, and though their professional lives sometimes coincide if they happen to be booked at the same venue, Lizzie said that most times they are 'ships that pass in the night'. So the off peak winter months are not just time for creating next year's shows but for having family time to regenerate relationships.

Lizzie, who has had offers of performing in the USA and on the continent, is keen to expand into these markets in the future but at the moment is thoroughly enjoying her trips around the UK.

Her home base, in a larger caravan, is in Norfolk.

Natural Healing Techniques Available In South Spain (1999)

No-one will deny that music forms a part of our very being. In our Western society it is forefront in our culture. Music in all its forms is played, talked about, even idolised, and it would be very unusual to go for any length of time without hearing it in some form or another. We have it played all the time, on the radio, TV, videos. We have record players, tape players and now take portable cassettes and iPods with us in cars, planes, on foot or even push-bike or motorcycle.

Why do we need music? Even without our sophisticated means of creating and transmitting it, we watch and listen to live music without amplification. Musicians in both sophisticated and primitive society are sought after and revered for their ability to create sound.

Music itself creates mood. It appeals to certain parts of our mind. It stirs the soul as well as the intellect. Research has shown that certain tones, notes and harmonics can make us happy, sad, frightened, angry, excited or relaxed. A simple example is the musical scores used in films, the atmospheric music played in restaurants, the 'muzac' in shopping malls.

When people want to get a message across they find that it makes more impact through song, hence advertising jingles. Even successful poetry or prose does not have such a wide-reaching appeal as a song. A well-produced recording draws together not just a singer - the human voice with its own range of tone - but one or more instruments which can in turn impart their own tonality and can effectively harmonise with each other and the voice.

Scientific research and history have proven the power of music on our senses. Music has always been and will continue to be used to influence people, to sway their emotions, to lead them to war or peace. The bagpipes and trumpet have led men into battle. The swirl of the pipes with its eerie tones fortified the advance and scared the foe. The strident note of the trumpet is a call to battle, or when mellowed, is used for the last post.

From ancient to modern times, people singing hymns in religious ceremonies are using the power of the voice to centre themselves and unite with others to focus on a communal thought, the prayer.

When music became mass produced in record form in the sixties and large concerts of pop music were performed all over the Western world, young people were led to hysteria. ie. Beatlemania. In more recent years the message, in songs for Band Aid, reached out and inspired millions to give to the needy in far-off lands.

Music then, is a powerful tool, and it can be used very successfully to help us tune in our own minds and bodies, not just to help ourselves but each other and the world.

The human voice and musical instruments produce different notes in a range of tonal qualities and all of these notes are produced by vibration - either of a string, or air through a pipe or a vocal chord and this vibration affects not just our ear drums but other parts of our body. The value of music in meditation and healing has been known and used for many centuries in eastern cultures but Western scientists and doctors have also done much research on the subject. Using sophisticated equipment to measure and document changes in the body, they have discovered, amongst other things, that certain notes and resonances, for example in vowel sounds, can and do affect different organs.

The idea that disease or illness is disharmony within the body is not a new one and work with music to re-resonate the body organs to 'retune' them has proved very successful. Many well-known doctors and scientists have used musical methods related to ancient Tibetan over-toning with amazing results. Experiments on cancer and HIV patients are showing that cell structure can be altered through music therapy and destruction halted.

Each person has their own note, their own vibration, and it is this that they subconsciously use when they 'tune in' to others. It is our sound and vibration that attracts or repels. When we are in love, we feel that we are in complete harmony with the other person. When we cannot agree, disharmony prevails. If we learn to tune our own vibrations to as many others as possible, life becomes easier as relationships improve.

Hand in glove with sound is movement. A couple of years ago there was a market craze for the little figures that 'danced' when they picked up certain sound vibrations. Sold in forms such as flower or Coke cans, placed next to a tape player or radio they moved in time with the rhythm. They can be used as an example of how the human body also responds to vibrations.

We talk about the rhythm of life. Movement means life. Every living thing is moving all the time. The body needs movement to stimulate the flow of hormones, to exercise the internal and external organs, to 'keep fit'. Our movements express our feelings, ie. jumping for joy, shaking with anger, cowering in fear. This is our natural body language and our immediate physical response to a thought.

We can also use controlled movement to centre ourselves and direct our thoughts. Movement can aid concentration and awareness. Daily exercises that are common in the East in places such as China and Japan, not only help the body but prepare the mind to centre on the day's work ahead. Performed en-masse, they enhance the bonding effect of working together.

Folk dancing, where people perform certain set movements in unity, brings a great feeling of togetherness and generates an enormous amount of energy and enjoyment. We feel the excitement of dancing 'in step' with another human being. Even watching other people dance harmoniously together brings satisfaction – hence the popularity of programs such as *Come Dancing* or skating couples such as Jayne Torvill and Christopher Dean.

Movement in meditation brings awareness of the body's chakras – the centres of energy at certain points of the anatomy. Dance therapy is used for healing and, used in conjunction with music, is a way of creating energy and keeping the mind, spirit and body in harmony. Learning to breath correctly and to use and control your own body rhythm counteracts stress and gives a feeling of general wellbeing.

Another very important factor in how we feel about ourselves is related to colour. We all know that we feel better when the sun shines. Our spirits lift and we have more energy and positive thoughts. We want to be outside, feeling not only the warmth of the sun but the light of its rays. This light brings out the colour in all around us and every colour has its own vibration that is more fully activated when it is lit up. Flowers open when the sun's rays are on them, giving out their vibration and everything feels more alive.

If we bring flowers into a room we are bringing in a living colour. It is traditional to bring flowers to the sick – their colours bring energy and life. They are used to enhance special occasions such as weddings, birthdays etc, and as a homage to the passing of life at a funeral. Using coloured glass in a window is another way of using 'living' colour, as the tones change with the strength of the sun's rays. It brings a special radiance to a building or room and is an effect used in many places of worship. We are individually drawn to certain colours and again it is because they are on our wavelength or vibration in the same way that we relate to music. As different musical notes affect us, so do colours and they too can heal and guide us when used correctly, or aggravate us if not. If we feel that colours clash, it is because their vibrations are not in harmony with each other or with us. Some people feel happy wearing colours that others cannot abide.

Colour has been used for healing through the ages, from the Egyptians to the Greeks and to Isaac Newton who worked with the seven colours he found in the prism. This relates to the rainbow and the same seven colours therein. (Seven is a number continuously repeated in the universe, ie Seven Wonders of the World, Seven Seas).

The seven rainbow colours are: red, orange, yellow, green, blue, indigo and violet. Colours each have their own vibrationary wavelengths. Red vibrates at the lowest frequency while violet at the highest. Red, orange and yellow are warm, magnetic colours while blue, indigo and violet are cool and sedate. Green is the balance in between.

Through the ages, artists have painted people, especially saints and angels. Those relating to a higher spiritual plane are painted with halos or auras of light around them. Clairvoyants are able to see auras of different colours around people and Kirlian photography enables us to photograph the flow of energy around all things and to record changes in this energy.

The seven colour rays are related to different aspects of life and the chakras within us and effect certain parts of the body.

The red ray is the colour of life and activates the adrenals and stimulates the emotions and sexual responses.

The orange ray is the spirit of health and purity, controls the splenic centre, affects the gonads and assists assimilation and circulation.

The yellow ray is the spirit of knowledge and wisdom. It stimulates the solar plexus, the great brain of the nervous system. It affects the pancreas, liver and spleen.

The green ray is the spirit of evolution and stimulates the thymus gland and heart centre and balances our emotions.

The blue ray is the spirit of truth. It affects the throat centre, the thyroid and is antiseptic. (note the colours used in antiseptic mouthwashes etc)

The indigo ray is the spirit of power and knowledge and is linked to the brow centre.

The violet ray, the spirit of sacrifice and of high ideals, is linked to the crown centre at the top of the head.

We make simple associations with colours: red is the colour of life, pink is the colour of love and affection (pink hearts for Valentine's day), orange is for vitality and health, green for relaxing, giving and receiving, yellow for stimulating ideas and knowledge, blue for loyalty and trust, purple and violet for spiritual colours. When we understand the vibrations that colours give out and how they affect us, then we can use them constructively in our environment, in what we wear and how we decorate our homes, to bring out the best in ourselves. For example, pink can subdue the aggressive, green relaxes and yellow can bring clarity of thought and inspiration.

Many people find going for a walk amongst the natural colours of nature helps to calm them down and relax them. This is the combination of looking upon restful colours and breathing in their energy. The movement we use in walking helps us open our senses to these. Using filters or coloured glass to direct coloured rays onto ourselves can have a healing effect and coloured herbal oils have also proved therapeutic. As with music, colour is related to numbers and letters and we can use our given name and birthdate to work out what colours we best relate to, which we have most of in our auras and those we need to tune into to give ourselves a more balanced perspective.

In Northern Europe healing centres with therapists skilled in music, movement and colour therapy are well established, but not so in the South of Spain. However, a French woman, Fabienne Gaite is working to establish the 'Institute del Sol' in a suitable location in this area. Fabienne's involvement with various methods of healing have spanned most of her life-time. From a young age, she realised she had intuition and healing powers. Her love of music and singing led her to write her own material and use her powerful, resonant voice to reach out to others. Having trained as a physical education teacher, Fabienne was aware of the physiological effects of movement but came to realise how much music also affected the body and mind.

After extensive world travel, where she studied music and movement in many cultures, she decided to take further studies in healing through sound, colour and movement. After meeting Fabien Maman, a world authority who has academies in many countries, she attended a Reiki Natural Healing course and then went to Switzerland to work with healing and music master Joakim Marz to build her own monochord.

This instrument dates back to the time of Pythagoras when it was used to clarify the interaction between mathematics and music. Originally it had only one string which Pythagoras likened to the Universe, a string stretching between Heaven and Earth. He worked with the monochord to find his law of harmonic intervals which he applied to other aspects of nature. Nowadays, the monochord can be made with 26 strings, all tuned to the same note but providing a powerful resonance when playing a chord. Fabienne's instrument also encompasses the koto, set up on the reverse side of the monochord which can be swivelled on its supporting axis.

The koto has 13 strings which are tuned separately. The sound created by both instruments is ideal for meditation and creativity. Using various musical keys, the monochord can be tuned to help heal different parts of the body and to create harmonic support for meditational therapy.

Fabienne gives private healing sessions but has begun to conduct week-end workshops in South Spain. Her last workshop was held at *La Solana*, a country house hotel near San Roque. The hotel is set in stately gardens in a hillside area with an outlook of green, rural surroundings. An old Spanish estate, the house has many large rooms with traditional, heavy, wooden Spanish furniture and a centre courtyard made interesting not only by the trees and shrubs planted there but the placement of the present owner's iron work sculptures.

A large circular sunroom at the rear of the house has a cane ceiling, tiled floor with pile rugs and soft furnishings placed on the perimeter. The effect is of light and space and being part of the surrounding greenery.

In her last weekend workshop at La Solana, Fabienne used the calm setting plus her monochord and voice to help the group become aware of themselves. In order to do this, she used music and movement with meditation to bring a feeling of inner peace and harmony. In this relaxed, receptive state, guided imagery was employed to enable the group to centre and direct their energies, to overcome whatever problems they may have been facing. The ability to think clearly and calmly is one that most of us lack when we are under pressure.

The group worked together, interacting to give mutual support and tune in to each others' vibrations. There were four sessions per day, starting at 10am through to 5pm, with breaks for coffee, tea and lunch. It was very noticeable after each session how the group had unwound and relaxed, beginning to relate more fully to each other. By the end of the weekend a great feeling of peace, harmony and positive energy prevailed.

The setting at La Solana is conducive to this type of work and there is a possibility of further workshops there with a view to it becoming a centre where people can come, not only to heal themselves, but to meet others who can give inspiration and guidance. However, at present, to enable her to expand her work, Fabienne wishes to travel further afield to use her creative and healing powers in other centres. She is open to suggestions and welcomes contact from people who may be interested in offering appropriate locations to carry out her work.

Fabienne feels that a focal point is needed where scientists, healers and people already known to do research on all levels, can come together and share their knowledge and create an opportunity for local people to contribute their ideas so that everyone can benefit. She has already received an offer of support from Joakim Marz, the music therapist and instrument maker, who would be prepared to travel to South Spain to conduct monochord building workshops. Other international healers, musicians and artists are interested in coming to share their knowledge.

Reference books;
<u>Know Yourself through Colour</u>
Marie Louise Lacy, Aquarian Press 1989
<u>The Miracle of Colour Healing</u> Vicky Wall, Aquarian Press 1990
<u>Healing Sounds</u>
Jonathon Goldman, Element Books Ltd 1992

A Plethora Of Peters (Printed in *Discover Gibraltar* Nov 1994)

Has it ever occurred to you just how many men named Peter there are in and around Gibraltar? In all the many countries and communities I have lived, I have never come across such an abundance.

And yet, on enquiry into the origin and attached meaning of the name, the reason may be easier to understand in connection with Gibraltar for Peter means 'Rock'.

Originally a Greek word and translated as Petrus in Latin, Jesus gave the name of Peter to Simon, son of Jonah saying 'I shall name you Peter and on this rock I will build my church'.

Peter appealed to the medieval church more than any other apostle, therefore the name Peter was popular as a Christian name in many countries. It was introduced to England by the Normans and soon became a favourite.

However, the Reformation struck a blow to its usage as it was associated with the papacy and in the 17th and 18th century it became uncommon and regarded as old fashioned. It is thought that its return to popularity came after J.M. Barrie wrote the book Peter Pan in 1904, a story about a little boy who never grew up.

Another book, written by a Canadian born US professor, L.J. Peter, was entitled The Peter Principle and subtitled 'Why Things Always Go Wrong'. It stated that in a hierarchy every employee tends to rise to the level of his incompetence, i.e. a person who does his job well is promoted until he reaches one he can't cope with and there he sticks.

So, do we have a large number of Peters in Gibraltar because it attracts rocky, solid types, or a bunch of little boys who will never grow up, or a load of incompetents?

Maybe the Peter you know falls into one or other of these groups or maybe a combination.

Looking around at the ones I know, I think I'd be too petrified to say.

* * *

There was a young man called Pete
Who didn't know what to eat
Should he have a bun,
Or more than just one?
But still be able to fit into his seat

* * *

A flautist once blew on her flute
Came out with a rooty-toot-toot
She opened her eyes
Wide in surprise
And actually looked rather cute

Woad At The Wharf

Few people realise that the last weekend in August used to be a very important date on our calendar. In Celtic times it was Lughnasa, the time to celebrate the first fruits of summer, rather like a modern-day harvest festival. At Lughnasa, the tribes would gather for a political assembly but also to enjoy many other aspects of their Celtic life, so art, crafts, music, storytelling and displays of physical prowess were included.

In Leeds, at the Granary Wharf Centre, a similar festival was held to reconstruct some of the Celtic culture which is part of our own British Heritage. The event was co-organised by Sarah Mawson, from the *Ruadin Reivers Gaelic War Band*, and Peter Mosby from the *Embers Celtic Centre*. Peter also sponsored the festival by bringing well known electric Celtic bands such as Iona and Gaelforce to perform at the *Leeds Irish Centre* on the Friday night, and Celtic harpist Fiona Davidson and F.O.S. Bros (traditional Scottish and Irish music) in the onsite marquee on Saturday and Sunday. Also appearing twice daily was the *Sacred Flame Fire Theatre* and Irish dancers from the *Heather Smith School of Dancing*.

Sarah Mawson, of *Ruadain Reivers* (Red Raiders), was responsible for co-ordinating the battle re-enactment groups, archery, and the display of arts and crafts and storytelling in the 'village'. All activities adhered to a strict code formulated by research into authentic modes of behaviour and dress. Because of Sarah's degree in archeology and Celtic Art she is able to advise the various participants on their costume and kit. The battles re-enacted may have been real or legendary. The combatants, including women, put all their energies into 'killing' or being 'killed', thankfully to rise again for another battle elsewhere. Three groups attending the festival and involved in the battle re-enactments were; Sudeyinger from Glasgow, Yddraig from Stoke on Trent, and the Wolves of Andred from Tunbridge Wells.

The whole festival, over the two days, attracted a fair attendance but the mid-city site was not an ideal setting for photographic authenticity, or even working space. What the budding *Celtic Heritage Society* would like is to eventually purchase a rural site upon which to construct a permanent display and battlefield, a living history village incorporating hillforts and churches. This, like other historic villages in England, would enable the general public and school parties to study the Celtic way of life and to realise an awareness of the culture's place in our history.

At present (1993) the Ruadin Reivers, as a *Celtic Enactment Society*, travel all over Britain to present their knowledge of the culture. They have a wide ranging experience of battles, demonstrations and talks for national festivals, museums, schools, media and charity events.

To Celebrate Millennium In The Mississippi Mud

Y'all come to Cajun country where the gumbo's hot and spicy
And the swamp boats are a-burbling down among the cypress trees
There's jambalaya and catfish with a little touch of filé
And shrimps all wrapped in bacon by the belle of Cajun queens

Now the chainsaw's been a-buzzing and the wood-pile's getting higher
And the oil lamps are all planted to light us on our way
Through the trees the folks are coming, bringing love, bringing laughter
For we're all here together on this very special day

Y'all bring the crackers and a bunch of roman candles
For fixing for a party and we're gonna do it good
While they're dancing down in Sydney, in New York and in London
We're in Louisiana in the Mississippi mud

There'll be alligators rocking as the Zydaco plays louder
And the Spanish moss is swinging to the hopping Cajun beat
The wood duck quack in chorus while the ibis dance the two step
And the fish blow fancy bubbles from the bottom of the creek

We'll be knocking back the bourbon and opening the champagne
For we're gonna have a good time, come hurricane or flood
Bring on Y2K or earthquake, we'll include them in the party
As we stomp in the New Year in the Mississippi mud
We're all at Miss Debby's in the Mississippi mud
Yes, we'll celebrate millennium in the Mississippi mud

Port Vincent, LA (Geaud's Country),
31 December 1999

I met Debby Anselmo in South West Africa in the 1970s and we promised that we would meet up for Millennium from wherever we were in the world. I was in Spain and she was back in Louisiana.

Highway 49

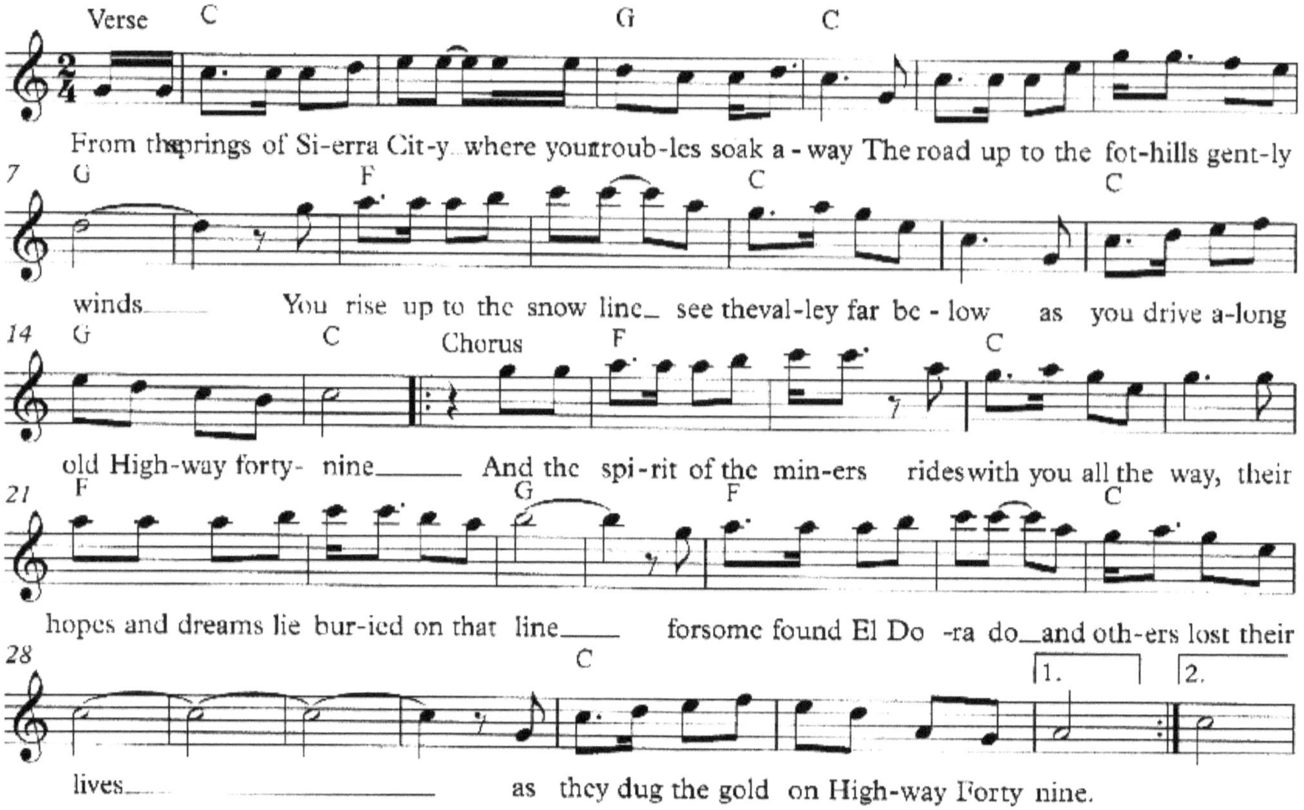
Verse
C G C
From thesprings of Si-erra Cit-y where youtroub-les soak a - way The road up to the fot-hills gent-ly
7 G F C C
winds You rise up to the snow line_ see theval-ley far be - low as you drive a-long
14 G C Chorus F C
old High-way forty- nine And the spi-rit of the min-ers rides with you all the way, their
21 F G F C
hopes and dreams lie bur-ied on that line forsome found El Do -ra do_and oth-ers lost their
28 C 1. 2.
lives as they dug the gold on High-way Forty nine.

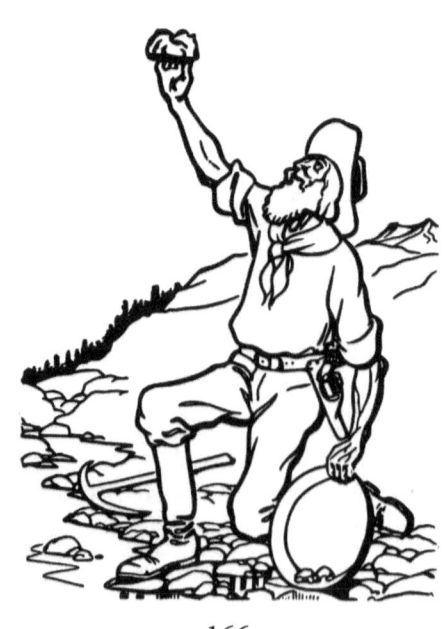

From the springs of Sierra city where your troubles soak away
The road up to the foothills gently winds
You climb up to the snowline, see the valley far below
As you drive along old highway 49

Chorus
And the spirit of the miners rides with you all the way
Their hopes and dreams are buried on that line
For some found El Dorado and others lost their lives
As they dug the dirt on highway 49

It all began in January 1848,
A day men will remember for all time
For better or for worse it put Coloma on the map
And made a start of highway 49

You can see the scattered ruins and remains of industry
In camps among the Ponderosa pines
And the feats of engineering had men borrowing far below
In tunnels under highway 49
Chorus

They came from England and from China, Australia and Spain
In hopes to see them golden nuggets shine
There were men of many colours, religions, race and creed
To try their luck on highway 49

And the women who came with them were worth their weight in gold
For they battled all the hardships they would find
Bore children and bore troubles through drought and fire and flood
And made a home on Highway 49
Chorus

On the streets of Mariposa you'll hear echoes of the past
In songs and stories flowing with the wine
There's some who found the motherlode be it gold or peace of mind
At that turning point on Highway 49
Chorus
Last line repeated with long held 'lives' finish on major chord

I visited America in 2000 and was fortunate to be loaned a Chevy 'truck' to go for a drive in California. I followed Highway 49 and learnt about the goldrush in 1849 which inspired this song.

El Camino De Santiago – The Way Of Saint James (2000)

The Camino de Santiago is a pilgrimage route which commenced in the 9th century following the miraculous discovery of the tomb of St. James in Ira Flavia, Galicia.

St James, one of the Apostles of Jesus was martyred when beheaded on Herod's orders in AD44. His body was recovered by his disciples and transported by ship to Galicia where his remains were buried and lost.

When discovered by the hermit, Pelayo, some 800 years later, they were sanctified and gave rise to the construction of a church on the site of a monastery, Sancti Jacobi. Due to the influx of pilgrims and trade, a town developed around the monastic complex to become what we now call Santiago de Compostela. A cathedral grew with the town, acquiring numerous additions in the following centuries and today there are many magnificent examples of medieval architecture.

The route of the pilgrims varied. Most came from Northern Europe through France, crossing the Pyrenees at varying points and meeting on entering Northern Spain. Some came from England via ship to the northern Spanish coast and others sailed to Lisbon, Portugal and then walked North.

Gradually the tracks acquired hostels and hospitals and by the 12th century guides were written to aid the travellers as to where to find food, lodging and good water en route and how to avoid bandits.

Traditional pilgrims' clothing was a wide-brimmed hat, a cloak and a wooden staff or crook, a leather pouch and a drinking gourd. When a pilgrim reached Santiago he received a scallop shell which he would then carry home on his hat, cloak or pouch, this being visible proof of completion of the Way. From the 15th Century pilgrims received a compostelana, a certificate of completion, of their journey.

Originally, pilgrims were monks or other religious people and for a while it became popular for members of the gentry to undertake the pilgrimage but by the 17th century, pilgrims were of a lower rank; clerics, craftsmen and country folk, drawn to pilgrimage by a combination of piety and a thirst for adventure. In some cases felons were given a choice; prison or 'walk the Way'.

Pilgrimage provided inspiration for songs, music, poems and stories. Music provided a way of communication and entertainment along the Way and even today pilgrims sing while walking. The Santiago streets ring with the sound of hurdy gurdys, bagpipes and many other instruments. *The Portico de la Gloria* (Glory Gate) in the Cathedral has carvings of 24 elders holding traditional instruments symbolizing the harmony of the world.

Today *El Camino de Santiago* is seen as a challenge as well as a religious pilgrimage. Thousands of people from many different countries and walks of life stream continuously into the welcoming streets of Santiago and their reasons for doing so are many and varied. They arrive all year round but mainly during the summer months of vacation and many carry a scallop shell to, as well as from, Santiago. Now a compostelana is needed from where you begin your journey. This is a card which you have stamped along the route to prove that you have walked or horse-ridden a minimum of l00kms or bicycled a minimum of 200kms. This card will prove your authenticity as a pilgrim and entitle you to stay at the refugios along the Way and to receive a discount on bus, train or air tickets out of Santiago at the completion of your pilgrimage.

During my trip to Galicia in 2000 on my BMW I parked it at a campsite at Portomarin, due east of Santiago and walked for two and a half days to get a Compostelana, along part of the *French Way*. It was a delightful experience and I wrote the following poem.

Buen Camino

Murmurings in the gentle dark of pre-dawn
As the pilgrims pack their few possessions
For another day's travel
On the Camino shapes shuffle by in the morning mist
More heard than seen
The tapping of staffs and tinkling of swinging cockleshells
Signalling their pace
As the mist lifts and sunlight shows
Heads raise, smiles blossom and the greeting rings out
'Buen Camino'

The swish and whir of wheels as cyclists pass
Pedal pushing into the distance
Milestones marking pilgrim's progress
Lead the body with shell-like signs
While stone crosses, chapels and churches
Inspire and encourage the spirit
'Buen Camino'

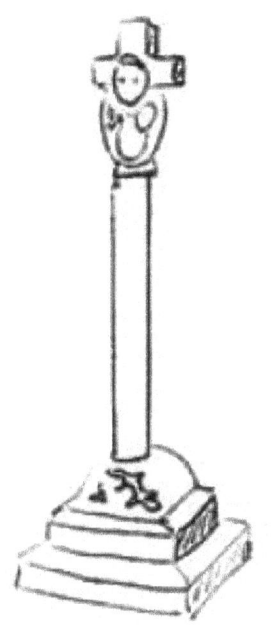

Heat sneaks into the midday
Feet are dipped into cool fuentes, streams or laundry wells
Bliss to peel off socks and shoes and spread troubled toes
Gather to share a drink or joke, queue for a stamp
On the Compostalana
'Buen Camino'

The rural land shows its varied faces
Solemn stony walls, ragged flags of maize
Pine trees and oaks, tall resinous eucalyptus
Or the sickly sweet smell of cow-dung
Women working - herding cows, tossing hay or selling berries
Their ruddy faces seamed with wrinkles
'Buen Camino'

How far to the refugio?
Does it matter? We walk 'til we arrive
Flowers fixed to staffs, faces laughing, feet limping
The day ends with a crush of bodies
All shapes and sizes, every age and nationality
After months, weeks or only days
They are united in common aim
And lie alongside each other in exhausted sleep
'Buen Camino'

The morning brings a shower of rain
Coloured capes over the moving masses
The final few kilometers and the holy spires appear
For the first to espy – King for the day!
The camino winds through the outskirts where
Roaring jets disturb the ear and car fumes foul the nose
The trickle, stream and flood of pilgrims flow directly
To the welcoming centre, Santiago.
Thrilling, thronging, musicians playing
Its stone-flagged, narrow streets leading us past
A multitude of ancient buildings
To the gigantic cathedral – St James' repose
Through the *Gate of Glory* – tears of joy as triumphant fingers
Fill the worn indentation in the marble pillar
We're here!
'Buen Camino'

Santiago, Galicia, Spain, July 2000

A Walk North (2001)

After the enormous effort of the WIMA rally (*Women's International Motorcycle Association*) held in Spain 2001, I decided to wind down by tackling the Portuguese route of the *Camino de Santiago*, starting at Porto and heading north for some 220kms. I had walked a 100kms of the original French route in July 2000. It is the ancient path of a famous pilgrimage to the supposed repository of the remains of St James in Santiago de Compostela-Galicia.

The French route, which enters Spain via the Pyrenees and heads west, is believed to be, according to some peoples' research (including Shirley MacLaine's) on ley lines and therefore a path of immense spiritual force, enabling self-revelation during the hardships of those who complete at least 100kms of it on foot (preferably a lot more). I must admit that I have no spiritual or religious aspirations. I simply enjoy walking and was looking forward to having the company of my sister, Anne, along the track but this time from Portugal on a lesser-used route.

We left Castellar early on Tuesday morning after the rally ended on Sunday. Monday I had spent preparing/repairing the bike. The 'Find the faults' exercise at the rally, using my BMW as a model had been very useful for me to pin point a number of things that needed attention. (I had heard it murmured that some of the participants thought it would never run again – such little faith.)

The August heat caught up with us by mid-afternoon when we stopped for a while to cool down and refresh ourselves by a river somewhere in Extramadura. Then it was on up to near the Portuguese border where we found an ideal camping spot amongst pine trees with a small stream as a washing place. I was amazed to discover that it was the first time in her life that Anne had been camping. On our Moroccan trip three years earlier we had stayed in hostels. However, she survived and we arrived in Porto at midday on Wednesday to try and find some information on starting the route and to obtain the first stamp in our record books to prove the authenticity of our walk. We had little luck in the town centre but were finally given a telephone number to call. This call was made by our Portuguese speaking friend, Judy, who, with her husband Alby, was offering us hospitality for the night and garaging the trusty BMW while we continued on foot.

So, next morning Judy dropped us off at our start point in Moreira on her way to work. We walked from 9am to 2.30pm and found ourselves in Vila de Conde where we just missed the banks and, as I had left the pin number of my card behind, we decided to stay the night and go to the bank the next morning. It is an interesting town with a Roman aqueduct and tranquil fishing port and we enjoyed our stay, especially ogling the gorgeous young waiter in the pizza bar. In the bank next day we fortunately found some cash between us to change as in Portugal they only accept cards in machines, not over the counter. A fact worth remembering.

Our first day's walk had been in pleasant weather on mainly tarred roads and we were following directions from an English guide book which were somewhat frustrating. The next day's walk was similar and we ended it in Barcelos, another Roman city which had some grand buildings and a legend about a cock. Luckily we had encountered the yellow arrows of the official Camino along the way so were able to follow them which made direction finding a lot easier and also took us on more wild footpaths.

The third day proved tough – over mountain tracks in exhausting heat though the sound of fiesta music from mountain villages echoed around us and lifted our spirits. It was a long, hard day's walk (32kms) made worse by Anne being assaulted by a teenager on our last kilometer into town. Fortunately he was unable to snatch anything from her well-hidden purse but she fell heavily in the attack and was badly bruised and shaken. I had only been seconds ahead and was alerted by her screams but the boy had run away by the time I reached her.

We spent a somewhat sleepless night disturbed by church bells in the very picturesque town of Ponte de Lima and continued the next day into a beautiful bright morning to climb more mountains on the road to Valenca. Unfortunately we overstretched ourselves that day and by the end of our 35km march Anne's right ankle was swollen and painful.

The next day we crossed into Galicia past the Cathedral of Tui where many pilgrims join the route at the 100km mark. Anne was in a great deal of pain and that evening limped into Porino where I asked at the council offices for directions to the medical clinic. In Galicia pilgrims are treated like royalty; we were taken by police car to the clinic and then on to the hospital in Vigo for an X-ray. As Anne is over 50 they thought she may have other problems like osteoporosis. However it proved to be a bad sprain and she was advised to give it total rest. We stayed the night in a sports hall where two local firemen brought her a mattress and I went with one in their fire engine to get the medication while Anne and the other sat and chatted in English and Spanish respectively only understanding each other by inflection, nods and smiles.

Much to Anne's enormous disappointment I insisted that we take the train back to Porto to collect my bike and take her to Santiago to catch her bus and plane back to the UK. She didn't have enough holiday time to give her ankle the required rest before continuing on foot. She had completed 120kms of our planned 220 so had achieved more than many who only aim for the final 100.

We retrieved the bike and had a couple of days touring the beautiful green Galician countryside seeing ancient Celtic sites, old mills and waterfalls and part of the spectacular west coast before spending a day in Santiago itself; full of splendid architecture but seething with pilgrims who only served to remind Anne of her inability to get there on foot. When I left her at the bus station she was still in pain and, in fact, her ankle took several weeks to heal in the UK.

After a day attending a Celtic festival I returned to Porino where I left my bike with the firemen and completed the walk (over much less stressful terrain) in 3½ days, encountering a day of rain and many more pilgrims on that last 'easy' 100kms. It was a lovely walk but I missed Anne's humorous company.

From Santiago I returned by train and bus to my bike in Porino and rode down through Portugal stopping at Gois where the 2nd biggest rally in Portugal is held (Faro is the biggest). After my solitary walk and ride the sound and sight of so many people was disconcerting so I only stayed one night before continuing my ride home to Castellar.

The whole trip was hardly a relaxing one but was an enjoyable contrast to the WIMA rally and I look forward to following another Camino route with Anne in the future.

Next time we'll take it easy.

Damp Day on the Danube

Written on my way back to Germany from the Czech Republic in the 1990s. It was raining.

If You Want To See A Tree

I first visited Sweden in 1968 by motorcycle. My lasting impression of the country was that it had many, many trees. When I next visited in 2003 my first impression was verified, for, lo and behold, I saw even more trees plus lakes and streams.

But I discovered a far more interesting thing appertaining to that country – the mythical creature called the Näcken. This, in Swedish folklore is a shape-changing phenomena which appears often as a beautiful young man who plays fiddle, naked, in the rushing streams. (See picture on next page) His music is so melodic that it draws the interest of passersby who come closer to listen and when they are near enough he grabs one (preferably a sweet young maiden), pulls them under water and sucks their blood. Apparently this is because he is a fallen angel and a sufficient amount of good Christian blood will redeem him.

I wrote this song while being driven around parts of that country, sightseeing. I saw many trees, lakes and streams but unfortunately I didn't see or hear any Näcken! But I wrote this song.

If you want to see a tree go to Sweden
They have a lot of trees up there
The spruce and the fir and the pretty silver birch
If you look around you'll see them everywhere
Hej hej hej, hej hej hej, hej hej hej, hej hej

If you want to see a lake go to Sweden
The have a lot of lakes up there
The rivers and the streams and the channels in between
Of water they have plenty to spare
Hej hej hej, hej hej hej, hej hej hej, hej hej

If you want to see a fiddler go to Sweden
For they have a lot of fiddlers there
But if you hear the Näcken play you will never get away
For he'll suck your blood and take you to his lair
Hej hej hej, hej hej hej, hej hej hej, hej hej

If you want to see an elk go to Sweden
They have a lot of elks up there
But by day they're hard to find as in the woods they hide
They're running from the wolves and the bears
Hej hej hej, hej hej hej, hej hej hej, hej hej

So, if you want to see a tree go to Sweden
They have a lot of trees up there
The spruce and the fir and the pretty silver birch
If you look around you'll see them everywhere
Hej hej hej, hej hej hej, hej hej hej, hej hej

'Hej' is Swedish for hello.

Näcken ("The Water Sprite") by
Ernst Josephson, 1884

The Overlander

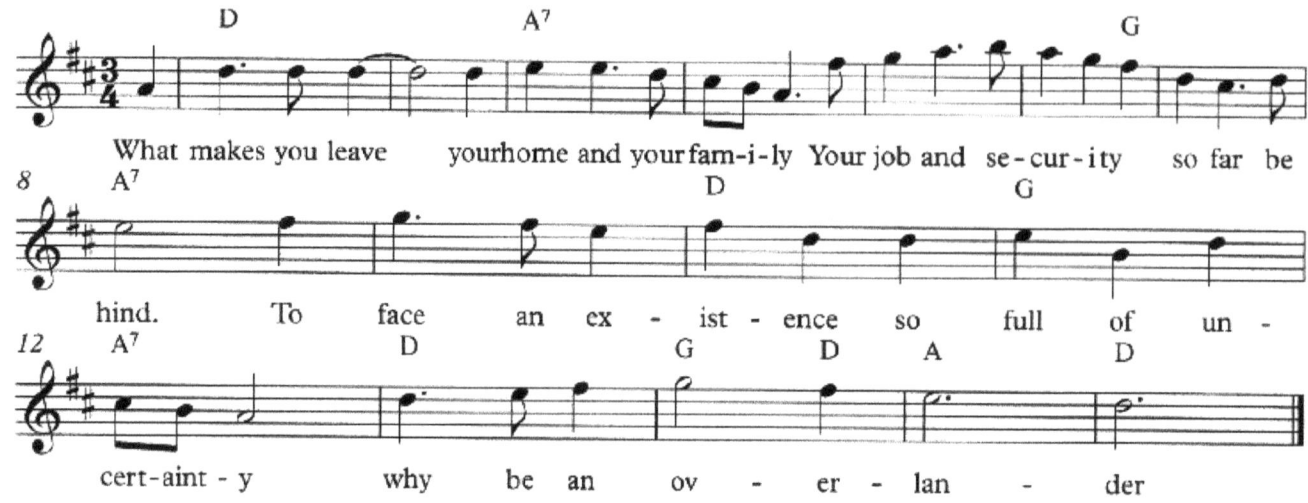

Who or What is an Overlander?

An Overlander is the term given to someone who travels to and through various continents by road rather than by ship or plane, in a vehicle such as a 4 wheel drive, car, truck, on a motorcycle or bicycle, or even by foot. There may be ship or plane travel included if an ocean has to be crossed, ie in my overland trip from Europe to Australia I had to transport myself and motorcycle by plane from Nepal to Thailand as it was politically impossible to ride through Myanmar. I also had to catch ferries to and through the islands of Indonesia and my bike went by sea from East Timor to Darwin, Australia, while I had to fly.

In my earlier overland trip from England to South Africa it necessitated a ferry from UK to Tangiers, North Africa to start the southern journey through the African countries to Cape Town, South Africa.

During both these journeys I was asked many times about my reasons for my travel and other Overlanders were likewise questioned. This song is my answer.

What makes you leave your home and your family
Your job and security, so far behind
To face an existence full of uncertainty?
Why be an Overlander?

To travel the world and see all its wonders
Its places and people and cultures distinct
To lose fear of the unknown, put faith in humanity
That's being an Overlander

But don't you feel lonely, lost and bewildered?
How do you know which way to go?
There are so many dangers in all those strange places
Where you are an Overlander

Yes, at times I feel lonely, lost and bewildered
Often confused not knowing the way
But someone or something will happen to change things
And help out an Overlander

The problems you face are outnumbered by pleasures
Life never is easy at home or abroad
But learning to trust is one of life's treasures
In being an Overlander

Forget all the images painted by media
And open your heart and mind to the world
A smile is the only weapon expedient
In the pack of the Overlander

So I'll keep on my way across the great continents
To see many wonders both big and small
I'll help where I can and share out my knowledge
While being an Overlander

So raise up your glasses and toast all the travellers
We who have chosen to wander afar
And those left at home who keep us connected
Here's to you and the Overlanders

Written in Katmandu, Nepal, while on my overland trip Spain to Australia, 2005-2007.

The Overlanders in Pokhara, Nepal, 2006

This is a group of motorcycle Overlanders that I met during my trip, who were gathered in Nepal at various stages of their journey. Most were from Europe heading East to India or even beyond, some had completed their journey and were about to fly home.

I was the oldest amongst this group, having recently celebrated my 60th birthday in India. Most motorcycle Overlanders I met were aged between 20-45 and were travelling for a variety of reasons; some to take up jobs in another country or to be volunteers, some to ride out a long held dream to visit these exotic countries and one man who had recently lost his wife was doing the journey from the UK to India in her honour as they had talked about doing the trip together before her early death.

Other Overlanders I met in 4 wheel drives included older, retired couples who had the time and money to explore the world.

A website which gives helpful information for Overlanders is; www.HorizonsUnlimited.com

Birthdays I Will Always Remember (60th)

In 2005, the year of my 60th, I was on my overland trip between Spain and Australia and was not sure how long it would take and what country I would be in on the day. However, as November approached I realised that I would be in Northern India.

My nephew, Steve, and his Indian wife, Trupti, lived in Rishikesh and that seemed an ideal place to be but then I discovered that Rishikesh was a 'dry' town and therefore alcohol was not officially allowed and wouldn't be served in any hotel there, so I had to look further afield in the area to find a suitable venue for the celebrations and to accommodate friends and family who would be attending. Riding around the picturesque region, in the southern Himalayas, I found Mussoorie, another hill town, and, in it, an old colonial hotel, the Kasmananda Palace, which proved to be ideal *and* happy to take my booking for dinner (with alcohol) and rooms overnight. So, on the day of the 21st November, I and my invited guests arrived. My sister, Anne (Steve's mum) from England, Frank Reiser my motorcycle friend, from Germany (bringing with him much needed spares for my bike,) Steve and Trupti from Rishikesh, Elke and Chris, a Belgian overlanding couple I had travelled with for a while in Pakistan, riding their Yamaha Teneres, and Ingo, a German overlander I had met in Baluchistan, riding his BMW.

I had bought a long dress from the market for the occasion and wore jewels given to me by some girls in Pakistan so I felt a very glamourous sixty-year-old. The hotel was grand and had been used by the colonial English when escaping the summer heat on the plains. It was also a hunting lodge and had antlers and skins on the walls and a wide winding staircase. We had a wonderful Indian dinner with wine and spirit my sister had brought, duty free, on the plane journey over and we could buy local beer. Chris and Elke had written a song for and about me which they sang amidst much laughter and applause and we all had a great time before retiring to our luxury accommodation. The next morning we had breakfast on the terrace which afforded magnificent views of the Himalayan peaks. Then checking out we returned to our various cheaper digs in other parts; Frank and Anne back to Europe, Steve and Trupti home to Rishikesh while we overlanders continued on our various routes east.

Bent Crash Bar Song (Oops and I've fallen off again!)

In 2005 I swapped my old BMW for a Suzuki DR650 to make the overland trip between Spain and Australia. Although the bike was lighter in weight it was distributed differently and packing it the same as I had the BMW made the bike very unstable. Although lowered, the height and weight was still difficult to balance and I was always falling off.

While staying at a hostel in southern India I was looking at the bruises on my body and wrote this song to explain them! However I did make the journey to Australia – 81,000kms (21 months) without serious injury to myself and the bike……. but wouldn't attempt such a long ride again!!

In Pakistan the truck is slow the road is long and straight
But he decides to make a turn just as I overtake
In the dirt along the roadside I use heavily my brakes
Oops! and I've fallen off again!

Now there's an uphill mountain track with lots of rocks and water
To keep the throttle open now I know I really oughta
But the right turn in the middle well it takes a bit a thought, ahh!
Oops! and I've fallen off again!

In Rajma there's an accident, the traffic's in a queue
I keep along the inside lane as that's the thing to do
But a big truck clips my panniers as he tries to do it too
Oops! and I've fallen off again!

To navigate in Poona town you have to be right cluey
In case of misdirection I may have to make a uey
I have to turn, I'm wrong again, I must admit it's true eeee!
Oops! and I've fallen off again!

The track is very muddy as it rained the night before
And just about my turning point is parked a red rickshaw
I didn't think I'd make it and right now I'm very sure
Oops! And I've fallen off again!

The houseboats on the backwaters are really very grand
And riding alongside I have my camera in my hand
While looking for a photo shot I didn't see the sand!
Oops! And I've fallen off again!

This bike is an enduro and it has endured a lot
Off road it is a superstar and I am just a clot
How many times I've dropped it now I really have forgot
Oops! And I've fallen off again!
Ooops and I've fallen off AGAIN!!!!

A Bump in the Road (2005)

I was in the campsite in Islamabad, Pakistan. Many other Overlanders were there, some motorcyclists, like myself, others in Landrovers or campervans and some cyclists. A real mixture of nationalities. I had been practising my Spanish on a group in a campervan from that country and they, like me, were heading up the Karakoram highway toward the Chinese border. They left early one morning and I left the next day.

It was fine weather and the route led out north cutting across a hilly area, through Murree before meeting up with the busy main north road. In the hills I noticed some fallen rocks on the road and thought it odd that they hadn't been cleared since the last rainy season. I carried on to meet the main highway so joining the traffic then later while passing through a busy town, I was surprised to see many fallen houses. Oh, I thought maybe there is demolition for a new development.

The road gradually wound upwards alongside the Indus River and then suddenly I saw a campervan coming toward me flashing its lights and tooting the horn and I realised it was the Spanish group. We both stopped and I said, 'What are you doing coming back?'

'Linda, there is an earthquake! The road ahead is blocked and we are returning to Islamabad.'

Apparently the hostel they stayed in overnight had collapsed early that morning and several people were seriously injured. They were visibly upset.

'Didn't you feel it?' they said, 'And the shocks are ongoing.'

Of course I was riding a bike with a big single thumping engine and anything I felt I took just to be a bump in the road.

'I'll be OK on the bike,' I said, sure that I would be able to get round any blockages. Bidding them farewell, I continued higher up the mountain road.

Finally I stopped to have a bite to eat and a man stopped his car and came rushing up to me.

'What are you doing here?'

'I'm just riding north,' I said.

'You must find somewhere safe to stay. There has been a huge earthquake. I will lead you to the next town.'

I started to follow his car but then he stopped as a crowd of people came toward him waving. It appeared that they were relatives and one of the party had been killed in the earthquake.

Leaving him with his distraught family, I continued on until I reached the town of Bataram and decided to stop and camp by the road. On the left side was a steep bank and on the right a large hotel built on the edge of a chasm over the Indus valley. I put up my tent and was immediately surrounded by a group of young men who said they were employees of the hotel but had all run out on the road when the earthquake shook the building.

We all decided to walk into town to buy something to eat. On the way we passed the hospital which had mainly collapsed and the patients were outside in the open on their beds.

In the town the shops were open with their wares on the street. Every time a tremor shook everyone ran away from the buildings. We bought some food and walked back where I had my tent. I had a camping stove so we cooked and shared out what we had. The boys advised me to move my tent as there were boulders above it which could shake loose and fall, so I put it up on the other side of the road in the hotel forecourt.

It was beginning to rain and the boys had no shelter so, inadequate though it was, I gave them my bike cover to huddle beneath.

That night there were many more tremors and I could hear tinkling of glass from the shattered hotel windows. Although I didn't feel afraid for myself, as I was flat on the ground, I was worried my bike might fall over. If the whole cliff broke away with the hotel we were gone anyway.

The next day I carried on through the town. When I stopped to take a very few photos on my tiny camera the people came rushing up to ask if I was from the BBC! People were wandering around and shortly out of town the road was blocked with huge boulders which even I could not go around.

I had to go back to Islamabad but decided to take an alternative route. Little did I realise, until I saw the road blocked with trucks and cars trying to negotiate boulders that I was riding into the absolute epicenter of the earthquake, Mazafarad. Hardly a building was standing and the army were trying to organise the chaos.

I spent the night camped on the pavement listening to the sound of feet passing all night as people from their collapsed homes in the surrounding villages walked in to get help.

Finally I made it out of town and down to Islamabad. Aid trucks were on their way up but were being ambushed by desperate people.

When I arrived in the city I went to the Australian embassy to see if I could help in any way but was told they didn't want amateurs, only people skilled in search and rescue. So, I waited two weeks until the roads were re-opened and then left in company with two other motorcyclists to head north again, this time via the Swat valley. The aftershocks kept coming and the destruction all over northern Pakistan was immense; thousands left homeless.

Certainly an experience I shall never forget. Funnily enough I never felt afraid for myself but had the deepest sympathy for the people affected and the tragedy that the rest of the world mostly ignored.

Elephant Walk

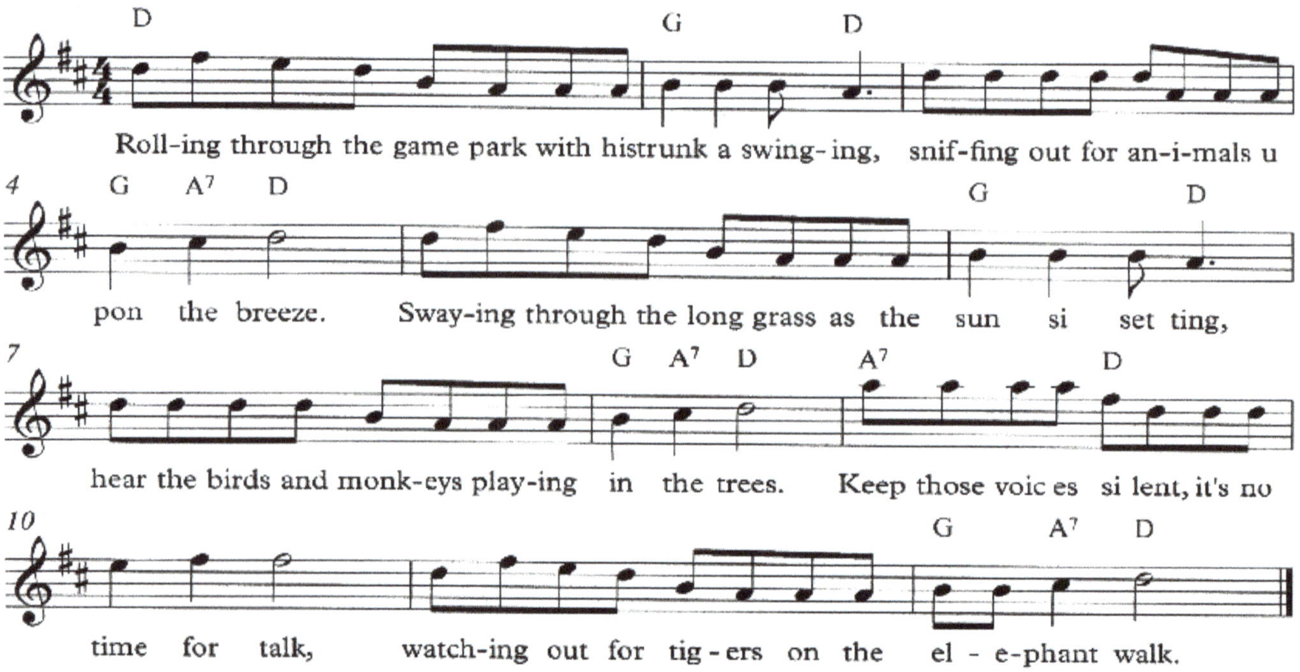
D G D
Roll-ing through the game park with histrunk a swing-ing, snif-fing out for an-i-mals u
4 G A7 D G D
pon the breeze. Sway-ing through the long grass as the sun si set ting,
7 G A7 D A7 D
hear the birds and monk-eys play-ing in the trees. Keep those voic es si lent, it's no
10 G A7 D
time for talk, watch-ing out for tig - ers on the el - e-phant walk.

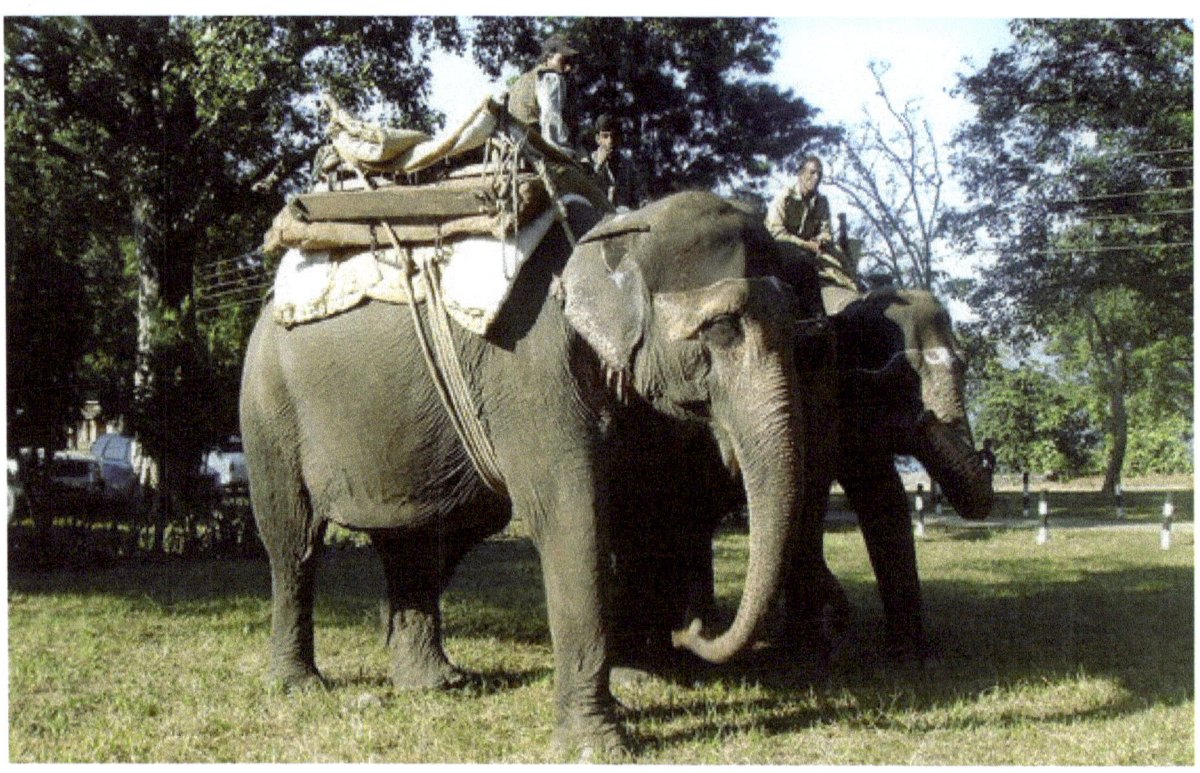

Rolling through the game park, with his trunk a swinging
Sniffing out for animals upon the breeze
Swaying through the long grass, as the sun is setting
Hear the birds and monkeys playing in the trees
Keep those voices silent, it's no time for talk
Watching out for tigers on the elephant walk
Um, um

Wading through the river, see the turtle swimming
Looking out for crocodiles among the rocks
Up upon the far bank, hog and deer are running
Get a wink or two from the sly, old fox
Keep those voices silent, it's no time for talk
Watching out for tigers on the elephant walk
Um, um

Back toward the compound as the day is ending
Hear some growls and trumpeting among the trees
Dismounting from the elephant, our legs unbending
Time for a chapatti and a cup of tea
Hear the people chatter, now it's time for talk
Recounting all our sightings on the elephant walk
Feeling mighty seasick, I'm as white as chalk
And we didn't see a tiger on the elephant walk
No, there were no bloody tigers on the elephant walk!!
Um, um

During my overland trip on my 650 Suzuki (2005-7) I spent a few months in India and a German friend, Frank Reiser, flew over for my 60th birthday. During that time we went to a game park to see tigers. This song is the result.

The KL Blues

My view of KL from the 23rd floor.

I got the KL blues riding in the pouring rain
It's coming down so hard I just can't see a thing
Hear the thunder clap, see the lightning flash
I'm sure I'll drown, if I don't crash
Got the KL blues riding in the pouring rain

I got the KL blues lost in the traffic lanes
I've been going round and round all day
Is it this way or is it that
I just can't read this bloody map
I've got the KL blues lost in the traffic lanes

I've got the KL blues sitting in a high rise flat
With three locks out front, you can be sure of that
Jump in the lift but watch that door
For it won't hang around for you no more
I've got the KL blues sitting in a high rise flat

I've got the KL blues hearing that traffic roar
Night and day it makes your eardrums sore
If you don't have that double glaze
You'll be deaf well before old age
I've got the KL blues hearing that traffic roar

I've got the KL Blues looking for my motorbike
I could have sworn I parked it here last night
I thought that I was here before
But it seems I'm on another floor
I've got the KL Blues looking for my motorbike

I've got the KL blues but soon I'll be on my way
There really is no reason left to stay
The bike is fixed and the visa's through
And Choo's flat is painted too
So I'll pack my bags and bid you all 'Good day'

In 2006, on my overland trip I stayed in Kuala Lumpar, Malaysia, waiting for my visa for Indonesia. As the song suggests, it was quite an experience!

Police Problem In Indonesia (2006)

I had just spent a couple of weeks in Kuala Lumpar waiting for my Indonesian visa. When it was ready I went to the embassy to collect it and while there, I made enquiries about the situation there regarding bringing foreign bikes into the country. I had seen on the Horizons Unlimited travelers website that recently an Australian overlander had taken his bike over on the ferry to Sumatra and, when he arrived, though he had the travel carnet, he was told that he couldn't bring the bike in and, after much argument (during which I believe he lost his temper) he had to return to Malaysia on the next ferry.

The official at the embassy said that, as I had the papers, all should be well but admitted that they didn't really know how things were 'on the ground' over there. All I could do was hope for the best. Great!

So, I took the ferry from Melaka to Dumai, the bike squeezed in between the passenger seats. When the boat docked the bike was unloaded and I was pretty conspicuous as I wheeled it to the custom's area. I was told to wait while they investigated my paperwork and left alone I brought out my fiddle (bought in Thailand) and played for a while. I had already decided that I would keep away from the police, if possible, in regard to the other traveller's problem. However, when the official came back with my custom's papers he informed me that the police were on their way to talk to me. When they arrived I was told to follow them to the police station.

En route a man on a motorcycle came riding up along-side shouting, 'Please Missus, I am an English teacher, please come to my school and give a lesson.'

'I can't,' I said. 'I am being escorted to the police station.'

'Then I'll come with you,' he replied and so we all arrived at the police station and this man acted as an interpreter for me as the police officer had very little English. I was told that they were confiscating my bike as it wasn't allowed into Indonesia.

It was getting late so the teacher kindly invited me to stay at his house and I could go back in the morning to begin negotiations. He suggested I tried to bribe them, as that was the usual way.

The next morning I returned to the police station. The chief was more interested in playing video games of the combat variety on his computer than talking to me. He said, 'You have to go back to Malaysia.'

I said, 'It will cost me money to return on the boat. Surely it is better if I pay the equivalent of that fare to you and you let me go.'

No, that plan didn't work. He said only officials in Jakarta could allow me in. 'But Jakata is on the next island of Java and we are here.' Surely he could contact their office.

Finally, after hours of talking, me desperately keeping a smile on my face, and being polite while I was seething inside, he told me that I could go and see another higher official in the town of Pakenbura which was 200kms away.

'You can catch a bus there,' he said.

There was one leaving on Monday morning. So, after spending the weekend giving English lessons for my new friend I caught the bus and arrived that evening and commenced looking for somewhere to stay the night. I was aided by a young man who saw me alight and decided to be my helper. He told me that he knew who I was as there had already been an article about me in the local paper!

After staying in a small hotel my 'helper' came back to show me the way to the police station where I found the appropriate official. Thank goodness this man could speak perfect English. He had been trained in Holland and understood my problem. Taking my paperwork he photocopied everything and contacted Jakarta and, in a short while, came back with an official letter to show to the police in Dumai and which I could keep as it gave full permission for me to ride my bike anywhere in Indonesia.

When I arrived back in Dumai the next day, it was all smiles and handshakes and photos all round. After saying a grateful farewell to the teacher and his family I took off and hadn't gone but half a kilometer when I was stopped by another policeman to whom I cheerfully showed my permission and was finally allowed on my way. I was never stopped again by police in the whole of the rest of the Indonesian islands.

Lesson learnt: Keep a smile on your face and never give up.

On The Shore Labuan Poh (2006)

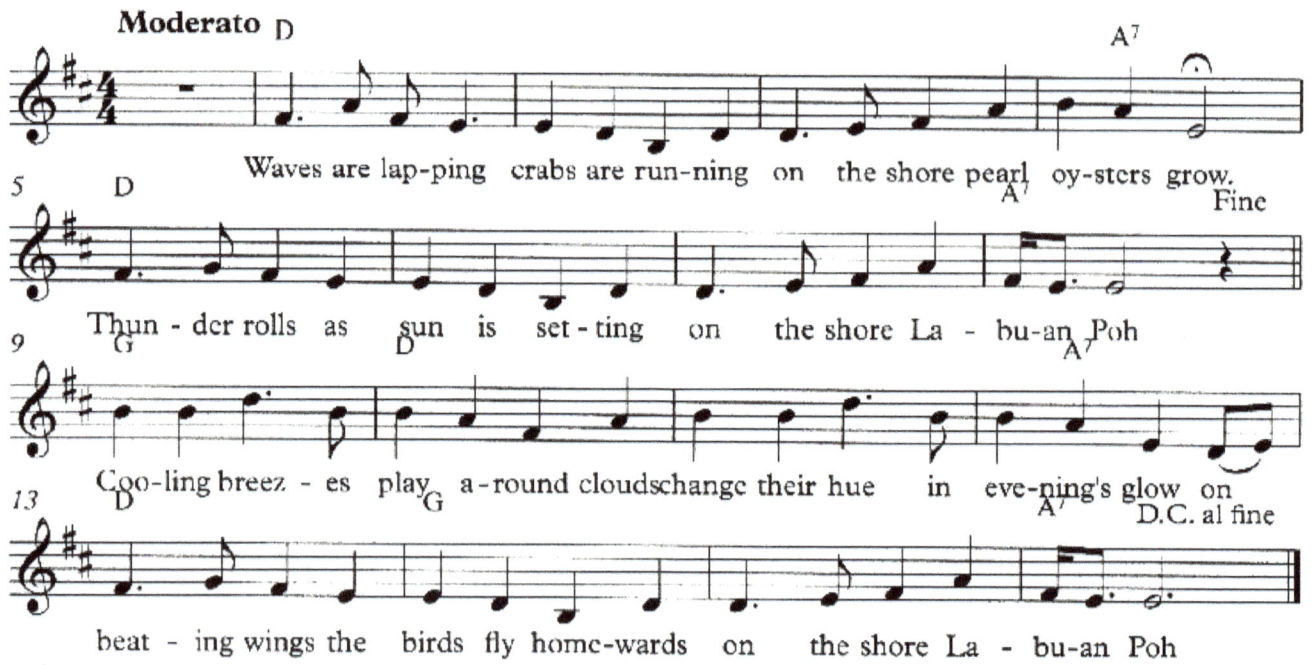

Waves are lapping, crabs are running
In the bay pearl oysters grow
Thunder rolls as sun is setting
On the shore Labuan Poh

Fishing boats lay at their mooring
Bobbing with the ebb and flow
Palm trees wave along the shoreline
On the shore Labuan Poh

Cooling breezes play around me
Clouds change their hue in evenings glow
On beating wings the birds fly homeward
On the beach Labuan Poh

Waves are lapping, crabs are running
In the bay pearl oysters grow
And I feel at peace just for a moment
On the shore Labuan Poh
Yes, I feel at peace on this Lombok island
On the shore Labuan Poh.

During my overland trip, 2005-7 I rode through the Indonesian islands and made a stop in Lombok at a small village, Labuan Poh where I went for a walk on the beach one evening and wrote this song.

On my return visit 10 years later, looking for the hostel where I had stayed, to my amazement, the owner rushed into the street shouting 'Mrs Linda!'. He had recognised me, even though it was years later and I was on a scooter instead of a motorbike.

Ode To Indonesia
(September – December 2006)

Smoke from craters and from forest
Clouds my view and dims my eyes
When it clears I find a country
Full of beauty and surprise

Volcanic mountains clothed in jungle
Sandy beach and azure sea
Ancient temples, mosques a-calling
As this country calls to me

Tough Sumatra, Batak domain
Cow horn houses, lazy lake
Oran Utang swing through jungles
Diminishing for progress´ sake

Java with its teeming millions
Spread twixt town and country fair
Jakarta, Jogja and cool Malang
With students laughter in the air

Flowering flame trees, bougainvillea
Frangipani scent the dead
Padi and palm in verdant valleys
Volcanic clouds drift overhead

Every village is a picture
In every field a photo lies
Lily ponds and waterfalls
Whilst at night the starry skies

Bali with its Hindu temples
Ex-pat enclaves, tourist price
Stunning sunsets, misty mountains
Scarecrows flapping midst the rice

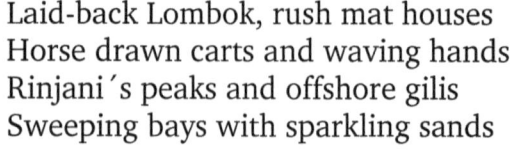

Laid-back Lombok, rush mat houses
Horse drawn carts and waving hands
Rinjani´s peaks and offshore gilis
Sweeping bays with sparkling sands

Sumbawas´road runs like a ribbon
West to East it gently winds
Stilted houses, fish farms, mountains
Grace the view on either side

Each twist and turn shows Flores beauty
Fruit and flowers line the way
Pearl farms increase the islands wealth
And tourists dive in crystal bays

Volcanic lakes that change their colours
Bright woven cloth with patterns rare
Dark skinned folk with smiling faces
In fields and forests everywhere

Eucalyptus now appears
As jungle thins on eastern slopes
The border crossed, the road shows views
Of sparkling sea along the coast

Dilli bows now to the dollar
East Timor in uneasy peace
Gun toting guards from many nations
Homes in tents and UN police

Indonesia now behind me
Its many faces turned away
As New Year points a different path
I hope that I´ll return some day.

Dili, 2006

Epitaph for Larry, The Sheepskin Seat Cover (2007)

From the freezing cold north of Pakistan

To the tropical heat of Timor

You have been my constant companion

Over rough roads and smooth through India,

Nepal, Laos, Malaysia and Indonesia

You have protected my nether regions from heat and cold

And tried valiantly to save me from callouses

You have suffered the pollution of Indian traffic

That turned your snowy locks into black tangles

Been washed and dried many times

And endured the indignity of shrinking

Larry, I sincerely appreciate all your efforts

To save me from the excruciating discomfort of Suzy's seat.

I thank you from the bottom of my bottom

Be assured that you will be sorely missed

Rest in Peace

The DR 650 Suzuki that I rode from Europe to Australia had the most uncomfortable seat. Indeed it had been cut down to help lower the height of the bike. When in Northern Pakistan I rode through a small village and saw they had some sheep skins out to dry on the road. I stopped and bought one. When I returned to the campsite in Islamabad, I cut it down and tried to cure it with my urine. Then I washed it and attached it to my seat. It was an improvement!

When I reached Timor and was bringing the bike to Australia I knew I couldn't bring it in so I had a service for Larry and said these few words while I cremated him in the garden. We had a couple of sparkler fireworks and I played a tune on the whistle.

Baa Baa Bach (Wales, 2009)

Baa baa Bach, the rain is falling down
The clouds are lying low upon the Beacons
The fern is changing colour, the broom has lost its bloom
Winds chase away the summer that is fleeting

Baa baa Bach, put on your winter coat
Not long before the snow lies in the valleys
The ponies are a huddling, the pheasants slow their flight
The children jump the puddles in their wellies

Baa baa bach, pile the wood stocks high
Bring out the harp and music for the chorus
Card the wool and spin it, close the curtains tight
Its time to join the family round the fire

In 2009 before coming back to Australia I spent some time in South Wales with a friend. It was autumn and so this song was born describing that feeling.

Patience

There are times we must be patient
Let the world turn as it may
Just lay back and let it happen
Leave it for another day

We may try and push for progress
Hit our head against the wall
We must learn to take life easy
Does it matter after all?

For there's always tomorrow
Be it laughter or sorrow
The sun will rise and set
If we win some or lose some
Under bright skies or rainstorm
We can only do our best

So relax, go with the day's flow
For it's clear for all to see
That impatience only stresses
Just smile and let it be.

The Arctic Ale

In 2010 I decided to sell up and leave Spain, after sixteen years of mixed experiences there, and began preparing for a journey from North to South America. To this end I bought a motorcycle on eBay, a 250 Kawasaki Super Sherpa. The seller was Christopher Bowen in Pennsylvania and I flew over to pick up the bike.

I discovered that Chris was a craft brewer and he was selling the bike to aid the funding a very interesting project. He wanted to brew a special beer in the Arctic Circle. The story behind this beer is really extraordinary.

It is a well-known fact that Lord Franklin led an expedition in 1845 to find the North West Passage and that he and his two ships with 129 men were lost. The ship had become icebound on the Victoria Straight near King Edward Island in the Canadian Arctic. Franklin and his men were not seen again despite an initial search for them.

In 1848 Lady Jane Franklin persuaded Queen Victoria to send out another expedition to find out what had happened to her husband and his men. To this end four ships under Commander Belcher were ordered to go.

In those days it was believed that to help combat scurvy sailors should drink a strong, hoppy ale as a supplement. To find a beer suitable, a competition was initiated in the centre of brewing- Burton-on-Trent, Staffordshire. At that time there were approximately fifty breweries in the town and its beer was exported worldwide. The winner of the competition was Allsops and they produced a beer which was 11 percent alcohol and capable of withstanding extreme low temperatures. It was named Arctic Ale.

However, due to extreme winter conditions Belcher's expedition failed and he had to turn back leaving some of his ships trapped in the ice; the men were brought back on the other ships but the beer remained.

In 1875 another batch of Arctic Ale was brewed for the expedition to the Arctic led by Sir George Nares.

About a hundred years later some ships were recovered when ice had melted and bottles of beer, believed to be from the Belcher expedition were recovered. Chris Bowen managed to procure a bottle and analyze it. He was determined to replicate the brew but do it under very different circumstances. His idea was to import some hops from England and take them and other ingredients up into the Arctic circle in North America. There with local water he would brew his own Arctic Ale.

Being a motorcycle enthusiast he and two friends were going to ride their BMWs and the other team members were driving his truck with the ingredients and brewing equipment. They also included two Russian women filmmakers to record the trip.

Chris succeeded with this project, made the film and came over to England to do talks on it. One place that he had to visit was Allsops in Burton on Trent and there they gave him a tour of the cellars and presented him with a bottle of the original Arctic Ale.

The following song I wrote for Chris and it was included in his film.

Brew The Arctic Ale (Linda Bick & Traditional)

It was homeward bound one night on the deep
Swinging in my hammock I fell asleep
I dreamed a dream which I thought was true
Concerning Franklin and his gallant crew

And so went the song and the stories of old
In Baffin Bay last seen we were told
For the North West Passage he searched in vain
His ships and his men were ne'er seen again

But his wife was determined, she would not give in
She wanted to know just where they had been
She called on Queen Vic and the Admiralty
To search one more time in that cold Northern sea

Under Belcher five ships were commissioned to go
Sailing out in the ice, wind and snow
And to keep the men happy, hearty and hale
A search went out for a good British Ale

Find an Arctic Ale, me boys
Find an Arctic Ale

In Burton the breweries competed to see
Who could come up with the best recipe
Then Allsopps produced one they said could not fail
They brewed it and called it Arctic Ale

Brew the Arctic Ale, me boys
Brew the Arctic Ale

So victualled the ships set out on their quest
To find trace of Franklin they must do their best
But the winter was bitter, filled Belcher with fear
Four ships were abandoned along with the beer

They lost the Arctic Ale, me boys
They lost the Arctic Ale

Many years passed 'til the ice lost it's grip
And a bottle was found in the hold of one ship
Its discovery put fire in the heart of one man
To study its contents and try once again

To brew the Arctic Ale, me boys
To brew the Arctic Ale

Here's luck to bold Chris to his Arctic Team
As he rides North to fulfill his dream
With BMs and brew kit he surely can't fail

To brew the Arctic Ale, me boys
To brew the Arctic Ale

Yes, with BMs and brew kit
Our Chris did not fail
He brewed the Arctic Ale, me boys
He brewed the Arctic Ale

Leaving On A Sherpa (Linda Bick & John Denver)

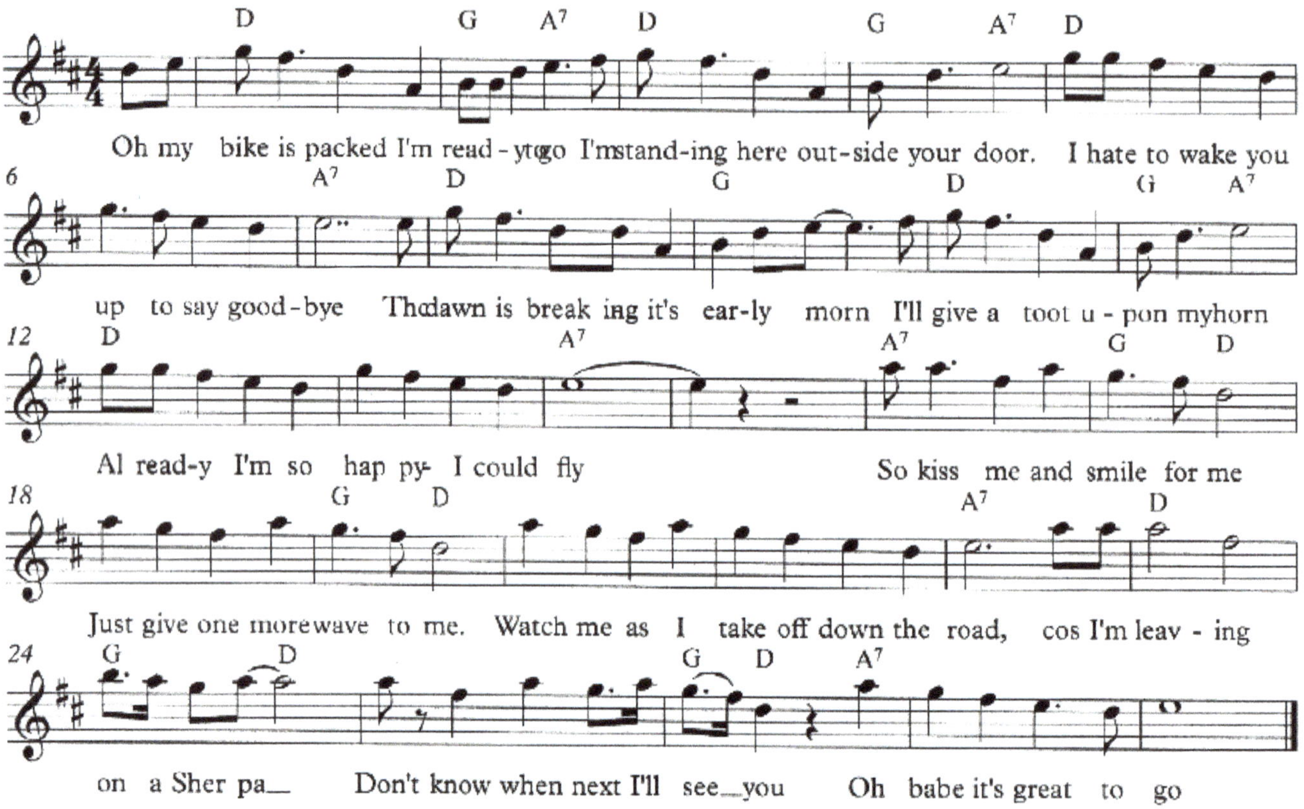

D G A7 D G A7 D
Oh my bike is packed I'm read - y to go I'm stand-ing here out-side your door. I hate to wake you
6 A7 D G D G A7
up to say good-bye The dawn is break ing it's ear-ly morn I'll give a toot u - pon my horn
12 D A7 A7 G D
Al read-y I'm so hap py I could fly So kiss me and smile for me
18 G D A7 D
Just give one more wave to me. Watch me as I take off down the road, cos I'm leav - ing
24 G D G D A7
on a Sher pa Don't know when next I'll see you Oh babe it's great to go

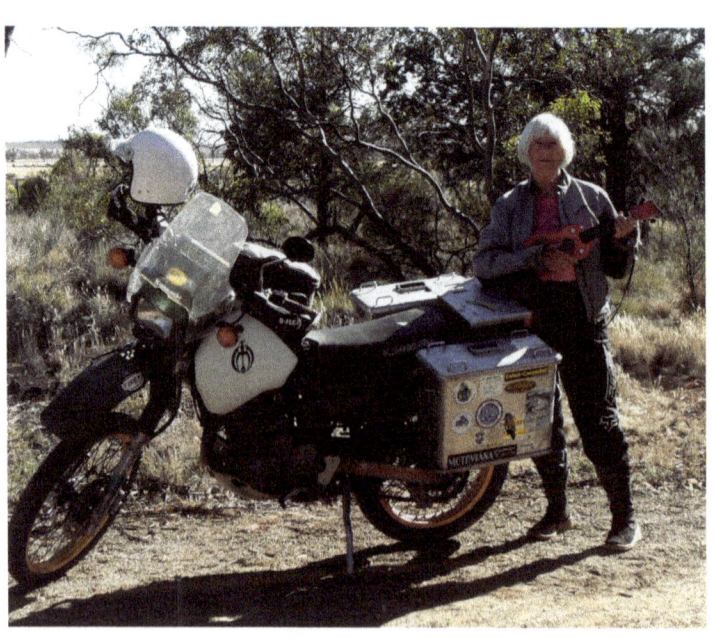

Oh my bike is packed, I'm ready to go
I'm standing here outside your door
I hate to wake you up to say goodbye
The dawn is breaking it's early morn
I'll give a toot upon my horn
Already I'm so happy I could fly

Chorus
So kiss me and smile for me
Just give one more wave to me
Watch me as I take off down the road
Cos I'm leaving on a Sherpa
Don't know when next I'll see ya
Oh, babe, it's great to go

There's so many times I've played around
In folkie bands around the towns
I tell you now, it's the greatest thing
Every country road and highway too
Every continent that I've been through
I play my old tin whistle and I sing

Chorus

Now the time has come to leave you
One more time now let me kiss you
Wave goodbye 'cos now I'm on my way
I dream about the days to come
When I am out there on my own
For one more time I'll smile at you and say

Chorus

Parody of *Leaving on a Jet Plane* that I wrote when I owned a Kawasaki Sherpa. About 2012.

Beginning Again (2012)

It's not easy, beginning again
The mind tends to relive the past
Memory is strong and relentless
Harping back …
If only…I should have…
Why did this happen to me?
Loss of love, belongings, home or family
All leave a vacuum
To fill it one needs strength
And help --- but kind and gentle
The pain is overwhelming and
Self-hatred and despair can lead to destruction
The final solution

It's not easy to find a way forward
Others suggest…
'You should…' 'Why don't you….?'
Often they become impatient
The answer to them is obvious
But still the mind twists and turns
What can I do? I can't go on
How can I put the past behind? The present seems hopeless
Nightmares persist, energy fades
To climb out of the deep dark hole into the light
Is a long, slow haul
There is no simple solution
No magic wand
Ultimately it is our own mind that must change
By whatever means

No, it is not easy beginning again
Take heart though
It CAN happen

Back Into The Light

Down, down, down I go
Nothing fits, delusions grow
What is it that makes the turn
A ray of light, a kindly word?
Then up I come, like a flower unfurled
And I bloom again

Two Chairs

Two chairs, why only two?
There used to be four, or even more.
Where are the rest? Wait I'll make a guess;
Under the vine on the verandah wide.
We had a party. It was outside.
The chairs indoors they had to go
Out. 'Out!' we cried. 'The wine must flow!
And we need a seat under the shade
Where the table is already laid.'
So now in the kitchen only two remain.
They're standing firm in their usual domain

* * *

The Bed

They were married just before the outbreak of WW2. In their heady honeymoon days their newly bought iron framed, deep metal sprung bed was well used and took pride of place not only in their meagre flat but in their giggling daytime recollections of nighttime raptures.

But he was called up. For long stretches of lonely nights she lay solo and frustrated, holding him close in her dreams and waking to find herself tangled in the bed clothes, on her own.

After the war, from which he fortunately returned, the bed was moved with them to a modest, two up, two down semi-detached house in the suburbs. Sunday mornings would find them snuggled with the kids in the bed, warding off the pillow fights.

The next move took them overseas- the bed was big and cumbersome but they felt it part of their lives and could not leave it behind. As years went by the springs sagged and even with a new mattress it became hopelessly dipped in the middle.

Then the husband died and his widow soldiered on. In the small apartment the bed was too big and totally unnecessary for her solo life but she felt it still part of her memories of him.

Finally enough was enough, she could no longer stay abroad and returned to England. The bed was unceremoniously turned out onto the street for the rubbish men to collect. Scrap iron- but oh, how well it had served!

Port Lincoln My Home (1986/2011)

Gulf waters flowing out to the sea
Fishermen casting their lines hopefully
A circling seagull dives for his prey
Boats bobbing gently on a warm summer's day
In crystal clear waters the tuna fish swim
The fishing fleet anxious to harvest them in
A pelican hungrily waits for his share
His appetite keened by the clear Lincoln air

Chorus:
Port Lincoln my home, surrounded by sea
Your clouds and your rainbows blend enchantingly
Port Lincoln my home, where I want to be
Your kinship and kindness a haven for me

Sand covered islands in sea azure blue
Green sweeping coastline panoramic in view
And solitude found at the top of a hill
Where Flinder's first vision remains with us still
On shell studded beaches you may wander along
With only the sound of the bush-birds sweet song
You may wander down many a dusty bush track
Port Lincoln's quiet beauty will soon call you back

Chorus x 2

Originally written as a poem when visiting Port Lincoln on an Arts Council tour in the 1980s. When I came to live here I added the chorus and now it is a favourite of the town.

Winner of FAME Award 2012

Table Tennis (2012)

Now there's a game we love to play, it's table tennis
Where there's a will there is a way, for table tennis
We'll leave the housework far behind, for action of a different kind
It's good for body and for mind, it's table tennis

Who cares if the floors aren't clean, we're at table tennis
We need to be there for our team, at table tennis
The washing can wait, the grass can grow, let someone else go out and mow
For there's a place that we must go, it's table tennis

We're there on Wednesday afternoon, at table tennis
Listening to that ping-pong tune, at table tennis
There's laughter loud, a shriek or two, a raffle prize, trip to the loo
Can you think of anything better to do than table tennis?
No there's nothing better for us to do than play table tennis!

Written for Ladies Wednesday Afternoon Table Tennis
in Port Lincoln.

Community House (2012)

It's in a little back street, so you'd hardly know it's there
But signs on the wall in mosaic lend a certain flair
The door is always open, the kettle always on
And a smile of welcome to make you feel at home
There's courses, talks a- plenty and laughter in the air
Or an open invitation to just pull up a chair
'To foster a sense of belonging' is what it's all about
'Our place' around the corner
Port Lincoln's Community House.

The Men's Shed

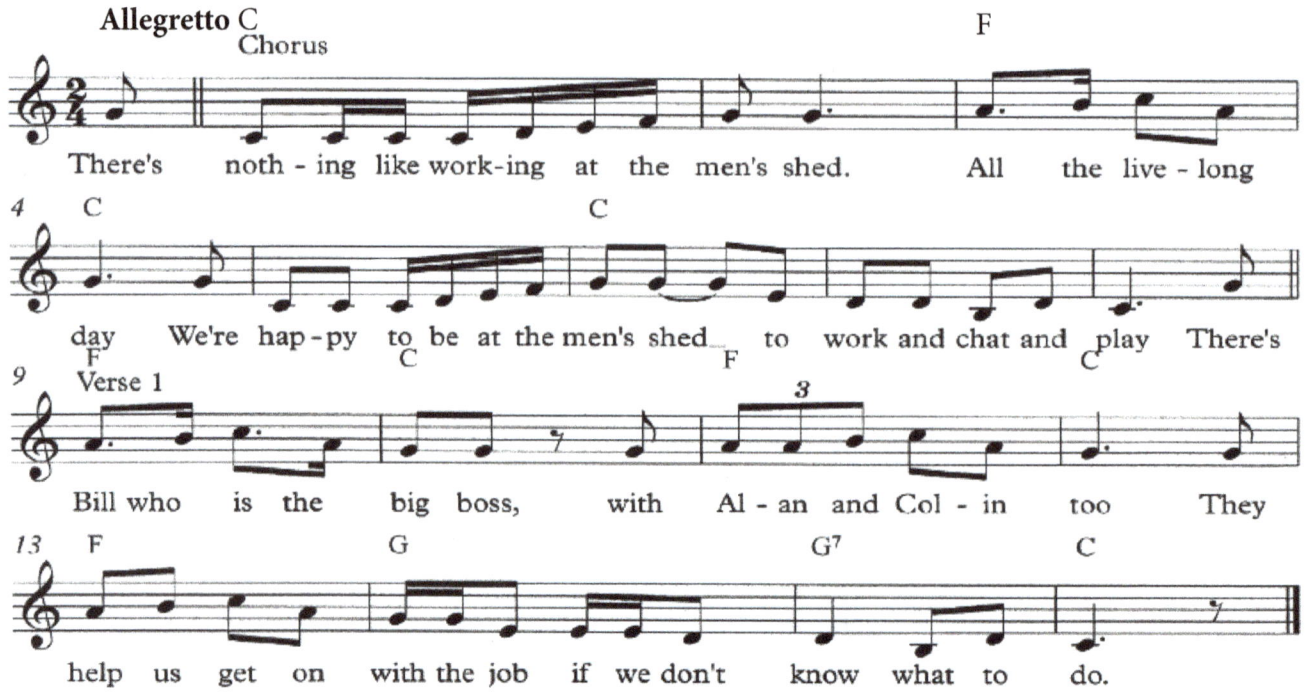

An Overlander was visiting and came to give a talk at the Men's Shed, circa 2018.

Chorus:
There's nothing like working at the men's shed
All the live long day
We're happy to be at the men's shed
To work and chat and play

There's Bill who is the big boss
With Alan and Colin too
They help us get on with the job
If we don't know what to do
Murray holds the welding torch
And Vaughn the sanding disc
Jurgen knows the ropes alright
And can teach us how to twist

Chorus

If you want a leadlight window
Or a pretty picture too
Ernie is the one to ask
He's an artist through and through
When its tea time at the men's shed
We stop for drinks and jokes
Maybe a blessing from the priest
And games for the younger blokes

Chorus

There's drills and saws and fancy tools
You must put them back in place
Or George will chase you with his broom
And you'll be in disgrace

Chorus x 2

I am lucky to be included as a member of Port Lincoln's Men's Shed so I can use all their equipment and share a cup of tea with the 'boys'!

Addiction (2012)

With Thursdays 'Times' the fun begins, I start to make a plan
With eager eyes and hopeful heart the classifieds I scan
Out comes the magnifying glass and map the route must bear in mind
The time each sale will begin, and what I will likely find

Come Saturday morning I hit the road, no breakfast before I start
It's the early bird that catches the worm so I'm up with the lark
Some let you in before the time, some make you wait a while
Some greet you with a confident grin, some with a nervous smile
Trash or treasure, jewels or junk it's I who must decide
Is it a matter of need or want or am I just out for the ride

There really is a need, of course for folks to buy things new
For how else would we re-cyclers do just what we do
It's great that people change their minds, body size or taste
So we can make the most of what would otherwise go to waste

Though I now have furnished my whole house
Each Saturday I'm up without fail
For I've now become an addict of
The weekly Garage Sale

Self-explanatory I think.

May Peace and Love Be With You

Zakaria Saad is a pharmacist who came to live and work in Australia. On an online game site he met Edyta Gradowska, who lived in Poland. They recognised in each other a compatible intelligence and so, during some holidays Zakaria flew to Poland to meet Edyta face to face. They fell in love and Edyta came to live with him in Australia. To comply with Australian immigration law they married within the mandatory six months. And the civil ceremony was held in Port Lincoln. A few months later they had a Coptic Christian service in Melbourne to satisfy Zakaria's parents in Egypt.

At the civil ceremony on Monday 29 April 2013, I sang these words for them.

You have come from distant countries
Left your friends and folk behind
Settled here in South Australia
A new life for to find
May peace and love be with you all the way

You're learning a different language
In place and culture new
Finding friends among the people
Who want to know you too
May peace and love be with you all the way

From the busy streets of Cairo
Or Bialystok's coloured walls
You are here in love united
Let your dreams encompass all
May peace and love be with you all the way

Zakaria and Edyta
Welcome to our land
Let Australia be your shelter
And Port Lincoln be your home
May peace and love be with you all the way

Song of the Endeavour (9 Feb 2012 night watch on board)

Allegretto

Oh shi-ver me tim-ber and hoist up me sails I'm leav-ing the coal yards be-hind. I'm bound for the south sea far far a-way and who knows what trea-sure I'll find me boys. Who knows what trea-sure I'll find. We'll fol-low the stars and bright plan-et too, we'll track their path from be-low and new land we'll find to claim for our King and chart them where-e-ver we go me boys and chart them where-e-ver we go

212

Chorus
Shiver me timbers and hoist up me sails
I'm leaving the coal-yards behind
I'm bound for the South Seas, far, far away
And who knows what treasures we'll find, me boys
who knows what treasure we'll find

We'll follow the stars and bright planets too
We'll track their path from below
And new lands we'll find to claim for our King
And chart them wherever we go, me boys
and chart them wherever we go

The cat is seldom out of the bag
Captain Cook is strong but he's fair
And Banks with his passion for science and plants
Has plenty of money to spare, me boys
has plenty of money to spare

Chorus

We've beef stew and sauerkraut and plenty of ale
What more could a sailor boy need?
We'll swing in our hammocks and stitch well the sails
For a fair wind will give us Godspeed, me boys
a fair wind will give us Godspeed

So, shiver me timbers and hoist up me sails
I'm leaving the coal yards behind
I'm bound for the South Seas, far, far away
And who knows what reassures we'll find, me boys
who knows what treasures we'll find

A replica of Captain Cook's ship, the Endeavour, came to Port Lincoln in 2012 and I took a course to be a guide, mainly so my folk group could sing on it. I had to stay on board one night and, having learnt its history, wrote this song.

The Trolley in the Trees (July 2012)

A transportable house is situated on a block a few miles out of the country town. It has some outbuildings nearby: stables and sheds. Ripples move on a small swimming pool and a kitchen garden growing a variety of herbs is near the dwelling. A Hills Hoist turns creaking, empty in the breeze. Nearby amongst the gum trees a washing trolley is found, clothes in it jumbled and half dried...

His big truck was parked outside the pub, large as life, dwarfing the cars that were parked either side.

As I entered I saw him immediately at his usual place at the bar but instead of hearing his boisterous laugh, he sat there is silence, head bowed over, face in hands. On the bar in front of him was an empty schooner, sides still sliding froth, signs of a swift disposal.

'Hey Bluey, what's up?' I said, slapping him jovially on the back.

He turned slowly, his blue, normally twinkling eyes now red-rimmed and dull, his ginger hair dishevelled and a good two-days' growth of stubble on his chin.

'She's bloody gone,' he grunted.

'Who's gone? Where?'

'Dolly, the missus, she's gone.'

'What, off to Sydney to visit her Mum again?'

'No, you dickhead, gone gone, left me,' and he sniffed, dangerously close to tears.

Embarrassed, I ventured, 'Praps for just a short while?'

'Na, good and proper this time.'

He jerked his head up. 'Hey, Billy, a couple of schooners here mate,' he shouted.

I remained silent while the barman served us then waited.

Bluey took a large gulp of his beer. I watched as he reached into the chest pocket of his checked shirt for his fags, lit one and breathed out, his beer gut straining against the buttons and over his Harley Davidson belt-buckle holding up his faded blue jeans.

Once more in control he continued. 'Got home this arvo, bloody late again - hell of a trip. When I left Brisbane it was pissing down, could hardly see the road, even with the wipers going full whack. Got outa that lot, then had two blowouts on the Hay Plain. Two!! Still bloody raining and I got soaked out there fixing 'em. That set me back. I was calling Dolly on the mobile to say I'd be late but no flaming signal and when I got to Tailem Bend and tried again there was just a message. So, carried on as fast as I could, off-loaded in Adelaide and then on here. Got to the house. Quiet as a mouse. None of that diddly-dee stuff she usually has playing - bloody stuff! Like a bit of Slim meself, John Williamson or even Ted, bloody Egan but that Celtic stuff gets on me tits.

'Anyhows, I go inside and nothing. Quiet as the grave, could hear a pin drop or a rat shit, or whatever,'

"Dolly!" I shouts. "Where is ya?"

'Then I noticed half the gear in the lounge is missing. I went into the bedroom, wardrobes empty, suitcases gone. Went into the kitchen and looked around and there was the note.

'Shoulda seen it coming, I spose,' he sighed. 'She's been whinging for months now. I'm always away or down the pub with me mates. Nowhere for her to go, nothing to do. Well she was the bloody one who wanted a 'home among the gum trees'.' He used his fingers to make inverted commas, dropping his ash on the floor.'she didn't like living in Mile End, said it wasn't posh enough.

"Get a block of land," she said, "in a nice little country town."

'Well we did, didn't we. Slaved me guts out to buy the acres. Got the transportable, then she wants a horse, a stable, a swimming pool, blah, blah. I'm supposed to go trucking half way round Oz and then come back and spend me days off building. Well, sod that! Got to have a bit of relaxation.'

He took another huge gulp, draining the glass, and held it up to indicate another round. I swiftly got out my wallet to pay.

'Yeh,' I said, 'but she went off for a visit to her Mum in Sydney and came back saying she hated big cities'.

'Well, there's no bloody pleasing 'em,' he snorted, 'but it's even worse!'

He turned and glared at me, eyes flashing.

'Yes, it gets worse,' he said. 'I read the note. She said she'd found someone else, someone who 'really appreciated' her and she's gone off with him. Just packed her bags, just like that and she didn't even hang the bloody washing out!'

A scientist set out to lie
His discovery was pie in the sky
He said that all ills
Would be cured by his pills
But in fact you would probably die

A guard dog once sat down on strike
He simply refused to bite
When a burgler came in
He just watched with a grin
As the thief ran off into the night

The Desert Breathes (May 2012)

Tarmac scars the blood red earth where barefoot limbs once trod
Desert oaks sway in the breeze dancing for a different God
The eagle soars on high, a hopping mouse to spy
And the desert breathes

Cloud castles build 'gainst azure blue, then gently float away
Shade shortens as the sun climbs high to warm another day
The lizard basks at ease and through the shady trees
The desert breathes

Though 'oer the land the tourists swarm in their buses cars and vans
Their presence cannot overcome this ancient, sacred land
Their lives are but a single day where Tjkjurrpa holds sway
And the desert breathes

With lazy gait the camels stroll through buffel grass and dunes
The kangaroo and emu run....but action slows at noon
But in winter's chill they're running still
And the desert breathes

Katachuka with its many heads, Uluru's crouching form
Colours changing red and gold at sunset and at dawn
Wet season's green, seldom seen
And the desert breathes

Written whilst on a trip out to the Red Centre in Australia.

Lament for the Nauo Nation

Tell me what can we do when they've taken the land
Bush tucker and water denied
We can't live on handouts of sugar and flour
They've taken our living and pride, they've taken our living and pride

The whalers and sealers first came to our shores
Built huts and lived in the bay
They looked to the sea for their livelihood
Did little to upset out ways
But then came the settlers in search of a life
That meant taking the land for their own
They cleared it and brought in their woolly white sheep
No more could we be left alone, no more could we be left alone

Now where is our water, our bush kangaroo
Our berries and cherries and beans
With the loss of our lakes and swamp fishing grounds
We must find food by some other means, we must find food by some other means

A young white boy has fallen, our spears found their mark
At last we have had to reply
We raided his hut when we had not enough
But with his death peace also will die
Though our spears attack many their guns have more might
Their troopers are stronger it seems
We've been poisoned and whipped, hunted and shot
Our former life only in dreams, our former life only in dreams

Tell me what can we do when they've taken the land
Bush tucker and water denied
We can't live on handouts of sugar and flour
They've taken our living and pride, they've taken our living and pride

Written about an incident that occurred on the lower Eyre Peninsula in the early days of settlement when a young white boy was attacked when guarding a food store.

A Walk in Wilpena Pound (2013)

Within the tent walls I lie cocooned
Darkness persists but the sounds of dawn approaching
Gradually awake me
First a raucous crow calls
Then the multi-toned warbling of the magpies
Laterly a cackling kookaburra
As light creeps gently into the morning come the human sounds
Tents unzipping
Childish laughter leading to the bathrooms
I emerge to see the cliff tops glowing red in the sun's first rays
Euros and wallabies hop hopefully near the campers
Reviving their fires for a warming cuppa
After dressing and a few morsels of muesli
I leave the campsite to track the trailhead
Then off, led by the blue markers
Over dry creek beds with tangled roots and twigs
Scaling fallen tree trunks that form graceful arches across the path
Their limbs a home for a myriad of insect life
Further on I pass blackened fir trees denoting a past fire but
New growth abounds
The slight incline through the low scrub now steepens
And soon boulders appear and the path becomes vertical
Muscles strain to pull limbs upward
Breath shortens, lungs expanding
A break, for heaven's sake!
As I gasp, perched on a rock ledge
Taking in the magnificence of the rearward view
Two red-shirted, be-sticked Germans pass
Living up to my expectations
Throughout the world I have witnessed
Tutonic bush-walking pace
As the tortoise beat the hare by its slow persistence
So my erratic progress is again overtaken
Their back-packed rear ends are soon lost behind the
Torturous rocks ahead and the sound of clicking sticks diminishes
At last the shoulder is reached
Shall I continue to the peak?
It is another 1.8 kms – my aching limbs decline

It is said that the Adnyamathanha people prefer that
Visitors do not climb to the summit in deference to
Their tradition
Excuse enough for me
As I look up to the peak I play a whistle tune for the mountain
Si beg, si mor
Then I start the slow descent to the Pound
A well-trodden track, an easy walk
Though the heat is rising a cool breeze dances
Through the bush
And soothes me
During a break for a sip of water and another tune
A yellow bird comes down to investigate the sound
Head cocked he listens
Then flies off to fetch his mate
They both depart as the tune ends
At length I am in the Pound- the ground is flat
Tall trees surround me
Their trunks shining silver or scribbled with grey bark
More coloured birds fly amongst the grey-green leaves
A parakeet, a red headed robin
At last the Hills Homestead is reached
Time for another rest but yet another climb
To a view-point where the sloping sides of the Pound
Depict the bodies of the man-eating serpents
The Dreamtime legend of how the Pound was formed
The last few kilometers follow the Heysen Trail
And a cool creek bed, water flowing
Mirroring the white trunks of the River Gums
At last I finish the trail but
The trail has also finished me
By 6pm I am snug in my down cocoon
And my sheltering tent
What challenges will tomorrow bring?

Wilpena Pound is in the Flinders Ranges
in South Australia.

Poetry Through A Lens

In 2013 the Port Lincoln Camera Club and Eyre Writers Inc combined to present a booklet of photographs with poetry written in response, and poems with photographs taken in response. The following are my poems that were included in the publication.

Gravestone
in repsonse

Were you happy, Dinah
On that isolated isle?
Your infamous father
Finally turning from alcohol
To the Holy Book
Christianity your education
For a life where farming and fishing
Brought a precarious living
Yet you survived
Not only survived but surely thrived
To bring into the world ten children
Beloved mother
They were your bounty

Gravestone photograph by
Pam Hewstone

The Love of Your Life
in response

A necessary evil or a necessary good
Depends which way you look at it – if you ever would
It always hits your pocket, 'specially if it hits a post
And its regular 'doctors' visits dent the bankcard most
But the feeling of elation as you cross the open plain
Lets you know that all your spending has not been in vain
Climbing over passes and speeding down the hills
Brings laughter to your lips, lets you throw away the pills
And in early morning traffic when you're moving very slow
You can listen to Deane Williams on local radio
With a personalised rego you know just where you are
In the love of your life – your own dear motor car.

The Love of Your Life photograph by Andrew DeLaine

Rusting Heap
in response

Where did you go to my lovely
When you were out on the road
All dressed in your sparkling paint job
Seeing your chromed headlights glow
You were born in '37
The very best of your breed
With a 60 horsepower engine
You could reach a respectable speed
The family all gasped with pleasure
For they could all fit inside
On seats upholstered in leather
And a boot both deep and wide
You triumphantly followed the highways
And dirt tracks you conquered with ease
Your suspension smoothed out the potholes
As you flashed past paddocks and trees
But now you lie unattended
Your body riddled with rust
Windows broken and tyres denuded
Your interior covered in dust
But you remember those days of glory
When your pinions and axles were greased
Maybe someone will come and restore you
Or simply leave you in peace
La, la, la, la, la, la. La
La, la, la
La, la,
La

Rusting Heap photo by Denise Easton

Busy Port
in response

Hey Warren, what d'ya reckon, mate
I think you're next to go
I see they're loading up real fast
And soon they'll need a tow

There's been a bumper crop this year
With all the silos full
They can't on load it fast enough
They'll be looking for a pull

I tell you, mate, when season's done
I'd like a little rest
After all, there's only three of us
And we can only do our best

Me funnel's due a paint job
And me engine's running rough
Another week or two at this rate
And I reckon I've had enough

So, off you go, our Warren
I see you're first in line
Go get that next big grain ship
I know you'll manage fine

Busy Port photograph by Steve Sykes

Nearly There

Kick, kick, kick I go
I think I'm nearly there
That lily pad can't be that far
Then I'll come up for air

Mum said I should learn to swim
Underwater for, you see
I can hide when birds fly low
Looking for their tea

But, my goodness, I feel a hiccup come
Can I hold my breath?
If I surface with that Ibis near
It could mean an untimely death

The Land Of Smiles

Where golden buddhas hide among the hills. The orchid and the lotus show their bloom
Giant trees with buttress roots, fern and bracken underfoot Now you know you're in the land of smiles.
Will you laze upon a southern beach or let northern hot springs bathe your feet
Mango lassies cool Chang beer all you need is offered here when you come into the land of smiles.

Where golden buddhas hide among the hills
The orchid and the lotus show their blooms
Giant trees with buttress roots, fern and bracken underfoot
Now you know you're in the land of smiles

Waterfalls that spring from every hill
And dead, dry caves that house the good luck shrines
Night time cool and daytime heat, markets form on every street
Now you know you're in the land of smiles

Will you laze upon a southern beach
Or let northern hot springs bathe your feet
Mango lassies, cool Chang beer
All you need is offered here
When you come into the land of smiles

Gentle people live their lives at ease
Ignore the Falang's needless speedy pace
So where'er you go, go with the flow
Feel the peaceful feeling grow
And take your time to see the land of smiles
You're always welcome in the land of smiles
So come again into the land of smiles

Thailand is a lovely country which I have explored by motorcycle a couple of times and hope to go back. It is known in the tourist trade as the Land of Smiles and I wrote this while I was there in 2014. Having lost my driving licence for 3 months in Oz, I spent the time in Thailand.

Get On With It (2014)

Chorus
Get on with it, let's get on with it
Let's make a brand new start
Get on with it, let's get on with it
And feel it from the heart

We've had to learn the hard way but we can start anew
We all can give our very best and see what we can do
It's no good always laying blame at each other's door
Telling tales and pointing bones, it's all been done before

Chorus

Let's be done with recrimination, let's be done with laying blame
Let each new generation be done with calling names
For we CAN live together in peaceful harmony
A true reconciliation between you and me

If we get on with it, let's get on with it
Pull down the wall of hate
With a bit more understanding
You will be my Aussie mate

Written for a school to sing on Reconciliation Day.

An Island Interlude (2015)

Swishing of bicycle wheels peddling past on quiet island roads weaving through salty lakes
The squeal of the gulls or the caw-caw of crows pierces through the peace
Osprey ride the wind or build seaside stacks of gathered twigs
Small furry quokkas hop, snakes slide and the king skink slinks into the scrub
Little left of the cruel past – aboriginals or foreign nationals interned in the Quod or in rust coloured houses by the bay
Lighthouses, once vital to a ship's safe passage now fascinate the visitors
'See the view from the top!'
Or you may delve deep into the sand covered gun tunnels
Army barracks, dismantled defences, rusty rail tracks – a reminder of WW2
Now pleasure boats and walking trails abound
Segway tours, ice cream, cappuccino, tasty pies and boutique beers
Perth's towering buildings sit in a haze on the horizon across the bay
There let them stay
Peaceful Rottnest is a world away

I was fortunate enough to spend a few days on Rottnest Island.

A Rottnest Island quokka.

A Christmas Story

It was a clear, bright night on the hills above Bethlehem; the ground was white with frost and it was bitterly cold.

Maurie, Micky and Minnie lay snuggled together in their little nest in a tree trunk waiting for their parents, two other field mice, to come home from their foraging and feed them.

Micky was impatient, he poked his little head out of the nest, nose and whiskers quivering, to look over the fields.

Yes! In the distance he saw them hopping toward him but, horror of horrors, just as they neared the nest, out of the sky a large hawk swooped and with a grab of his extended claws, plucked Micky's parents from the ground and bore them aloft and away!

Micky was horrified. No parents, no dinner! He turned and explained the situation to Maurie and Minnie who, for a moment sat in stunned silence.

Minnie, the practical one said, 'Well boys, it's no use just sitting here we need to go out and search for food.'

So, one by one they crawled out, over the lip of the knot hole in the trunk, jumped down onto the ground and hopped hopefully down the hillside.

They saw a group of shepherds sitting around a fire, their sheep nearby. The trio of mice smelt cooking so approached, mouths watering.

Just as they neared the group there was a bit of a commotion and the shepherds were pointing upward at the sky.

A huge flapping of wings, a trumpeting sound and a bunch of angels appeared singing and saying

'We bring you tidings of great joy.'

Micky, Maurie and Minnie stared in amazement but were more interested in the food in the pot on the fire.

As they crept toward it there was another blast on a trumpet, the sheep jumped in fright and one of them landed heavily on Maurie, his hoof crushing the life out of the little fella.

'Oh no,' cried Minnie, 'we must get out of here.'

They looked up into the sky again and the angels had disappeared but a bright star was shining over the town of Bethlehem lying below in the valley.

'We must go there,' said Minnie. 'There must be some place we can find some tucker.'

Sadly leaving behind the poor bleeding body of Maurie, Micky and Minnie hopped on down the hillside toward the lights of the town.

There was a good deal of commotion there too, especially at the pub.

Apparently a census was being held and people were travelling, mainly by horse or donkey, in between towns, staying at the various hostelries.

Micky and Minnie carefully bypassed the animal hooves outside and made their way into the pub. There was a warm and friendly atmosphere; the ale was flowing and people were chatting and supping from their large tankards.

'Quick,' said Minnie. 'Through that door, it must be to the kitchen.' Sure enough this room was filled with all kinds of food and Micky, spotting a bowl of cereal, made straight for it.

'What's this!' A loud cry from a very large and angry looking chef. 'I'll have no mice in my kitchen!'

Wielding a long, very sharp knife he dashed toward them and, with one clean swipe, decapitated poor Micky.

'Aaaah', Minnie squealed and raced for the back door. Outside on the back step she sat quivering and tears began to flow. In a matter of one hour she had lost her whole family and she was also very hungry.

Finally, pulling herself together she wiped away her tears, looked around her and realised that the large star that she had seen before was shining brightly right overhead. She looked across at a stable door and there seemed to be a number of people entering it; not in the jovial fashion of the crowd in the bar but quietly. And a strange smell of incense pervaded.

She timidly approached the stable door and inside were many people and animals looking at something. Very carefully she manoeuvred her way through their feet and came to the front of the crowd.

There was a shabby looking couple, the woman in a blue shawl, kneeling next to a manger and, strangely, also peering into this receptacle were three richly-costumed men, with crowns on. One of them was black! Interesting, smelly packages lay around.

The shepherds from the hillside were pushing their way in and some of the angels were singing harmoniously in the background with harps and bells. Sheep, donkeys and a cow or two shuffled around.

'What on earth are they looking at?' Minnie thought and hopped nearer. She ran right up the side of the manger and peered through the straw.

There lay a little baby wrapped in a sheet.

'So,' thought Minnie, 'what is it doing here?'

Then the baby turned his face toward her and gave her the most radiant smile. His whole head had a sort of brightness about it and Minnie felt a glow of happiness come over her.

The angels sang 'Unto us a child is born, unto us a son is given, 'Halleluja' and, in amongst them she thought she saw the ghostly, smiling faces of her recently lost family.

And that is how poor, orphaned Minnie found Jesus.

Harvest Time (1980s/2015)

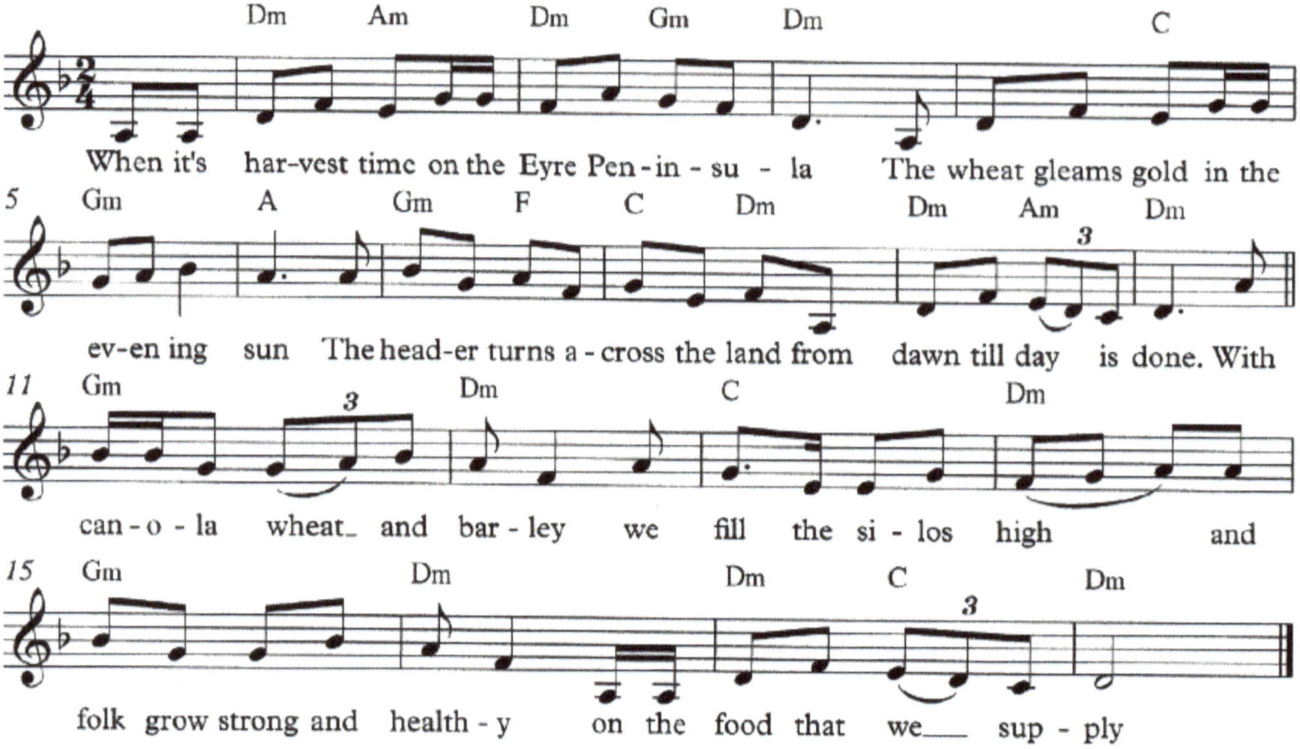
Dm Am Dm Gm Dm C
When it's har-vest time on the Eyre Pen - in - su - la The wheat gleams gold in the
5 Gm A Gm F C Dm Dm Am Dm
ev-en ing sun The head-er turns a - cross the land from dawn till day is done. With
11 Gm Dm C Dm
can - o - la wheat_ and bar - ley we fill the si - los high and
15 Gm Dm Dm C Dm
folk grow strong and health - y on the food that we___ sup - ply

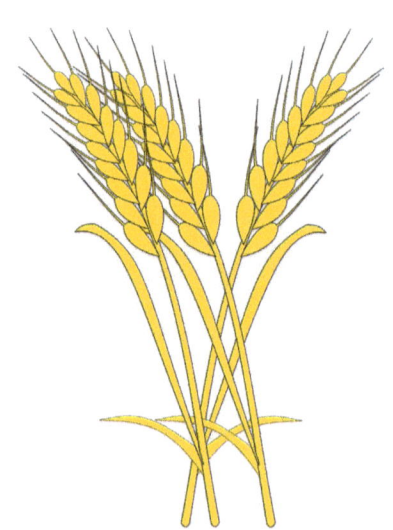

When it's harvest time on the Eyre Peninsula
The wheat gleams gold in the evening sun
The header turns across the land
From dawn til day is done

Chorus:
With canola, wheat and barley
We'll fill the silos high...
And folk grow strong and healthy
On the food that we supply

It's up each morn when the cock is crowing
We'll pack our lunch and on our way
The tractor chugs both back and forth
All through the summer's day

Chorus

And when the harvest is all gathered
And Christmas time is drawing near
We'll raise our glasses high and toast
The coming of New Year

Chorus x 2

Originally written in the 1980s to accompany a Morris dance we were doing with kids in Victoria, it has been adapted for the Eyre Peninsular, as there are harvests everywhere!

Incident in the Andes

In 2015 I was trying to get to Sucre, Bolivia to spend my 70th birthday with friends there. I bought a 125 Yamaha in Santiago, Chile, spent a few weeks touring that country and was now about to climb into the Andes to enter Bolivia.

I started the climb from sea level at Arica, just south of the Peruvian border. The road led steeply away from the coast, giving spectacular views of the shoreline. The little bike was handling the climb well and I stopped for coffee in the small hillside village of Putra then continued to the Chile/Bolivian border with spectacular mountain views en route.

There was a long queue of trucks as this is the main road that Bolivians use to take their goods to and from the sea ports in Chile. The weather was deteriorating and by the time I reached the border offices it was sleeting and very cold. There was a two hour wait while people were being processed not helped by the power going down interrupting computer entries.

Finally I was free to go and was hoping to make the 200km ride to the next town before dark to find somewhere to stay as the weather wasn't conducive to camping. However, I needed fuel so stopped at the service station to fill up. I had to wait for the power to come on to start the pumps as there had been another interruption. Although it was cold and raining the attendant would not allow me to wait inside!

Much later than I had hoped I was able to go and started off in the cold and wet but what was happening? The bike was missing and would only do 40kph. Had they put the wrong fuel in the tank? The light was fading, the rain was falling and there were many trucks overtaking me. I felt very vunerable and knew that it was not a good idea to be out on the road but it was still a long way to the next town and no sign of any habitation, just a few llamas wandering around in the bleak landscape.

Eventually I came across a small building which looked like a llama hut. Desperate to get off the road I stopped and tried the door - locked - however there was some shelter offered beside the building in a small low-walled yard. I parked the bike, unloaded the tent and started to erect it. As the rain was falling the tent filled with water before I could get the flysheet on. Shivering with cold I couldn't locate my cup so looking around, I found a small empty plastic drink bottle and cut off the top with my penknife to use it as a scoop to take the water out before putting in my Thermorest and sleeping bag.

Feeling sick with the altitude and exhausted after the day's activities I crawled into my bag, fully clothed, put my motorcycle jacket on top and finally slept, hoping that the bike would survive the rain.

The next morning it had stopped raining so I quickly packed up. The bike started - God bless her- and I slowly rode to Patasamaya, the small town on the main road to La Paz. There I first found breakfast in a small café before looking for a mechanic to reset the carburetor needle for altitude and to add new fuel. After that both I and the bike performed a lot better and I made good time to La Paz. Thus ended probably the most memorable camping experience I have ever had!

Birthdays I Will Always Remember (70th)

My 70th birthday I was determined to spend in South America as that was the one continent I hadn't explored by motorbike. Whilst living in Spain I had met some musicians from Bolivia who were touring Europe, playing their panpipes etc. in the street. They were three brothers; two had returned to their home in Sucre and I had kept in touch by email. Sucre seemed an appropriate place to be that year on my trip around Chile, Bolivia and Argentina so I contacted Lenin, the younger brother.

'I am coming to Sucre this November to play music with you on my 70th birthday,' I told him.

His reply was, 'It is very high here, you will get altitude sickness.'

A little later I emailed again from Chile, 'I am coming to Sucre to be with you and your family on my birthday 21st November. I am riding there on my motorbike.'

His reply was, 'The roads are bad; it is dangerous for you to ride a motorbike here.'

It was getting closer to the date and, not having had a positive reply, I emailed, 'I really would like to play music with you on my 70th birthday but if this is a problem for you and your family then I won't come. Please let me know as soon as possible.'

The reply was, 'We are expecting you and my mother is very happy to have you here. She is making a cake.'

So, I rode up over the high Andes – with only mild altitude effects – and arrived in Sucre where I was welcomed with open arms by Lenin, Edwardo and the whole family. I gave their mother money to buy food for the celebrations and the boys money for beer.

The morning of my birthday I was called down to breakfast where the boys played 'happy birthday' and the birthday cake came out. In the evening there was a BBQ in the back yard with all the family plus friends and neighbours and I had a go at playing the pan-pipes myself. I had brought with me my lagerphone and whistle so we played some Celtic tunes too. It was a great time on that day and all the time I was in Sucre with these wonderful people.

Border Control (2017)

In 2017 my friend Choo, a Chinese Malaysian woman I met while working in Gibraltar, invited me to her 50th birthday party. Although living in Gibraltar herself her family all lived in Malaysia and her sister had organised a big party in a hotel in Butterworth. It was a great excuse for me to take a trip there so I flew to Penang, hired a motorcycle and after the party did quite an extensive tour of the northern part of Malaysia catching up with Nor, the head of the Malaysian sector of the Women's International Motorcycle Association and she introduced me to many interesting people.

It was flying back to Australia when the problem began; at Adelaide airport customs.

All I had with me was my red rucksack over-wrapped in Penang to attach my lagerphone, and a small day pack which I was wearing. After a long wait in the queue through immigration and approaching customs an official asked me if I would mind having a sniffer dog around my luggage. 'Not at all,' I said, quite happy that I had no illegal items. So, I stood there confidently while the dog circled my rucksack on the trolley but then came to a rest behind me in the region of my small daypack.

'Please bring that over here,' I was ordered, so I took off the backpack and laid it on the table. Just general things like my address book, purse, hanky, spectacles and whistles came out but then they shook it upside down and out rolled two small nuts.

'What are these?' the lady customs official enquired, looking accusative.

I looked at them puzzled and then remembered that while out in the country on a walk with Nor she picked up a couple of nuts and explained that, as kids, they used them to play knucklebones, or five stones, as we called them in the UK. I took them from her and played with them and then must have put them in my pack.

'This is serious,' the woman said sternly. 'No plant material allowed in.'

Seeing my rucksack she said 'Please put this on the table, we must inspect this too'

Well, I thought, it just contains my dirty clothes and my sleeping bag but, as they drew these things out, there also appeared a rotten hard-boiled egg, teeming with maggots, attached to a floppy, artificial flower.

'Oh my goodness!' the woman exclaimed just as a beetle came out rushing across the table and disappearing somewhere on the floor. I stood there horrified. Surely I was going to be locked up now.

'What an earth is this?' she asked, very accusingly.

Then I explained: While riding with Nor over to the east coast we had met some other motorcyclists who invited us with them to a traditional Malaysian wedding. There were many people there, with lots of music and dancing and eating, all colourfully dressed and having a great time. Many photos were taken especially as I was the only European there. I met the bridal couple and then the bride's father proudly gifted me the flower with the boiled egg attached as it is a traditional symbol of fertility. Ignoring the idea of fertility I thought the egg would make a snack later so put the gift in my rucksack and forgot about it. I knew nothing about where the beetle came from. I explained these circumstances to the official and she went into a huddle with others and I was left to ponder my fate.

All this had taken some time and I wanted to go to the toilet.

'You will have to be escorted,' they told me, so I was taken there by a guard and had to come back via the sniffer dog.

Finally the lady customs official said, 'We could fine you $400 for bringing in plant life but we realise that it was inadvertent. You are expected to check all your luggage before taking the flight and you have signed a form to confirm that. However, we will let you off the fine but you will have to leave all your luggage here to be fumigated and that will cost you $100.'

'Oh yes,' I said. 'I had to have my drum done before.'

One of the other officials, on hearing that said, 'Oh yes, I remember you!'

A few years before, I had brought some musical instruments back from Europe including my bodhran which had a Spanish goat skin which wasn't allowed to enter until I had it fumigated. This man was obviously the one who took my $100. I was now a marked woman!

So, I left everything behind and walked out into the cold Adelaide morning without even a jacket, as it had been strapped to my rucksack. A few days later they rang to say I could pick it up. I will try and remember to check my bags in future as it is an expensive lesson and I'm sure I am now on their watch list.

The Ruin in the Bush

I am a lonely ruin, thinking back on my glory days when the family lived and played within my walls, when the land was lush, bringing in the grain and providing for the necessities of life.

My hearth glowed with wood fires in winter and the stove always had a kettle on the boil for tea.

I saw men gather for the harvest and for the shearing; their laughter and jokes out in the quarters.

But then the drought struck. I saw the misery in the master's eyes when the sheep had to be shot; no feed in the paddocks that had turned to desert.

How the missus cried as they bundled up their possessions, as she carefully wrapped her prized silver teapot, and took them to the city.

With no-one to maintain me, my roof fell in and my walls crumbled. Now all that is left is my lonely chimney.

Ode To A Faithful Friend - My Car, The Whippet (July 2017)

She little knew when we first met the places she would see
The roads she'd travel, rough and smooth across this vast country
At first the Flinders Ranges, Blinman and Wilpena
Through creek beds and gorges made her way, no barrier could stop her
The Yorke Peninsula another spot then down to Adelaide town
In city traffic made her way and even further down
To the Fleurieu and Mt Gambier, the limestone coast a cruise
The Coorong with its empty roads temptation to let loose
Her hidden passion for to fly, to glide along the route
But soon her wicked ways were seen by men in navy suits
Undaunted, next she forayed north to the Olgas and Uluru
For coloured sunsets, desert oaks, click sticks and didgeridoos
She ventured into New South Wales, the Murray River route a breeze
Saw paddle steamers move along beside the big gum trees
She carried books, guitars, a harp, ukulele, whistles and a drum
Cooking gear, tent and sleeping bag, for when the night-time comes
To meetings, folk clubs and festivals she faithfully carried on
Til at last her heart gave out though she bravely struggled home
Now her body has finally gone to that breaker's yard in the sky
She will always be fondly remembered and I will surely try
To show her replacement, Sunny, as good a time that we
Both had together
Whippet, my friend through thick and thin, my heartfelt thanks to thee

Birthdays I Will Always Remember (72nd)

On my 72nd I was in Uganda with my old schoolmate, Liz Humphries, whom I hadn't seen since the 1950s.

Liz and I had a shared history at the Whyteleafe County Grammar School for Girls. We were both nearly expelled after this incident on a field trip!

Our geography teacher decided to take the class on a walk on the downs after school and so we all trailed along behind her, Liz and I hardly listening. It transpired that the route she took was towards Riddlesdown where Liz lived and where there was a train station where I could catch the train back home to Sanderstead. Liz and I decided not to return back to school and continued to walk together to Riddlesdown, breaking away from the group but NOT informing the teacher.

The poor woman, imagine her distress getting back to school with two girls missing! Of course we didn't think about this and were amazed when the next day we were hauled up in front of the headmistress and given a huge telling off. For some reason I was deemed the instigator of this misdemeanour and was shut in the headmistress' book store all day. My parents were called and it was decided that, though I wouldn't be expelled, I would be put into another class so being distanced from Liz. Although we saw each other at the station we both found other best friends in our respective classes and shortly afterward Liz's father, who was in the army, was stationed in Germany so she left the school and I heard nothing from her until she found me on Facebook just a few years ago. When she said she was living in Uganda I asked if I could come over for a visit as it was a country that I couldn't visit during my Africa trip in 74/5 as Idi Amin was in control.

She was happy to host me and we renewed our friendship easily and had a great time during my three months exploration of Uganda.

Liz's birthday was within a few days of mine so we went out to celebrate with other friends, having a picnic by Lake Victoria. A BBQ and drinks and a few songs made it a very pleasant day to remember and I sadly left Uganda soon after, hoping that it won't be another 50 years before we see each other again.

Further birthdays to be planned…

Left to Right: Rita Bulegeya, Linda, Liz and Steven

Koonalda (May 2018)

The stars shine bright on this Nullabor night
as we watch the fire's gentle glow
And the sounds that we hear as the day disappears
are the birds as they fly to and fro
The sun gently set out there in the west
through the trees we watched it fall
And the breeze fell away and quietly lay
before the sound of the dingo's call

For out there in the bush far from the city's rush
we can tell how folk lived their lives
By sunrise and sunset they chose their rest
as they battled through wet and dry
Off the old highway it lies beneath western skies
A homestead now abandoned and sad
Amidst the wrecks of many cars from near and far
Koonalda shows the life it once had

In 2018 I crossed the Nullabor plain on route to attend an Adventure Film Festival and to take some film en route to put together a presentation. The other two girls involved were doing the filming with their cameras and drone while I wrote songs. We stayed at Koonalda which is on the old Eyre highway to the west and is an abandoned sheep station. As it used to be a fuel stop en route there are wrecks of many vehicles that did not make the journey on the very rough road there before the new sealed highway.

Nullabor Nymph (May 2018)

Have you seen the Nullabor nymph
You'll find out Eucla way
They say she lives out in the bush
And with the 'roos she'll play
The truckies all stop off there to try and get a glance
For they say she's young and beautiful
And her clothes are rather scant

She's not been seen since 1971
So we came to have a look
It might have been a mirage, they get them when it's hot
We caught a glimpse of some-one
We'll let you decide
Was it the nymph are have we all
Been taken for a ride?

I'd Rather be a Dag than a Doll (Tulloch/Bick 2019)

I'd rather be a dag than a doll
Rather be a bandit than his moll
Throw away my bra – god, I'm a star
I'd rather be a dag than a doll

I'd rather dungarees than a dress
Don't care if my hair's in a mess
Play my banjo in the street, with baccy in my teeth
I'd rather dungarees than a dress

I play my fiddle in the middle of the night
Don't care if it's wrong or right
Need to play a bluegrass tune 'neath that silvery moon
I play my fiddle in the middle of the night

I play my guitar to Ma and Pa
They reckon I'm gonna go far
This bluegrass has a beat you can play in your bare feet
I play my guitar to Ma and Pa

I'd rather play a bass than a flute
I'd rather be a heavy than just cute
I'll pluck the strings with glee so all can see
I'd rather play a bass than a flute

Written with Sue Tulloch on our way to the
Bluegrass workshops in Quorn 2018.

Going Down To Louisiana

Mardi Gras costumes at Mamou

Going down to Louisiana, going to New Orleans
Going down to Louisiana, going to New Orleans
Gonna meet Miss Debby there, she's the Mardi Gras queen

I'm going to Pat O'Brian's, for a Hurricane
I'm going to Pat O'Brian's, for a Hurricane
Hear then two piana girls play any tune you name

Going out to Lafayette, for the Celtic Bayou
Going out to Lafayette, for the Celtic Bayou
Drinking lots of Guinness there and playing Irish tunes

I'm going out to Mamou, gonna see that poulet run
Going out to Mamou, gonna see that poulet run
Do a two-step at Fred's lounge, sure gonna have some fun

Touring the plantations, on the Mississipi line
Touring the plantations, on the Mississip line
Gonna check them Creole houses with their colours so fine

Gonna ride that Greyhound, half way across the land
Gonna ride that Greyhound, half way across the land
And meet the kind of folk on it
I'd never understand!

In 2019 I went to visit my friend, Debby Anselmo in Louisiana and we had a great time together as noted in this song written in Cajun style.

Faraway Friends (1995)

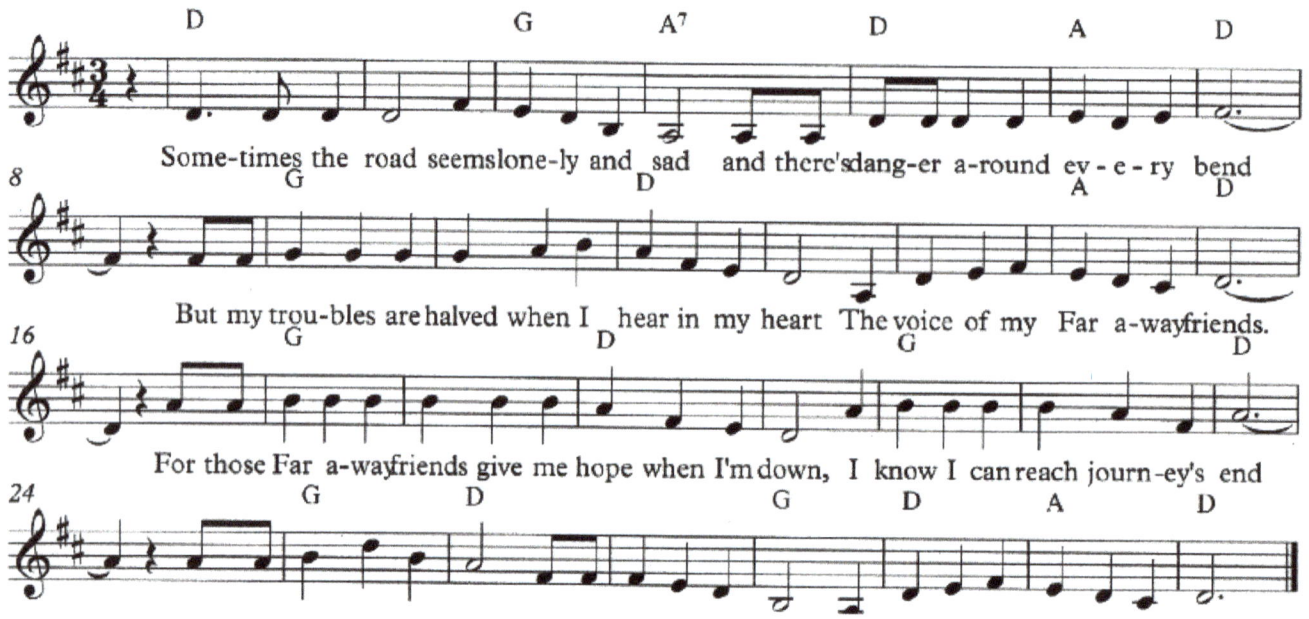

My friends were very far away at the time.
This was taken in Baluchistan in 2005.

Sometimes the road seems lonely and sad
And there's danger around every bend
But my troubles are halved when I hear in my heart
The voice of my faraway friends

Chorus:
Those faraway friends give me hope when I'm down
I know I can reach journey's end
There'll be laughter and light when I ride into town
And we are together again

Each place I go I take with me their smiles
The songs and the words that they've penned
To share out the love and the hopes and the dreams
Amongst other faraway friends

Chorus

There's times I'm not sure where I'm heading or why
And I don't seem to follow the trend
But I know more than once I've got back on the track
With the help of a faraway friend

Chorus

For all round the world I've scattered my life
Seen sights that would make the mind bend
But each trip's not complete unless I can meet
And make one more faraway friend

Chorus x 2

While walking alongside the river Thames in London, Ontario 1996 I was thinking about all the friends I had around the world and wrote this song for them.

Where Will We Be?

Our feet have stepped on countless shores
And many mountains climbed
New friends we've found in distant lands
And some we've left behind
We've tasted life's diversities
Seen happiness ebb and flow
When time slows down our restless feet
My friend, where will we go?

Will we accept a comfy couch
A normal, safe routine
When memories well recall the times
We took life to extremes
Our bodies may fail but will our minds
Shall exasperation show
As old age slowly narrows choice
My friend, where will we go?

For life has shown its different paths
Its cultures old and new
Will we return to family roots
To our place of birth be true
Or having given part of our hearts
Unto other lands
And made of web of 'foreign' friends
Who seem to understand
Can we decide which way to turn
For love and security
When time's turned the key to hold us fast
My friend, where will we be?

Castellar, Spain, 1998

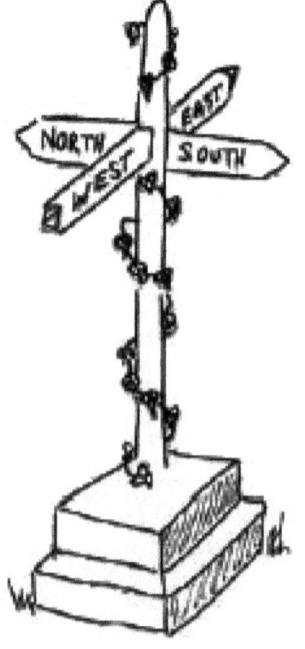

Whilst attending an art class in Jimena de la Frontera, Spain,
the teacher asked us to do a picture representing important things in our lives
– this is mine.

I hope you have enjoyed reading this book and will recommend it to your friends
– or even your enemies!

Please feel free to send comments and questions to casalinda2006@gmail.com or on Facebook at Linda Bick.
For more information check out Linda's websites:
www.lindab.id.au   www.haefale.de/linda

Other books by Linda, available on Amazon or direct from Linda:

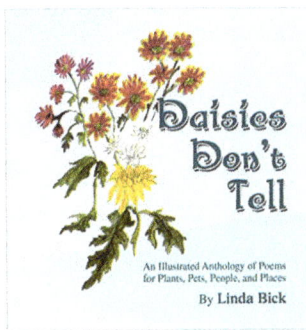
Daisies Don't Tell: An Illustrated Anthology of Poems for Plants, Pets, People and Places
by Linda Bick.
First published 2010.
2nd Edition 2020.

Where Angels Fear to Tread
by Linda Bootherstone.
First published 2009.
2nd Edition published 2015

ISBN: 978-1511561822

Three Wandering Poms
by Linda Bootherstone, Jacqueline Griffin and Angela Griffin.
Published 2014.

ISBN: 978-15003671-6-9

Into Africa With A Smile
by Linda Bootherstone
Published 2015

ISBN: 978-1517109905

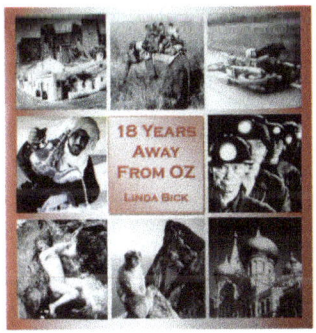
18 Years Away From Oz
Released 2012.

This CD features many of the songs in this book.

Tales of Tommy Tucker & Bo Peep
Released 2020.

This CD features two stories interwoven with traditional nursery rhymes.

For copies of these and Linda's other recordings, please email her at casalinda2006@gmail.com for **details of pricing and availability.**

www.ingramcontent.com/pod-product-compliance
Lightning Source LLC
Chambersburg PA
CBHW061132010526
44107CB00068B/2913